Censorship in Islamic Societies

Trevor Mostyn

Censorship in Islamic Societies

Saqi Books

British Library Cataloguing-in-Publication Data
A catalogue record for this book is available from the
British Library

ISBN 0 86356 041 5 (pb)
ISBN 0 86356 098 9 (hb)

Saqi Books
26 Westbourne Grove
London W2 5RH
www.saqibooks.com

To my wife, Julia

Acknowledgements

I would like to thank the following for so kindly reading and commenting on the manuscript, with the usual caveat that any errors remaining are entirely my own responsibility: Dr Peter Clark, the well-known translator of Arabic works; Prof. Charles Tripp at SOAS; Dr Derek Hopwood, former head of the Middle East Centre in Oxford; Baqer Moin, Head of the BBC Persian Service and Malise Ruthven, author of several outstanding books, not least *Islam in the World* (Penguin, 1984).

The most beautiful thing in the world is freedom of speech. (Diogenes 400–325BC.)

We must destroy the press, or the press will destroy us. (Cardinal Wolsey AD1475–1530.)

Contents

Introduction

The West divides many countries which are culturally Muslim into moderate countries which it likes and radical countries which it does not. The two favourite moderates, Egypt and Saudi Arabia, fell out of favour with Washington after their lukewarm response to the US-led coalition against terror after the attacks on the World Trade Centre and the Pentagon on 11 September 2001. As the veteran journalist David Hirst noted in the *Guardian* newspaper,[1] most of the suicidal hijackers were Egyptian or Saudi. Osama bin Laden's key advisers in his secretive al-Qaida Organization are Dr Ayman al-Zawahri and Sheikh Taseer Abdullah, both Egyptian. Both countries were accused unjustly of tolerance for terrorism and in both the US press belatedly saw lack of democracy and civic transparency as the causes of miltant Islamic tendencies. Until then a staunch friend of the West, Egypt's President Mubarak was now accused of using the state to provoke anti-western and anti-Israeli thinking.

His response was a single word, 'Palestine'. 'Palestine', he went on to say, 'generates over 50 per cent of the causes of terrorism and even when Palestine is not the cause, terrorism uses it for its own purposes ... Besides, terrorism has nothing to do with freedom of expression. For that exists in Egypt and most Arab countries.' It is, he argued, 'Israel that ignores the rulings of the judiciary, engages in mass murder and throws human rights to the wind.' Yet both Egypt and Saudi Arabia, as Hirst points out, condemned the bombing of Afghanistan while using it as a cover to oppress their own opponents. Precious little was done by either country to help the Palestinians. Having eased up in its fight against repression of suspected Islamic terrorists, Egypt renewed this repression after 11 September. According to the Egyptian Human Rights Organization this amounted to a kind of 'legislative violence' which, in the name of security, continually reduced the space for the pursuit of legitimate demands.[2]

Saudi Arabia began making widespread arrests in quarters considered sympathetic to Osama bin Laden while Prince Bandar, the Saudi ambassador to the USA, bitterly recalled how Britain had granted political asylum to Muhammad al- Mas'ari, the Saudi dissident who had waged a fax and email campaign against the abuse of power in Saudi Arabia. In Jordan the democratic experiment initiated by the late King Hussein, and which embraced fundamentalists, was being challenged by the new King Abdullah after 11 September. After suspending parliament he authorized a series of laws making it an offence to disseminate information considered 'defamatory, false, damaging to national unity or the reputation of the state, liable to incite crime, strikes, or meetings which are illegal or disturb public order'. The same development can be seen in Syria where the replacement of the late Hafez al-Asad by his son Bashar at first was welcomed as an era of political liberalization and reform. However, the blatantly political trial of two MPs a few weeks after the World Trade Centre bombing attracted little attention.[3]

But what is the role of Islam in these developments? Socialism and secularism have given way to political Islam in recent history, better understood or reviled in the West as 'Islamic fundamentalism'. Although the history of Islam has tended towards tolerance, political Islam often spurns such tolerance. The destruction by dynamite in March 2001 of the wonderful giant rock-hewn Buddhas at Bamiyan by the Afghan Taliban (but almost certainly ordered by Osama bin Laden and his Arab, Wahhabi disciples) reflected the most extreme expression of Islamic iconoclasm. Although serious Muslims have scant regard for the Taliban and Islamic scholars throughout the world begged these obscurantists to preserve the statues, the issue was soon forgotten after they were destroyed. Two and a half million refugees had been created by the Taliban and seven out of ten Afghan children orphaned by them.

The destruction of the World Trade Centre, the bombing campaign against Afghanistan that followed it and the sudden defeat of the Taliban entirely overshadowed these horrors. The whole issue of Islam's role in the modern world now dominated international thinking. Salman Rushdie noted in the *Guardian* that 'The only aspect of modernity in which the terrorists are interested is technology, which they see as a weapon that can be turned against its makers. If terrorism is to be defeated, the world of Islam must take on board the secularist–humanist principles on which the modern world is based, and without which their countries' freedom will remain a distant dream.'[4]

Looking at increasing pressures on the freedom of expression coming from, or else in response to, Islamic fundamentalists in Egypt, the Egyptian exile Nasr Hamid Abu Zayd told the *Guardian*:

These cases are proof of the failure of the mechanism of society. They show the contradictions of the ideology of the state, which used religion and the religious establishment when they are suitable to its ideology. It is understood that other forces can use it. Who pays the price? Freedom of thought. We all suffer. We've fallen into a hellish vicious circle. We're stuck between the rock of the state and the hard place of the fundamentalists.[5]

But on Tuesday, 13 November 2001, the day that the Northern Alliance of tribes marched on Kabul and other cities as the Taliban fled, music hit the streets of Afghan cities once again. The *Independent* newspaper's Justin Huggler in liberated Talogan sat by a bazzari stall listening to the recording of Ahmad Zaheer, the great Afghan singer, echoing from a cassette recorder. 'Today I have drunk too much, let me dream my dream,' he sang, 'Put me in a river of wine.' All of Afghanistan, wrote Huggler, 'was dreaming with him'.[6] Under the Taliban forbidden cassette tapes hung like pennants from telegraph wires.

This book will study freedom and its control, analysing certain landmarks such as the 1980 televised transmission in Britain of *Death of a Princess* (the execution of a Saudi princess for adultery), the execution for blasphemy in Khartoum of Mahmoud Muhammad Taha, the *fatwa* (legal ruling) issued by Ayatollah Khomeini declaring Salman Rushdie an apostate, the suffering in Pakistan today of women subjected to rape as victims of their own accusation, the banning of the gynaecologist and writer Taslima Nasrin's book *Lajja* for its sexual explicitness, and the forced annulment of the marriage of Egyptian Abu Zayd and his wife Ebtehal. Such incidents have fuelled Islamophobia and the arguments contained in articles such as Samuel Huntington's *The Clash of Civilizations*.[7]

The English writer Daniel Defoe discovered after his conviction for his *Short Way with Dissenters* in 1702 that prosecution was a valuable boost to sales. In Egypt writers have even been reported advertising *fatwa*s against their books in newspapers in order to publicize them. Where, as in Syria, censorship has been cautiously, albeit partially, lifted, the authorities have been surprised to discover that new freedoms do not lead to any sort of violent reaction but rather an increased sense of stability.

Hopefully, we are witnessing a catharsis in that Islam is an inclusive religion by its nature, traditionally more tolerant than Judaism and Christianity, and that the Islam of the next generation may enjoy a renaissance reminiscent of many of the great ages of Islam, not least the Golden Age of twelfth-century Spain.

One

The Islamic World Today

A coffin bearing the face of a boy
A book
Written on the belly of a crow
A wild beast hidden in a flower
A rock
Breathing with the lungs of a lunatic:
This is it
This is the Twentieth Century

(Adonis, 'A Mirror for the Twentieth Century',
from al-Udhari (ed.) *Victims of a Map*, Saqi Books, 1984.)

I remember wandering with my Algerian girlfriend Fatima through the lovely
Kasbah of Algiers in 1973. She had a beautiful face and flowing black hair and
she wore a mini-skirt from Paris. She was as far removed from a veiled woman
of the Kasbah as you could imagine. Young men in the winding, whitewashed
alleys muttered to each other, 'Look, your sister is betraying us' and 'This
Roumi [foreigner] is eating the bread of our house.' The crowd began to turn
in on us, so we moved away. As we left the Kasbah for the grand, white
stuccoed villas of *belle époque* Algiers, I began to feel that I was carrying the
burden of Europe's colonial stigma on my shoulders. Two decades later such
a stroll would become a death sentence. During the first year of the civil war
which began in 1991 two western journalists were stabbed to death, filming
inside the Kasbah. Few journalists, let alone foreign journalists, entered the
warren of alleys for several years after that.

Censorship in Algeria was taken for granted in Boumedienne's 1970s.
Fatima played Raina in Bernard Shaw's *Arms and the Man*, which the class I was
teaching was preparing to stage, but the university authorities panicked and

banned the play from being performed. When I posed to my class the absurd question 'Which of you is Arab and which Berber?' they replied as one, 'We are all Algerian, Sir.' But realizing that I was interested in this forbidden Berber culture, a group of Kabyle students invited me to a clandestine meeting in a nearby ice-cream parlour where they conspiratorially passed me documents in Tamahak and other Berber dialects.

The girls revealed their yearning for freedom in their essays. D.H. Lawrence's *Women in Love* generated rather tragic, erotic images among the girls while the boys puffed up their revolutionary credentials when we read Sean O'Casey's *Juno and the Paycock*. Both girls and boys knew all about human suffering. When I asked two twin girls whether they were always as happy as they seemed, they replied in unison, 'Oh, we have suffered, Sir. When we were seven our uncle and brother were taken out of our house in the mountains by the French paras and shot before our eyes.'

The cycle of violence prompted by a war in which a million died was to start again. The Algerian army's abortion in 1991 of a democratic process which was favouring Islamic fundamentalists was to lead to an appalling bloodletting by the *eradicateurs* in the army on one side and by self-styled Islamic militants on the other. The anti-Islamic Organization of Young Algerians proclaimed in 1995, 'For every woman killed for not wearing the veil we shoot three who wear it.'[1] The award-winning Algerian novelist and editor Tahar Djaout summed up the dilemma of the writer and thinker in the Islamic world today when he said, 'Silence is also death. If you speak you die. If you keep quiet you die. So speak and die.'[2] Djaout was himself shot outside his home in May 1993 and died in a coma a week later. One Islamist tract at the time listed thirty francophone journalists in Algeria sentenced to death; nine had been murdered so far.[3]

Algeria was defying the West as it always had done. In *Sexual Encounters in the Middle East* Derek Hopwood quotes Théophile Gautier,

> It is strange, we believe we have conquered Algeria and Algeria has conquered us. Our women already wear scarves interwoven with thread of gold, streaked with a thousand colours, which have served the Harem slaves... If this goes on, France will soon be Mahometan and we shall see the white domes of mosques rounding themselves on our horizons mingling with steeples.[4]

Bernard Shaw might easily have been speaking of attitudes to freedom of expression in Algeria over the past decade when he remarked that assassination was the extreme form of censorship. In the West the *fatwa* or 'legal ruling' against Salman Rushdie, translated as a 'death sentence' in the prurient, drama-obsessed western press, is the best-known reflection of this view. To some the image of *The Satanic Verses* being burnt before huge crowds in Bradford in 1989 seemed to justify the extreme Islamophobia that has affected western perceptions of Islam. These perceptions have been moulded by the Crusades of the eleventh and twelfth centuries, the Spanish Reconquest of the fifteenth century, the gung-ho image of Israeli pioneers engendered by books like *Exodus* by Leon Uris, Israel's subsequent belligerence, the Islamic revolution in Iran in 1979, the virtual destruction of Iraq since 1990 and the fear of a *Pax Talebana* that existed before 11 September 2001. We should not forget that the principle of freedom of the press in Britain dates only from the Glorious Revolution of 1688.

Contemporary Islamophobes must be bemused by the Islamic *fatwa* launched against the director of the European film *Corpus Christi* in which Jesus is portrayed as gay. Born miraculously of a virgin birth in the Qur'an as in the New Testament, an episode hauntingly and lovingly described in the Qur'an's *Sura Miriam* (Chapter of Mary), Jesus is arguably as important a figure as Muhammad in Islam. Some of the great Sufi poets certainly thought so. Muslims were equally shocked by the lack of fuss in the Christian world over Andres Serrano's painting *Piss Christ* of a crucifix immersed in urine. These images hark back to Nicolas Kazantzakis's book *The Last Temptation of Christ*, which portrayed Jesus giving in to sexual desire, or to recent pornographic videos in Europe showing St Teresa of Avila engaged in sexual acts. The Court of Human Rights in Strasbourg did, in fact, rule that the British government could suppress the video given the offence it caused Christians, but the court seemed to contradict this by also ruling that this did not give the British authorities a licence to restrict political speech.

It is, perhaps, a little ironical that Muslims in European countries complain so bitterly about being ridiculed in magazines like Britain's *Private Eye* and *Punch* when the Arab poetic tradition of ruthless satire is second to none. Britain's Lord Ahmed (Nassir) of Rotherham told a conference organized by the al-Khoei Foundation in London in 1999 that he had been lampooned for praying in strange ways and places in the House of Commons. He was not unduly pained by these satires – others pointed out, in any case, that *Punch* is owned by Muhammad al-Fayed, a Muslim, and that satire is a typically British sport. The problem in Lord Ahmed's case was that the stories put about were entirely invented.

Islam has traditionally been a tolerant and enlightened religion. Jews and Christians are protected under Islam as People of the Book (*ahl al-Kitab*) or people under covenant of protection (*dhimmis*). They were accorded freedom and toleration but had to pay the poll tax (*jizya*) and were in principle forbidden to bear arms, wear certain colours or build or repair their places of worship although such stipulations were not always strictly applied. Non-Muslim men could not marry Muslim women whereas Muslim men could marry non-Muslim women. Conversion from Islam to other religions was forbidden. In Islam blasphemy is a *hadd* offence, an offence against 'the boundaries' of God which cannot be settled by compensation. According to Ibn Taymiyya, a fourteenth-century fundamentalist, anyone defaming the Prophet must be executed even if he repents.

Nevertheless, Islam's essential tolerance towards non-Muslims is reflected in the Arabic version of Article 13 of the Universal Islamic Declaration of Human Rights[5] in which the Qur'anic *aya* (line) 'you have your religion and I have mine' is invoked. 'Say "O Unbelievers, I serve not what you serve and you are not serving what I serve, nor am I serving what you have served, neither are you serving what I serve. To you your religion and to me my religion".'[6] As Ann Elizabeth Mayer points out, the English version of this section looks quite neutral and innocuous, calling for a position in which 'all worldly power shall be considered as a sacred trust'.[7] However, in sharp contrast, she says, the same section in the Arabic version is an expression of a commitment to a society where all people will believe that God alone is the master of all creation.

Here is the sting. In a reply to charges of gross violations of human rights during a 1985 session of the UN Commission on Human Rights, the Iranian ambassador to the UN replied that:

> We do not pretend to respect human rights principles, because for us the Universal Declaration of Human Rights and its covenants are not the criteria for judgement and decision... Our aim is to follow the principles of Islam. We believe that capital punishment and other types of Islamic punishments cannot be considered as a form of torture.[8]

But the situation of freedom of expression throughout the world is a sorry one today; it is not the monopoly of societies which claim to be Islamic. According to the annual survey released by Freedom House in April 2000, 63 per cent of the world's countries restrict print and electronic journalists and 80 per cent of the world's people live in countries with a less than free press. Globally, only 69 countries have a free press, where the flow of information is unrestricted, 51 have a partly free news media and 66 countries have government control over print and broadcast systems. The Arab and the wider Islamic world have fared poorly. During the Lebanese civil war one of many jokes did the rounds. A dog decided to go to Syria to flee the civil war in Lebanon. A week later he returned to Beirut. 'What's the matter?' asked his canine companion in Beirut. 'Didn't you like Syria?' 'I liked it a lot. There was no fighting; the food was great. But after a while I wanted to bark.'[9]

The roots of tight control of thought in the Islamic world, it seems, lie in culture and in chronic threats to that culture from the West. Burdened with colonialism and neo-colonialism of which the creation and defensive-aggressive behaviour of Israel has been a landmark, the Islamic world has become increasingly cynical of the so-called benefits of western 'modernization'. The founder of the Muslim Brotherhood (the Ikhwan), Hasan al-Banna, wrote:

> They [the Europeans] imported their half-naked women into these regions, together with their liquors, their theatres, their dance halls, their amusements, their stories, their newspapers, their novels, their whims, their silly games, and their vices. Here they countenanced crimes they did not tolerate in their own countries, and decked out this frivolous strident world, reeking with sin and redolent with vice, to the eyes of the deluded, unsophisticated Muslims of wealth and prestige, and to those of rank and authority.[10]

This is a harsh indictment and one certainly influenced by Banna's own prejudices, but it is a *Weltanschauung* shared by many militant minorities throughout the Islamic world today. The same theme comes across in Hanif Kureishi's film *My Son the Fanatic* where a Bradford Muslim father is horrified by the radical fundamentalism of his son, who is in turn disgusted with his father's surrender to women and other symbols of western decadence.

Muslim writers recognize that freedoms exist in the West but believe that these are curtailed when it comes to Islam. The western media chills its readers with the threat of an 'Islamic Bomb' but never, say Muslim writers, with Jewish, Christian or Hindu bombs. Muslims who kill are terrorists while Christians who do so are 'militiamen'. Muslims are 'fundamentalist' while their Jewish counterparts are 'Orthodox'. A number of Muslim writers even believe that freedom of speech is permitted in the West on condition that it does not target Israel. When the twelve-year-old boy Muhammad al-Durra was shot by Israeli soldiers cowering in his father's arms near Gaza's Jewish Netzarim settlement in October 2000, some Israelis writers asked what he was doing there, the outrageous implication being that 'Anyway, he is only an Arab.' Had he been an Israeli child the scandal would have become for the western media a milestone in horror. In Britain when Bradford Muslims burn a book it makes headline news but we rarely read about the Shi'a community's enlightened al-Khoei Foundation which runs large inter-faith conferences from its headquarters (a former synagogue) in London's Queen's Park.

The Syrian poet Nizar Qabbani recognized that the Israelis have perfected tactics long lost to the stumbling Arab world, although Israel's brutal behaviour during the 'al-Aqsa' Intifada that started in October 2000 suggests that it may now be losing its public relations edge. Qabbani sees the Arabs as their own worst enemies. He wrote:

> Our enemies did not cross our borders
> They crept through our weaknesses like ants.
>
> We are a thick-skinned people
> with empty souls
> We spend our days practising witchcraft,
> Playing chess and sleeping.
> Are we the Nation by which God
> Blessed Mankind?
>
> Our desert oil could have become
> Daggers of flame and fire.
> We're a disgrace to our noble ancestors:
> We let our oil flow through the toes of whoredom."

Jordan's Prince Hasan noted at an al-Khoei Foundation conference on Islamic Responses to Racism in January 2001 that during Bosnia's recent nightmare more statements in its support came from the Vatican than from the entire Islamic community.

In the West freedom of expression exists, goes the argument, to liberate the creative self from the constraints and limits imposed by the community, yet it is this very community – this Arabic *umma* – which is so crucial to traditional Islamic society. At the same time Christianity and Islam do not share the tolerance of Buddhism, each imposing a comprehensive allegiance on their followers, but Islam does at least respect People of the Book – monotheists – who may flourish within the *Dar al-Islam* (The Abode of Islam) under certain conditions such as the obligation to pay the *jizya* tax. Muslims argue that respect for human rights has been taken for granted within the Islamic community since the plea of Omar ibn al-Khattab, Islam's second Caliph, 'Why do you enslave men since they were brought free out of the wombs of their mothers?'

Much publicity was given in the British press in 1999 to the way in which a British Muslim girl of Pakistani extraction, who refused to abort her child by her boyfriend, was strangled by her weeping mother and brother. They had loved the girl, it seems, but were convinced that they were only doing their duty according to traditional codes of honour. To the modern westerner who is brought up with few social constraints to 'do his or her own thing' this incident was both horrific and absurd, taking place as it did in the heart of a British city. At the root of the problem lies the Pakistani honour-code or *izzat*, which can take precedence over personal loyalties. It may have as little to do with Islam *per se* as female circumcision (clitoridectomy – originally a Pharaonic tradition) in Egypt and Sudan, but it is associated in the West with Islamic cultural tradition. The murders of young women who have lost their virginity, often through rape, may reflect pre-Islamic tribal society. Some writers suggest that honour-revenge has its roots in Assyrian laws starting in 1200 BC, which codified a woman's chastity as clan or family property.

Since the eighteenth century enlightened westerners increasingly believe that the ever-widening forms of expression developed over the past decades should be immune from government control. It is a tendency supported by liberals throughout the world from Voltaire's 'I disapprove of what you say, but I will defend to the death your right to say it'[12] to Oscar Wilde's quip that 'There is no such thing as a moral or an immoral book. Books are well written, or badly written.'[13] Well might Oscar laugh but it is a deadly serious topic. Why has such individualism apparently found so little favour in modern Islamic political society?

Islamic writings from the Qur'an and the Hadith onwards stress the importance of the community. Community freedom is more important than individual freedom. The sense of community – the concept of *umma* – reinforces patriarchism and family solidarity in Islamic society. But a more modern problem is the fact that most 'Islamic' states are ruled by totalitarian regimes. Even those like Egypt which pose as democracies are democracies in name only. Egypt's President Mubarak received an uncontested fourth six-year term as president with 94 per cent support in October 1999. Syria's late President Asad had recently beaten him to it with 99.98 per cent of the vote. In Iraq Saddam Hussein was similarly granted an open-ended contract, in his case to brutalize his people. Even Tunisia's presidential elections were a foregone conclusion. Qadhafi's so-called *Jamahariyya* (State of the Masses) in Libya is part of a curious fiction that they, the masses, are in power anyway so he simply has no need to be elected. Many Arabs accept all this as a sort of ghastly *faute de mieux*. The West, of course, acquiesces as it did when it overturned Musadeq's democratic experiment in Iran in the 1950s. The West treasures democracy at home but has usually found it an irritant in countries whose resources it needs to control and manipulate.

The problem with censorship in most developing countries today is summed up with some licence by Khaled Kishtainy in his book *Arab Political Humour*. 'My brief [at the Arab League's magazine *Arab Affairs*]', he writes, 'was that contributors should have absolute freedom to write anything they liked about the Arab world provided that they did not criticize or offend any of the twenty-three Arab states."[4] Since those days, says Adel Darwish, former Middle East editor of *Index on Censorship*, censorship of the Arab media has become a job-creation industry. 'Censors are given epithets such as Controller and if they are not seen to control the input of information they believe that they cannot justify their incomes.' Ironically, indirect censorship in London is almost as strict as in the countries from which such media organs have tried to escape but it is not always indirect. When the Lebanese editor Salim al-Louzi went to a family wedding in Beirut he was seized by an armed group and tortured to death, apparently for articles he had written in a London newspaper. It was believed that he had offended the Syrians.

I spent four years in the 1970s as Macmillan Publishers' Middle East manager, travelling throughout the Middle East from Iran to Morocco. The quirks of censorship and good commercial reasons to respect the censor were constant themes in my calculations. I had to identify why many of our educational books had been banned by the Saudi censor. This led me to arrange a curious meeting with the censor in Jeddah. I expected to meet a fundamentalist Saudi in a magnificent suite but the man I met turned out to be an enlightened, liberal, young Palestinian in a tiny office crammed to bursting point with banned books. He must have been the best read man in the Kingdom. He felt a great affection for the books he was obliged to ban and clearly had very little in common with the Wahhabi culture that condemned them. Nevertheless, in order to justify his job he would always be obliged to err on the side of caution. 'This is my job,' he said sadly, throwing up his arms. 'I wouldn't ban any of these books if I had the chance.'

Nevertheless, sanctimonious demagogy is much in vogue in Islamic society today. To take but one graphic example, early in 1999 a Dr Khodr Uraif accused the soft drinks company 7 Up of blasphemy in a Saudi local newspaper; the US-educated professor maintaining that seen from the rear the 7 Up logo closely resembled the word Allah in Arabic. The Saudi Minister of Commerce quickly asked the company to change its label. In an article in the *Guardian* the Middle East journalist David Hirst notes that there is a concordat in Saudi Arabia whereby the clerics endorse the regime's Islamic legitimacy, in return for which they can pontificate to their heart's content on such matters as whether a wife can wear jeans in front of her husband, for example. 'They never do what they should,' says Hirst, 'denounce tyranny, injustice, corruption."[5]

But the true future of Islam's struggle for self-expression may lie in Iran. Of Iran's population of 66 million, 89 per cent are Shi'i and 10 per cent Sunni. The Safavid Empire was created in the sixteenth century by Shah Ismail who made Shi'ism the state religion. Known as Persia until 1935, Iran became an Islamic republic in 1979 after the ruling Shah Reza Pahlavi was forced into exile. The focus of opposition, the Ayatollah Khomeini, returned to Tehran in an atmosphere of unbelievable triumph. However, conservative clerical forces subsequently crushed westernizing liberal elements. Militant Iranian students seized the US Embassy in Tehran on 4 November 1979 and held it until 20 January 1981. From 1980 to 1988, Iran fought a bloody, indecisive war with Iraq over disputed territory. Iran agreed to end the war after Iraq's President Saddam Hussein used chemical weapons against the Iraqi Kurdish village of Halbja.

The Ayatollah Khomeini's *fatwa* opining that Salman Rushdie was an apostate for writing his novel *The Satanic Verses* was a milestone in Islam's relationship with the West. In recent years Iranian pilgrims have used the Hajj to Mecca to make political statements attacking Israel, the West, and by implication the pro-western Saudi dynasty. In August 1987 the Saudis reported that 402 people, of whom 275 were Iranians, had been killed in disturbances resulting from political demonstrations.

However, the key current issue is how rapidly the country should open up to the modernizing influences of the outside world. The liberals are led by Iran's popular reformist President Muhammad Khatami; the hardliners by its supreme spiritual leader Ayatollah 'Ali Khamenei. The possibility of a rapprochement with the USA increased after the World Trade Centre was destroyed on 11 September 2001. Iran sent its condolences and the chant 'Death to America' was dropped from prayer services in the mosques.

When some months before Iran's Islamic Revolution in 1979 my employers, Macmillan Publishers, asked me to do a buy-back deal for a vanity book they wanted to publish on a member of the Iranian royal family, the young Tehran bookseller – a nephew of a member of Savak, the national security organization – who had rejoiced in such enterprises before, asked me with a smile: 'Will the book include her near-arrest in Switzerland on suspicion of carrying hashish?' No, I laughed, it would not be that sort of book at all. This was a brief 'Prague Spring' where one could see just how far the wheel had come full circle in Iran.

But such new freedoms were short-lived. During the 1980–8 Iran–Iraq War in which Iranian soldiers died horribly in their tens of thousands, Roger Cooper, an Iranophile, remembered a cleric giving a series of television sermons about the inadvisability of men and women sleeping naked in bed. Why? Because if there was an earthquake and the building collapsed naked men would fall upon naked women in the rooms below. Sexual mores play an important role with modern fundamentalists. According to the writer Hamid Naficy, in the Islamic system eyes are not passive organs, they are 'active, even invasive organs, whose gaze is also construed to be inherently aggressive'.[16] This notion, he points out, was condensed in the following quote by the Iranian Ayatollah 'Ali Meshkini: 'Looking is rape by means of the eyes ... whether the vulva admits or rejects it, that is, whether actual sexual intercourse takes place or not.'[17]

Khomeini's views on human rights seemed clear-cut and crude but he was responding to a volatile historic period in which his power-base was open to challenge. 'Criminals should not be tried,' he said. 'The trial of a criminal is against human rights. Human rights demand that we should have killed them in the first place when it became known that they were criminals.'[18] He called Amnesty International 'Travesty International'.[19] This, according to his biographer Baqer Moin, was a man who was so compassionate that he even avoided 'killing flies, instead gently persuading them with the fringe of his cloak to fly away'.[20]

Iran's first post-revolution Prime Minister Mehdi Bazargan tried desperately to establish the rule of law in Iran but Khomeini had a different agenda, says Moin.[21] When Khomeini fought Ayatollah Hossein 'Ali Montazeri, his student and friend and – at one stage – his nominated successor, in the period after the cease-fire with Iraq, Montazeri's pleas for respect for human rights fell on deaf ears. Khomeini believed that anyone who took up arms directly or indirectly against the Islamic government was liable to the death penalty. Says Moin, 'Whereas in defence of his arguments Montazeri cited examples of the clemency the Prophet had shown towards his enemies, to Khomeini it was the religious duty to follow the example of the Prophet's decisive action against the Jews of the Banu Quraiza.'[22]

Nevertheless, the tensions that developed between hardliners and pragmatists in Iran after Khomeini's death also engendered unexpected realities. In an extraordinary film called *Divorce Iranian Style* made in 1998 by Ziba Mir-Hosseini and Kim Longenotti we see clerical divorce judges quite out of their depths when confronted with passionate and extremely outspoken women seeking divorces from their husbands. They are shown at times shrieking in front of – but never at – the quiet judge in his clean white *thobe* and turban, at others almost flirting with him as they describe the sexual inadequacies of their husbands and accuse them of crimes of violence, accusations which they openly admit to the cameras, and in effect to the judge himself, to be false. The film, first shown in 1999, represented a sign of the times when the liberal tendency represented by President Khatami was making its big comeback. In later chapters I will look more closely at the significance and influence of post-revolutionary Iranian cinema.

Another example of a softening process in Iran was in late 1999 when some of pop art's greatest treasures, including Andy Warhol's 1973 silkscreen print of Mick Jagger and James Rosenquist's portrait of Marilyn Monroe, were being shown at the Museum of Contemporary Art in Tehran. 'Those who profess that we should try to preserve our eastern purity and shut our doors to keep out all the winds that blow from the west, well, these people are depriving our art from a universal language and means of expression,' said Gholamhossein Nami, a prominent Iranian artist.[23]

Challenges to the increasingly unpopular clerical regime came to a head in April 2000 during a controversial conference in Berlin. Organized as a forum for serious discussion, the agenda was hijacked by an Iranian man who stripped naked in protest against the Iranian regime and by an Iranian woman who registered her opposition by dancing before the assembly. Iranian conservatives saw the conference as representing the excess of reformists after their victory in parliamentary elections the previous February. Three Iranians who attended the meeting, two print journalists and one prize-winning female novelist, faced ten years in gaol for 'acting against national security and propagandizing against the regime'.

Ahmad Shamloo, one of Iran's most respected poets has been in trouble both before and after the Islamic revolution. In his poem 'Punishment' the atmosphere of terror is chilling:

In this place there is a maze of prisons
And in each prison a myriad of dungeons
And in each dungeon countless cells
And in each cell scores of men in irons.[24]

By 1994 forty-eight writers and journalists had been executed by revolutionary courts, including the 28-year old Said Soltanpour, who was abducted in front of his bride at his wedding and later shot, and the novelist Rahman Hatefi, who was left to bleed to death in prison after interrogators opened his veins. There were then a thousand Iranian intellectuals in prison and twice that many in exile.[25] The reports of Human Rights Watch and Amnesty International in 1999 made grisly reading. In Iran the head of the Revolutionary Guards Corps, General Yahya Rahim Safavi, set the tone in April 1998 when he said 'we are seeking to root out counter-revolutionaries wherever they are. We have to cut the throats of some and cut off the tongues of others.' A few days later he threatened, 'we will go after them when the time is ripe ... fruit has to be picked when it is ripe. The fruit is unripe now.' Flogging was reportedly imposed for a wide range of offences, at times in conjunction with the death sentence. Vahide Ghassemi, the co-accused of a German, Helmut Hofer, was reportedly sentenced to 100 lashes after being convicted of illicit sexual relations. The following month, in the town of Lahijan, Khosrow Ebrahimi was acquitted after he escaped from a pit in which he had been buried to the waist in order to be stoned to death for adultery. Many journalists and editors were imprisoned and their newspapers closed down. Others disappeared.

Meanwhile in 1999, the 15 Khordad Foundation increased to $3 million the reward for killing Salman Rushdie. In the month of November that year alone one journalist was found dead after advocating the separation of religion and state; the editor of the banned newspaper *Hezb-e Mellat-e Iran* and his wife were killed at home; several journalists seeking to establish an independent writers association simply 'disappeared'; and another journalist was executed for converting a Shi'i Muslim to Bahaism.

However, most see these horrors as the backlash of a flagging right wing. Khatami's efforts to normalize Iran's relations with the West and the USA by speaking out in support of fundamental human rights and the rule of law deserve careful study. Tens of new newspapers support Khatami today. Although many were closed down in 2001, the closures are unlikely to be permanent. Press freedom is at the heart of wider demands for liberalization. After the revolution in 1979 the then president, Bani Sadr, had antagonized the mullahs. Then the gruelling war with Iraq put any improvements on hold for many years and the issue of political freedom became marginalized. It is really only now that political reform is back on the agenda with Khatami's convincing victory in the February 2000 elections. Egypt has always claimed to be the beating heart of the Arab, if not the Islamic, world but it is enticing to argue that the real test for Islam as a political culture lies in the Iranian experience, a strange hybrid of democratic thinking and intolerance.

Even under Egypt's 1980 Press Law it is an offence to advocate opposition or hatred towards state institutions, or to publish abroad false or misleading news or information which could damage the interests of Egypt. Indeed, Egypt, despite its sophistication and great history, is astonishingly sensitive to criticism, as I was to learn to my cost when I returned to Cairo as a journalist in 1985. I felt the sting of censorship after I wrote an article for *The Economist* magazine about the Aga Khan's conference on urban planning in Cairo. In the article I had praised the government for revealing 'the rotten wood' of negligent urban planning. My fax to *The Economist* was seized by the Marriott Hotel's desk manager, who happened also to be a member of the *mukhabarat* (secret police). He promptly had me arrested for calling Egypt 'rotten wood'.

Although I had organized a press conference for the conference and was well connected, I did not wish to trouble my friends of the Aga Khan Foundation who were sipping coffee in the hotel and went happily to the police station, wearing jeans and a T-shirt and carrying no papers. The police muttered 'rotten wood' down the phone and ignored my attempts to explain and I was soon transferred by car to a dungeon beneath the *mukhabarat* headquarters, which I was to share for four hours with two frightened Palestinians. Rats squealed outside our door. At every point of my downward spiral that day I had heard the words 'rotten wood' repeated by each police group I was passed down to. So serious was my crime that nobody would listen to my protests although at midnight I was suddenly released through the intervention of the British ambassador. I was sorry to say goodbye to the Palestinians who had shared an orange with me and were lonely and frightened. They were also cautious with me when I spoke to them in Arabic, suspecting that I was a *mukhabarat* plant.

I returned to the Marriott to be welcomed by twenty friends at a great dinner to celebrate my release. It had all been an adventure for me but for Egyptians censorship is no joke at all. Alaa Hamed, a novelist and government tax official, was sacked and imprisoned in 1997 for publication of a book which a court judged immoral because it contained sexually explicit material. This followed years of harassment and summary imprisonment without sentence. The most absurd case had been in 1993 when the Egyptian Court of Appeal had ruled that the wife of Professor Nasr Hamid Abu Zayd must divorce him after he was judged to be an apostate from Islam for comments made in a book, and hence no longer allowed to be married to a Muslim woman, regardless of her wishes. Threatened with death for apostasy, the couple fled into exile in Europe.

In a further threat to liberties in Egypt which horrified liberals everywhere, on 30 June 2000 Dr Saad Eddin Ibrahim, a media-friendly political sociology professor at the American University in Cairo and head of the Ibn Khaldun Centre, a non-governmental organization, was arrested at gunpoint in his home in Cairo's Maadi suburb and held in police custody until his release in August. He was charged with 'spying for the USA', distributing propaganda, harming Egypt's reputation, voter registration fraud, international bribery and receiving foreign funds without government permission. All charges were widely considered to be entirely false. The national press launched a campaign of character assassination against him and despite support for him from the western press, Egyptian public opinion was persuaded that he was a western agent, a spy and a traitor. His real crime seems to have been forming an independent monitoring and observation team to assess the fairness of the then upcoming November 2000 parliamentary elections that President Mubarak was to win so overwhelmingly.

Attempts to please Egypt's puritan thought-police can have comic overtones. In Dr Nehad Selaiha's Arabic translation, Harold Pinter's four-scene play, *Mountain Language*, becomes a comedy of manners, says the Egyptian playwright Karim Alrawi. The word 'shit' is translated as 'shut up', 'shit-house' as 'dregs' and 'arse' as 'posterior'. Wherever possible the word 'fuck' is omitted entirely. 'She looks like a fucking intellectual' becomes 'I believe she associates with intellectuals, sons of dogs'. 'Can I fuck him? If I fuck him will everything be all right?' absurdly becomes 'Will this Mr Dokes lay with me? If he does, is everything all right?' This level on self-censorship, increasingly favoured in Egypt, entirely distorts the meaning of the play but it reflects an increasing trend in the Arabic and Islamic world today.[26] In British and Egyptian culture there are different levels of shockability. The Egyptian equivalent is as shocking to an Egyptian reader or audience as the British word is to a British audience. The use of the word 'fuck' in British publications is only forty years old. If an Arabic equivalent word had been used, the resonance of shockability would have been far greater and therefore not a valid translation.

Osama bin Laden's key advisers in his al-Qaida Organization were Dr Ayman al-Zawahri and Sheikh Taseer Abdullah, both Egyptian. Abdullah is reported to have said that he was hoping that his Islamic Jihad movement would forge an alliance with the Gama'a Islamiya led by Sheikh Omar 'Abd al-Raman, the blind Egyptian preacher jailed in America after being convicted for his role in the 1993 bombing of the World Trade Center. Another high-ranking Egyptian member is said to be Shawki al-Islambouli, a brother of the militant fundamentalist who assassinated President Sadat in 1981. The fact that most of bin Laden's closest people are Egyptian may reflect the extent of Egyptian President Mubarak's success in expelling his Islamic opponents. Bin Laden's eldest son married Sheikh Abdullah's daughter in February 2001. Muhammad Atta, the man US investigators suspect of having coordinated the 11 September 2001 attacks on New York and Washington, was also Egyptian. Significantly, Egyptian Islamists massacred 60 foreign tourists near Luxor in 1997.

It is in the realms of religion rather than politics that the deepest problems lie. Like the *fatwa*s against Salman Rushdie and against Taslima Nasrin in Bangladesh, absurdities such as the hounding of Abu Zayd are making a mockery of contemporary Islam. Some modern Muslim writers blame Salman Rushdie for sparking off the witch-hunt by so-called Islamists against writers. Suffice it to say that booksellers at book-fairs in the Arab world, in Cairo and Sharjah for example, but particularly in Kuwait, are seeing increasing numbers of their books banned. Even the great classical writers of the region like Jalal ad-Din Rumi are not immune. Copies of Rumi's Sufi poetry that had been displayed at the Sharjah book-fair were banned at the subsequent Kuwait book-fair in early 2001. The censor has to justify his or her job. The Arabic translator Peter Clark ran a British Council exhibition of British books in the Islamic World in 1988. Although the choice of books had been punctilious and cautious the censors withdrew two books after a long, painstaking search. They clearly had problems carrying out their task but would have been vulnerable had they censored no books at all.

Sensitivities go far beyond the era of the Prophet Muhammad since Muslims consider themselves heirs to the biblical tradition that started with the prophet Abraham (the Muslim Ibrahim). Mixing spoken word with music can be a satisfying way of bringing in the audiences, but it is not without its perils. The English oboist Jeremy Polmear contrasts his experience in London with a tour of the Gulf states.

> It was our very first concert with words. We were performing in a church, and Jenny Agutter moved into the pulpit for one item, Keith Waterhouse's witty parody of the story of Noah's Ark ('And the Lord said unto Noah, where is the Ark which I commanded thee to build? And Noah said unto the Lord, Verily, I have had three carpenters off sick ...'). There were three priests sitting in the front row. Were the next few minutes going to be deeply embarrassing? As it turned out they thought it very funny so everything was all right, but I realized that by adding words to our recitals we were entering a different world ... That same item did give us trouble later, on a tour of the Gulf States, where the authorities were not happy in spite of our contention that the satire was directed at English builders, not the Lord. So we took it out. As Billie Whitelaw, who was reading on that occasion, observed 'it's a good piece, but it's not worth a whipping'.[27]

Humour has been one of the first victims of censorship in Islamic society.

Both before and since the murder of Palestinian cartoonist Naji el-'Ali in 1987 many cartoonists around the world have been killed because of their work. On 2 July 1993, Asaf Koçak, a 34-year-old cartoonist, was burned to death in the city of Sivas in Turkey when thousands of Muslim fundamentalists staged a protest against 'progressive' artists participating in a festival. They set fire to their hotel. Koçak, a humanist who used his cartoons to fight illiteracy, exploitation, fundamentalism, torture and injustice, was one of thirty-six people killed.

In 1995 Guerrovi Brahim, a cartoonist for the pro-government Algerian daily *El Moudjahid*, was kidnapped and executed. Severe but lesser sanctions against cartoonists and those who publish them have included floggings and long terms of imprisonment. In 1992, Manouchehr Karimzadeh was sentenced by Iran's revolutionary court to fifty lashes, one year in prison and a fine of 500,000 rials for a cartoon the authorities claimed bore an unacceptably close resemblance to Ayatollah Khomeini. After he had served the sentence, he was retried and a further ten-year sentence was imposed; although he was quietly released after two years (see Chapter 5).

TWO

The Islamic World Confronts the Monster West

After the 1991 Gulf War I was invited by the European Commission to create and run a programme called Med Media, which was inspired by a dangerous breakdown in understanding between Europe and its mainly Arab neighbours. This breakdown was highlighted by the war, itself a mirror of centuries of misunderstanding and conflict between Islam and Christendom. As Europe draws together into an increasingly powerful union, Med Media aimed to reassure its increasingly vulnerable southern Mediterranean neighbours through the relationship between European Union (EU) and third country television, radio and newspaper networks. Med Media co-financed training projects, media workshops, media exchanges and television and radio co-productions.

The argument was that if economic unrest in countries like Algeria, Egypt and Turkey bred militant fundamentalism, unbalanced media coverage of such issues would itself inspire increasing bitterness rather than understanding. Today, we in the West only have to condemn the bombing of Iraq and the crippling sanctions we have imposed, or remind our leaders that one million Iraqis have died since the 1991 war, to provoke the pompous and irrelevant mantra that Saddam Hussein is an evil man. During that war 66,000 tonnes of bombs were dropped on Iraq and since the war 567,000 Iraqi civilians have died because of sanctions. Tens of thousands of Iraqis affected by the depleted uranium contained in a million allied shells dropped on Iraq are likely to contract cancer as a result. None of this can mask the horror of Saddam's regime. The execution on 15 March 1990 of the British-based freelance journalist Farzad Bazoft was a symbol of Baghdad's ghastly response to criticism. Bazoft had collected soil samples around a missile complex after an accident, hoping to shed light on Iraq's production of chemical weapons. His link with the UK's *Observer* newspaper did not save him.

During the early part of the Islamic revolution in neighbouring Iran I was strolling through the arched bazaars of the lovely Iranian town of Shiraz when

I glanced down at a pirated cassette of the anti-regime Islamic economist 'Ali Shariati. The cassette-seller looked up briefly and said quickly and bitterly, 'Shah ou-ra Kosht' (The Shah killed him). An imam was condemning the Shah within the nearby mosque, which had been surrounded by armoured cars. Earlier in the day a procession had been led through the streets by a man waving a bloodstained shirt. The government, it seemed, could put rings of steel around the mosques, but they could not stop word of mouth spreading by cassette sales. It was through the sale of these underground tapes that the Revolution was to take root. State-controlled media created an image of tranquillity and harmony, but the more people became disillusioned with what came from the state the faster they adopted the media of the underground.

From the emergence of audio cassette culture in the 1970s media superstars were made entirely on the basis of their output through cassettes. Indeed, many of these stars were never to be broadcast on the state media at all. As Haifaa Khalafallah explains in the journal *Index on Censorship*[1] banned films such as *Death of a Princess* (about the execution for adultery of a Saudi princess – see Chapter 12) and *Alexandria Why...?* were widely circulated in Saudi Arabia and the other Gulf states. The most popular films tended not to be those originally made for video but those that had attracted popular attention because they had been banned from public broadcasting.

The fame of the Egyptian singer Sheikh Imam Issa, who enjoyed a long partnership with the lyricist Fouad Najm, quickly surpassed that of other singers, and was regularly broadcast on hundreds of radio channels. From 1967 onwards the Imam–Najm duo became a magnate for oppositional culture in the Arab world. Under President Sadat the authorities tried hard to co-opt the duo but without success. In January 1969 they tried to plant hashish in his home. In May both men were taken to prison, beaten and put into a cell full of razor blades to encourage suicide. Their songs included lines like these:

> Toss the word into the dark shadow's womb
> So that Salma conceives and gives birth to light
> Which reveals our defects and burns us in flame
> Sting upon sting – we rise, stir and revel
> Circle around as you please, words, circle and spread.[2]

The Lebanese singer Marcel Khalifa popularized through audio cassettes songs stressing the need for Arab unity, social change and justice for women. The size of the audience of his 1981 Tunis concert – Beirut and Tunis were the only Arab cities in which he was permitted to perform in public[3] – was surpassed only by that of the extraordinary Egyptian phenomenon of the late Umm Kulthum.

During the 1960s Arabs from throughout the Arab world would tune into Nasser's speeches on the radio for hours on end but Nasser would never speak in public when she was performing. The young Umm Kulthum sang religious songs normally performed by males. She appeared dressed as a boy to avoid the disapproval her father could face for putting his daughter on stage. Other singers began to encourage Sheikh Ibrahim, her father, to move the family to Cairo, which was a centre of musical performance and commercial recording. Umm Kulthum adopted the modest yet rich and Europeanized dress of the wealthy Muslim ladies of the city. During the 1950s and 1960s she became a major cultural figure. She was passionately loyal to Nasser and, following Egypt's defeat in the 1967 war, launched a series of concerts to replenish the Egyptian treasury, beginning in Paris and continuing throughout the Arab world. When she died, she was called 'the voice and face of Egypt'.[4]

In September 1999 in Beirut Marcel Khalifa was accused of insulting Islam for incorporating lines from a Mahmoud Darwish poem based on verses from the Qur'an into a song he had recorded in 1995. An indictment was issued charging him with blasphemy. The original case had been filed in 1996 but the then Prime Minister, Rafiq al-Hariri, had ordered it to be dropped after widespread protests. Khalifa had responded 'whatever happens I will sing and sing and sing ... Nothing will close my mouth.' Ironically, his controversial lyrics were not about his own country at all. They were about the plight of the Arab peoples facing Israel. In 1999, most political and religious leaders in Lebanon, with the exception of the Sunni Mufti, attacked the charges and he was acquitted of them at the end of the year.

By the 1990s that astonishing breakthrough in communication, the Internet, was beginning to replace cassettes. Although Internet communication was launched in the 1960s as a tool of the US military that would operate even in the most severe nuclear war, it was not until after the US government opened it up to public use in the late 1980s that it became an indispensable form of communication for almost every household in developed countries. In 1995, there were some 56 million Internet users worldwide. By 2001 there were thought to be over 200 million. In many countries restrictions on the Internet have been imposed by governments in an attempt to limit the presence within their borders of information that they consider offensive or threatening. Besides this, large corporations control the development of the industry, again leaving developing countries submissive and in the cold. These obstacles block the free flow of information and the ability of individuals to benefit from the enormous potential of the Internet as a source of efficient, fast and democratic communication.

In December 1998 the Arab States Broadcasting Union (ABSU) rejected the membership application of the Qatari satellite television channel al-Jazeera, which was to become internationally famous after 11 September 2001, when it angered Arab countries by serving as a forum for opposition figures, according to the Egyptian newspaper *al-Akhbar*, but gave it six months 'to conform with the Arab media code of honour,' which 'promotes brotherhood between Arab nations'. However, many see such behaviour as an attempt to hold back the tide. The United Arab Emirates Information Minister, Sheikh Abdullah bin Zayed al-Nahayan, predicted in April 2000 that press censorship in the Gulf world would come to an end within five years because of increased Internet usage. 'You must examine the impact of staggering development and the growth of information technology on the laws on publications in the region,' he told a meeting of editors-in-chief of Gulf newspapers. 'Personally, I foresee an almost total collapse of censorship laws in five years. In five years, there will be more than 25 million Internet users in the Arab world ... In the face of this, censorship laws will become useless and ineffective.'[5]

At present, newspapers published in the six Gulf Cooperation Council (GCC) countries exercise a form of self-censorship, carefully avoiding issues linked to religion, moral issues or members of the region's ruling families. Media standards are often deplorable. But the sudden emergence of global technology has created a huge gap between old methods and new. Even Saudi Arabia has been unable to block use of the Internet while satellite dishes allow easy access to hundreds of international television channels.

Modern technology aside, disgust with the West and with the humiliations endured by developing countries not only encouraged censorship in the Islamic countries but it forced people to look elsewhere in their search for the truth. In her book *Islam and Democracy* the Moroccan sociologist Fatima Mernissi writes: 'The West that we believed to be anaesthetized by its luxury and libertinism opened up to emotions forgotten since the humanizing wave of 1968. An unforeseen Europe flashed onto Arab television screens: "*Kafir* [infidel] and humanist. Allah is Great", murmured 'Ali, one eye on his shoes, the other on the screen.' Mernissi describes the period following the crumbling of Berlin's '*hijab*' [veil, symbolising the 'wall'] just before the bombing of Baghdad in 1991 when Europeans

emerged from the Arab masses as promoters of the democratic credo... And then the powerful wave of universal hope raised by Europeans songs to freedom and the promise to condemn violence was rudely and brutally dashed by this war ...What they [nonplussed Arab masses] saw on their television screens was the appearance of another breed they had forgotten about ... old generals with kepis and medals just like those of the colonial army, generals who enumerated with pride the tons of bombs they had dropped on Baghdad. At moments of political crisis the whole merchant quarter of Suq al-Sabat comes to a halt around the televisions and the radios. [She quotes the merchant 'Ali saying] 'But the Americans with their machines – it's like the movies! Except that – God help us – it is our brothers who are the target. I have nightmares. My wife forbids me to look at the TV.'[6]

Modern Islamic figures are usually conscious of the need to pay lip-service to human rights and freedom of speech even if only in recognition that the international community demands this, but more traditional opposition to established authority can be considered *fitna* (sedition), a serious crime in Islam, and repressed in the name of the Islamic *umma*. During his short exile in Paris in 1978 Ayatollah Khomeini reassured a western journalist that 'an Islamic Republic is a democratic state in the true sense of the word ... everyone ... can voice their own opinion ... and the Islamic state will respond with logic to all the arguments put forward'.[7] It looked like a wonderful start for the new Iran but a year later he had changed his mind dramatically and made his views on criticism chillingly clear:

The clog-wearer and the turbaned have given you a chance. After each revolution several thousand of these corrupt elements are executed in public and burnt and the story is over. They are not allowed to publish newspapers. After so long the October Revolution still has no newspaper, except [the newspaper the state] wants. We will close all parties except the one, or a few, which act in a proper manner ...We all made mistakes. We thought we were dealing with human beings. It is evident we are not. We are dealing with wild animals. We will not tolerate them any more.[8]

This was a far cry from the much-admired 1906 constitution of Iran which guaranteed freedom of publication and the press and which had inspired many young, liberal Iranians to support Khomeini's revolution. Ironically, there is in fact no censorship of the press *per se* in Iran today but the Ministry of Culture and Guidance will happily prosecute and close down newspapers that publish articles that blaspheme. Under Article 513 of the criminal code, for example, insulting the Twelfth Imam, whose return to earth to usher in a period of perfect justice is awaited by pious Muslims, carries a possible death sentence. The Iranian Constitution proclaims that 'publications and the press are free to publish their ideas unless they are injurious to the founders of Islam or public rights' and 'freedom of publicity and propaganda in the Mass Media (radio and television) shall be insured on the basis of Islamic principles'. These controls spawned much protest and this came to a head in the student demonstrations of the summer of 1999. Students and intellectuals calling for basic freedoms were part of a development that had started with the constitutional revolution in 1906 and reached its high point in 1979. It could not be shrugged off. It should be borne in mind that even before the constitutional revolution the Qajar shahs had ruled 'by permission of the clergy'.

In early 2000 Arab film-makers were calling for the lifting of most forms of censorship and for the creation of an Arab version of Hollywood to boost the declining film industry and raise standards. The appeals came as Bahrain staged its first Arab film festival in April of that year. Film-makers told the press that censorship of films had to be reduced to give actors the opportunity to express their feelings. Without government support, the cinema industry in the Arab world – and the Gulf, in particular – would never grow, they believed. Los Angeles-based director Mustafa al-Aqqad called for the creation of a Hollywood-style production studio to give Arab cinema much needed encouragement. There was no lack of artistic ability, but what international films needed were an international language and advanced technology, he told the *Gulf Daily News*. 'The only problem would be that there are a lot of restrictions. There will be religious and social restrictions and those concerning the appearance of women on the big screen,' he added. 'I don't believe that funding would be a problem if officials and society became convinced of the importance of cinema as a means of entertainment, enlightenment and development.' Aqqad is known for his Hollywood-style, big-budget productions.

Nevertheless, like other forms of media in modern 'Islamic' societies, cinema has usually been used for propaganda purposes. The Iraqi press was never slow to put its own wretched case to anyone who would listen, particularly when sanctions imposed by the West began to lose their support. To celebrate, in January 2001, the tenth anniversary of the Gulf War, one of Iraq's most famous film-makers Abdul Salam al-Adhami made an epic film, *Hafr al-Batm*, using Iraqi soldiers as extras. *Hafr al-Batm* tells the story of a unit of Baghdadi conscripts who are buried alive by Allied troops. Al-Adhami was inspired by a CNN documentary in which US soldiers admitted bulldozing trenches full of surrendering soldiers during the rapid Allied advance into Kuwait. The film also showed British soldiers shooting dead Iraqi prisoners of war. 'My film will set the record straight,' he told the *Guardian* newspaper. 'I am proud to have been born here in the heart of the Arab homeland. Now it is time to tell the story of how we won the struggle.'[9]

But one cannot dispute the fact that the development of cinema can be a good yardstick from which to judge the development of a national ideology. Rose Issa and Sheila Whitaker's collection of essays, *Life and Art*,[10] on the subject illustrates this well. After the revolution Iranian cinema was accused of acting as a Pahlavi agent of western cultural imperialism. In August 1978 nearly 400 spectators perished in a deliberate fire in Abadan's Rex Cinema. By the time the Islamic government was installed the following January 180 cinemas nationwide had been destroyed (probably by Savak). During the first four years of the revolution some 513 films (mostly from the West) out of 898 foreign films were banned. Likewise, of 2,208 locally produced films 1,956 were denied exhibition permits. Nudity today is totally forbidden. Markers simply blocked off offensive parts of the female body when cutting confuses the narrative. Men are forbidden to look at women's hair and women are obliged to cover it.

Looking at sexual organs is condemned, whether directly, through a mirror or reflected in water (or, by extension, in the cinema). As one of Iran's most prominent directors, Dariush Mehrjui, remarked:

> In post-revolutionary cinema the religiously unlawful (*haram*) look does not exist. Women must be treated like one's own sister. Entertainers, actors and film makers were professionally liquidated. Film makers were threatened or arrested or simply fled the country. Sex, song and dance were omitted. There were constant references to religious topics, to the oppression by masters, to the rebellion of the oppressed against cruelty and to the fight against monarchic traditions.[11]

In a chapter in *Life and Art*, Hamid Naficy notes that although the 1982 regulations governing modesty condemn the use of women as commodities or as objects aimed at arousing sexual desires, in reality their role has been in constant flux. Immediately after the revolution came a period of self-censorship or the avoidance of using women in films at all. Women were housewives or mothers. Women were shown covering themselves even in front of close relatives. When women moved they had to show as little of their contours as possible. They had to be given static parts and avoid showing bodies below the head. A post-revolutionary film director underlined these practices, says Naficy, by saying that women in Islamic performing arts should be shown seated at all times so as to avoid drawing attention to their 'provocative walk', thereby allowing the audience to concentrate on the 'ideologies' inherent in the work.[12]

For the first six years after the revolution it was impossible to give a genuine portrayal of women.

Children were to play a key role in early post-revolutionary films in Iran. According to Hamid Naficy children were sometimes stand-ins for men in romantic stories, while male bonding itself was sometimes used to replace relations between men and women when even the woman's gaze had to be averted. *In Noqteh-e Za'f* (The Weak Point, 1983) directed by Muhammad Reza Alami, the relationship between a political activist and the security agent who captures him displays strong but deeply ambiguous sexual undercurrents in an Islamic society which severely punishes homosexuality or cross-dressing. Naficy notes that in the film the two men interact in 'boy-meets-girl-falls-in-love' formula films. They play soccer, passing the ball back and forth like two lovers. At the beach they sit side-by-side, gazing at the horizon while a wild horse gallops by and romantic music sets the scene.

We are now reaching the third phase of Iranian cinema, says Naficy, when women are beginning to play a strong part in leading roles as actresses and directors. Before the revolution Shahal Riahi was the only woman director of a feature film. Today there are a dozen women directors. In her early films Riahi shows women confined to the home to the extent that men are sent out to shop but in later films the women are strong and charismatic in contrast with the men who are weak. The *chador* (headscarf) in cinema was defended as not merely blocking the penetrating gaze of men. It was also seen as allowing women to use their own gaze 'judiciously'. Not easily controllable or subject to religious curfew, glances, even averted glances, became the most complicated and meaningful methods of communication between men and women.

After the Revolution women were portrayed as background figures at first. The 'averted look' technique was espoused; women were only filmed from a discreet side angle and did not look into the eye of the camera. But as time went on the averted look became more focused, sometimes charged with sexual desires. In 1982 the Farabi Cinema Foundation had been established as part of the Ministry of Islamic Culture and Moral Guidance to control the import and export of films and encourage the home-grown industry. Nevertheless, this has also helped to shake up the system and encourage film production to shoot up.

When the 1999 Cannes Film Festival awarded the Palme d'Or, its highest honour, to Abbas Kiarostami's *Taste of Cherry* the response was electric. The film's public debut had enjoyed standing ovations both before and after screening. It was the first time that the Palme d'Or had ever been given to Iran. Because the film concerned a man contemplating suicide, a taboo subject in Islam, it was forbidden a showing in Iran and was at first denied a permit to leave the country. But the Islamic Republic evidently soon realized that its film industry was an important asset that must not be sacrificed. Nevertheless, a polite kiss for Catherine Deneuve soon upset Kiarostami's home country. A strong fundamentalist reaction ensured that there was no welcoming reception when he returned home. He was whisked through Customs by a side door.

The emergence of satellite dishes is beginning to revolutionize the market and will have a big impact on government control; all depends on the direction that the liberalizing policies of Khatami's reform programme will take.

In the nineteenth century the great calls for Arab liberation from Ottoman domination during what is known as the 'Liberal Age' had come from intellectuals in Syrian towns like Aleppo. That enlightened period was a far cry from Syria's recent history when its media were almost entirely muzzled until the wind of change started with the death of President Asad in 2000. The partial lifting of censorship under his son Bashar was a much less frightening experience than the new government, always fearful of uprisings, had expected. When I launched the EU's Med Media Programme in 1991 the Syrian ambassador in London hesitated before giving me a visa, but when I pointed out that Syria should not remain out in the cold when its neighbours where all involved in the programme, he quickly relented and the Syrians from that moment onwards gave Med Media their fullest support. Syrian journalists who had never had to question anything before attended Med Media-financed seminars in London given by the maverick Gulf War correspondent John Simpson, the BBC Director-General John Birt and aggressive investigative journalists. They were even able to work discretely alongside Israeli journalists since Syria was preparing to negotiate Israel's possible withdrawal from the Golan Heights. It was clear that Syria was testing the waters of new media freedom through our programme.

But it has a long way to go. In her book *God has Ninety-nine Names* the American journalist Judith Miller notes some ambiguity in Syria's relationship with its writers. When the poet 'Ali Kanaan reads his poem 'Shards' to friends in Damascus in 1992 he reaches the line 'The king is made of glass, his castles are of clay. But in the henhouse, rights are luxuries.' When Miller asks him if the king refers to Asad the room falls silent. But he later confides to her that the poem is a protest against his own 'crime of silence' about government outrages. It had been refused publication in Syria, but was performed in Tunisia. A man she describes as 'Syria's Woody Allen', the comedian Duraid Lahham, tells Miller that his scriptwriter avoids censorship by the stratagem of criticizing previous regimes – 'our own regimes think they look good in comparison' – and by never mentioning venues.

All of my signs, streets, and names are fictitious ... I called the star of one of my films ArabCarlo: in *Borders*, a film about a young Arab who loses his passport and is trapped between two 'brotherly' Arab countries, the countries are called Eaststan, Westan, Norstan etc. ... I called the Arab League Allstan. Because there is so much corruption and tyranny in the Arab word, audiences in each country invariably believed my film to be about them.[13]

Sadallah Wannous's play *The Elephant or Lord of Ages* is clearly an attack on Syria's former president, Hafez al-Asad, and his police state. But when Peter Clark put this to a Syrian, the latter replied: 'It was written in 1969 so is not about Asad or his regime.' Clark's English translation was put on in 1997 in Damascus. Foreigners, Clark told me, were astonished by the daring of the words. It was another example, Clark noted, of 'licensed' or 'co-opted' art.

In Bahrain the censors insisted Lahham delete a line from his play *Wildflowers*. The offending passage referred, typically, to the relationship between God and Man in Islam. It was banned. Lahham is disparaging about Syrian media professionals. He told Miller, 'They outdo each other in poetic obsequiousness. One television producer shows five minutes of the president, so the next shows seven minutes the next night; the third fifteen minutes, and so on.' Mamduh Udwan, the Alawi playwright had had three plays banned in Syria and none published there. 'Anything but yes-men' he told Miller, 'are considered opposition. If you stick to what's allowed, you have no problems. But then again, you have no theatre.'[14]

Sadallah Wannous told Miller that Syrian officials tolerated some of his more critical work because it enabled them to show the West that Syrians enjoyed freedom of expression. 'My very existence is propaganda,' he told her. She had first met him in early 1992 after Syrian censors had banned his play *The Rape*. 'Do you know that *al-Thawra* and *al-Baath* newspapers are barred from even publishing my name?' he told her. 'Like Israel, I am an abstraction.' Miller notes that *The Rape*'s political sin was that it contained a sympathetic and hopeful dialogue between Wannous and an anti-Zionist Israeli psychiatrist. But she can't help noting that 'even he could not bring himself to create a sympathetic Jew who believed in Israel's right to exist'.[15]

In Saudi Arabia the media have barely advanced or liberalized at all. The Saudi rulers have been able to use their undreamed-of wealth to offer the people a new compact. Saudi Arabia produces almost nine million barrels a day, well over twice as much as Iran produces, and accounts for some 15 per cent of world supplies. As the *Guardian*'s David Hirst put it, 'modern forms of material wellbeing, development, education, lavish welfare services – in return for a complete surrender of modern forms of political participation'.[16] But lavish spending and corruption have instituted this compact. A London-based opposition publicist Saad Faqih calculates that 40 per cent of Saudi Arabia's national revenues find their way into Saud family pockets. 'This is a land of silence, a culture of silence,' a diplomat told Judith Miller. 'As the Saudis say, "Not everything known is said." Sins like corruption or sources of shame – suicide, mental illness, or AIDS – are all hidden away, discussed openly among themselves but rarely with strangers.'[17]

The environment in the Gulf differs considerably from the countries around the Mediterranean basin with predominantly Islamic cultures. These countries have, to a certain extent, mirrored developments in Europe but censorship is an ever-ready weapon in the hands of regimes to defend the state and the regime. Med Media had acted as a watchdog against censorship and an insurance against the manipulation of the media in the countries of the Near East and North Africa. After it was frozen by Brussels for internal political reasons the Palestinian media was soon muzzled by Arafat and his circle through financial manipulation and, if necessary, through violence. Hafez al-Barghouti's brave Ramallah-based newspaper *al-Hayat al-Jadida* (New Life) investigated taboo subjects such as child abuse and rape but was soon neutralized when Arafat bought it and made it an official organ of the Palestinian Authority (PA). Even Radwan Abu Ayyash, the chairman of the Palestinian Broadcasting Corporation (PBC), with whom we had worked exclusively on audio-visual projects, was soon having to defer to Arafat's faithful servant in Gaza, Hisham Mekke, a good networker with few media credentials who was to be assassinated in January 2001 by opponents who were accusing him of corruption.

The extremely popular and attractive young radio and television presenter Daniella Khalaf, whose radio talk shows broadcast from Ramallah allowed ordinary Palestinians to discuss their most intimate problems, decided not to return to the station after being temporarily expelled for allowing criticism of the brutality of the Palestinian security forces at Nablus's An-Najah University. Half Italian and the linchpin of Palestinian radio, she was no newcomer to suffering. Her father, when mayor of Ramallah, had had part of his foot blown off by right-wing Israeli terrorists. A deep believer in peace and understanding, however, she bore no bitterness. When I brought a young Israeli film-maker to visit the PBC in 1995 Daniella devoted most of the day to showing her Israeli visitor around the station.

Our initial anxiety was the threat from censorship and governmental opposition to the Med Media programme. When I visited Radio Nederland in Hilversum I was advised to bring top media professionals together into an initial seminar project in order to reassure them and their governments before the other, more daring projects began. It was a way of pre-empting censorship and it worked. But there were to be many disappointments. In Gaza I arranged a meeting with Chairman Arafat to explain the purpose of Med Media. Accompanied by Robert Krieg, a young German who had virtually created Radio Palestine through his Med Media-funded training programme and by Ola Tabari, a Palestinian actress and star of another Med Media project, Eli Sulayman's avant-garde *A Postponed Drama of Return*, we reached the beach-side villa at one in the morning. Within half an hour of haggling we were ushered into the Chairman's long office as all his advisers but Nabil Sha'th, his most prominent adviser, were ordered out.

Seated beside Arafat, I respected protocol and waited for him to speak. After some minutes Sha'th advised me to explain my mission. In simple English I explained that one of Med Media's goals was to lure back the stars of the Palestinian Diaspora to create a renaissance in the new Palestine. He did not look up from the faxes he was thumbing through. After ten minutes, on the point of standing up and taking a bitter leave, I mentioned the word 'television'. Arafat suddenly looked up, beaming. 'Television. Tell me more', he said. I turned to my colleague, Krieg, who described how the new television station would function and we were soon being photographed alongside a beaming Arafat. With profound disappointment I understood from that meeting that television for Arafat was merely a symbol of political power. His subsequent clamp-down on press and television was to support my fears. For all the wrong reasons Med Media was suddenly accepted.

In 2000 I visited the six GCC countries to study the possibility of emulating the Med Media formula. Eurogulf Media – not its real name – might be launched with a project on western media coverage of Islam and the Islamic and Arabic World, perhaps a seminar held by the Kuwait News Agency in Kuwait and led by GCC scholars and editors aimed at fifteen EU provincial editors from EU countries. The project would consider issues such as 'Is the West prejudiced against Islam and the Islamic and Arabic World?' focusing on the Crusades, the Reconquest of Spain in 1492, the creation of Israel in 1948 and the 1990–1 Gulf war. I soon discovered to what extent the GCC region felt neglected and bitter. Global communications are causing a serious tension between the old world of the media and the new. People expect dramatic changes, particularly in Saudi Arabia, over the coming years.

Locals in the Gulf are unwilling, on balance, to be newspaper reporters at all, while English language newspapers are usually edited by foreigners from the Indian sub-continent. It is their responsibility to write important editorials on behalf of peoples they barely know. As one Christian Indian editor who had only been in the Gulf for six months told me: 'They believe that they have independence but it is I who writes in my editorials what they are supposed to think on important political and cultural topics.' Besides this, GCC media professionals want local customs to be understood. The Gulf 'Honour Code', for example, may appear to a European journalist as a form of censorship but locals do not like to criticize top people in their countries because they are all linked by blood ties. The media in the Gulf remains dominated by the traditional Egyptian system of *taqlid* ('imitation'; the basing of legal decisions on the existing judgements of the four Sunni *madhabs* or schools of jurisprudence, but here meaning 'old-fashioned' and 'inefficient') by the locals. However, the sudden emergence of global technology has created a huge gap between the old methods and the new. It has been unable to block use of the Internet and satellite dishes allow access to international television channels.

While national broadcasting in Gulf countries tends to be wooden and dull, focusing on the comings and goings of rulers and government apparatchiks, anything from CNN to pornography is easily available anywhere. Censorship tends to amount to severe self-censorship. The Saudi Minister of the Interior, Prince Naif ibn 'Abd al-Aziz, told a Kuwaiti newspaper in 1985, 'As for freedom of speech for our newspapers, there are no written orders not to publish this or that, we have no censorship. Censorship comes only after publication.'

Nevertheless, Qatar's al-Jazeera Television (set up in Qatar in 1996 as the first Arab satellite channel specialising in news and discussion groups) has created a revolution of its own. It is run by Arab expatriates, many from the BBC after the BBC Arabic Service Television closed down when the Saudi-controlled Orbit refused to broadcast the words of the Saudi political dissident al-Masari's criticism of the Saudi regime in 1995. Al-Jazeera is highly professional and excels in controversial, adversarial talk-shows which some believe go beyond the limits of good, objective journalism. All Gulf Arabs switch on to al-Jazeera at the expense of local channels, which they will only watch for local news. Al-Jazeera has put Qatar on the map and although other Arab governments frequently withdraw their ambassadors in anger, other media organs are trying to copy al-Jazeera, above all Abu Dhabi Television which was set up at the same time.

'The Opposite Direction' on Tuesdays is al-Jazeera's television blockbuster, said to be the most controversial programme in the region. Two opposing figures debate (often acrimoniously) issues and answer viewers' questions. Such behaviour was unheard of in the region before. 'Top Secret' on the first Thursday of each month is investigative broadcast journalism dealing with issues veiled in official or private secrecy. Although censorship among the GCC states is widespread, self-censorship has become the order of the day. In Qatar censorship was lifted entirely in 1995 but along with this came a drastic reduction of government subsidies. A key victim was the once famed QANA news agency.

Specialist journalism barely exists. There does not appear to be a single expert on oil, gas or stock markets throughout the region. Bloomberg- or Reuters-training in these issues would be imperative. However, the GCC countries argue that the role of women in the media is improving. Even in Saudi Arabia where there is strict segregation and women may not drive, there are more female than male PhD holders, while in Kuwait, Bahrain and the other Gulf states women play important roles everywhere. Peter Clark was once told by an HSBC banker that private deposits in Gulf banks are larger for women than for men. Shari'a law guarantees women rights to possess money and women waste much less than men on wild living.

Good examples of successful Gulf women film-makers are Nujum Alghanem at Abu Dhabi Television, Lamia al-Humaidhy at the Kuwait News Agency (KUNA), Zawan al-Said, a private film-maker and cousin of Sultan Qaboos in Oman and Noura Sakkaf in Saudi Arabia (partly in London). A few good children's magazines are published in the region but much help is needed. *al-Majed* children's magazine in Kuwait seems outstanding but it is entirely run and edited by South Asians because locals regard it as beneath their dignity to write for children.

THREE

Islamic Tolerance and the Seeds of Despair

Jordan's Prince Hasan likes to tell the parable surrounding Vasco da Gama's arrival in 1498 on India's Malabar coast which was then ruled by a Jain king (the Jains will not kill any living creature). Da Gama ordered the king to expel or kill the region's many Jews. 'What is "kill"?', replied the puzzled king promptly.

> When the existence of the Church is threatened, she is released from the commandments of morality. With unity as the end, the use of every means is sanctified, even cunning, treachery, violence, simony, prison, death. For all order is for the sake of the community, and the individual must be sacrificed for the common good.
>
> (Dietrich von Nieheim, Bishop of Verden,
> *De Schismati Libri* III, 1411)

In his moving book *The Road to Mecca*, the Austrian Jewish convert to Islam, Muhammad Asad, describes himself seated in a snowbound hut of Afghanistan's Hindu Kush with villagers singing ballads, playing a lute and preparing coffee and a narguileh pipe. He suddenly bursts into a tirade against the hypocrisy and badness of many Muslims, saying 'And you are many, but your faith is small.' When he ends there is only the sound of the wind on the desert. His host, the hakim, pulls his sheepskin coat about him. After a long, long pause he turns to Asad and says quietly 'But – you are a Muslim' and after a pause, again, 'No, it is as I have said: you are a Muslim, only you don't know it yourself.'

I had much the same reaction from Muhammad al-Wazir, a Yemeni publisher and grandson of a former Imam of Yemen, when I spent several months with his family in Jeddah. In his view there should be no censorship in Islam and Shari'a punishments were all but impossible because in the true Islamic republic crime would not exist. 'What you see here is hypocrisy. True Islam can only come from the roots.'

Beneath the underlying Islamophobia that the West has adopted since the Berlin Wall fell in 1989 we know that Islam has always by its very essence been a tolerant religion, recognizing as it does the prophetic traditions of Judaism and Christianity. In the eleventh century the Crusaders, urged forward by Pope Urban II's crusader sermon on a hillside at Clermont, would descend on Syria and Palestine like odious birds of prey, at one stage of hunger roasting on spits (claims Stephen Runciman) the children of their Muslim vanquished.[2] According to most sources, when they took Jerusalem in 1099 they waded knee-deep in blood to the Holy Sepulchre to rejoice and sing their Te Deums. According to one chronicler the piles of Muslim dead were 'almost as high as the houses'. The synagogue in which the city's Jews were sheltering was set on fire to burn them alive while 'full of happiness and weeping with joy' the Crusaders went into the church. Before this massacre two Muslims had emerged from besieged Caesarea and approached the Patriarch and the Legate and asked them: 'Lords, you who are masters and doctors of the Christian law, why do you command your people to kill us, to invade our country, when it is written in your religion that no one must kill anyone who is in the image of your God, or carry off his goods?' The Patriarch replied: 'As to murder, we reply that he who fights to destroy the law of God must be killed in just vengeance.'[3] Christ had admonished his followers to love their enemies, the Crusaders, it seems, to exterminate them.

Islam had first come to the region with gestures of empathy and respect. When in 638 the Caliph Omar was guided through Jerusalem by the patriarch Sophronius, Omar refused to pray at the Anastasis, the place of the death and resurrection of Christ, for fear that if he had prayed at Christian shrines Muslims would have converted them into Islamic places of worship. When eventually he built his mosque it was on what Jews call the Temple Mount, the platform built by Herod for the Jewish temple. 'Once the Christians had surrendered', writes Karen Armstrong, 'there was no killing, no destruction of property, no burning of rival religious symbols, no expulsions or expropriations, and no attempt to force the inhabitants to embrace Islam.'[4]

There is an *aya* in the Qur'an which suggests that freedom is greatly cherished in Islam: 'O you who believe! If a miscreant comes to you with any news, ascertain the truth thereof, lest you harm people unwittingly and afterwards be filled with remorse for what you have done.' (Qur'an 49:6)

So the seeds of Islam's theoretical tolerance but increasing actual intolerance today lie in its populist, all-inclusive nature. Barbarians at the gates of the

Islamic world only had to proclaim: 'There is no god but God: Muhammad is the Prophet of God' to become Muslim. They could then promptly join the Islamic *umma* with all their cultural baggage. This openness led to an explosion of cultural energy but with this energy came also intense political instability. At times in Islam's confusing relationship with Christianity roles of tolerance and intolerance were reversed, the intolerance of the al-Muwahidun (Almohad) invaders of Spain in the twelfth century having an unexpected effect. The more intelligent of the Jewish and Mazarabic communities with their high intellectual traditions fled into Christian territory where they were welcomed by the enlightened sovereigns of Castille and Aragon. Among them were the Muslim Ibn Rushd (Averroes) and the Jewish Maimonedes. Alfonso VI was to encourage the Jews of Toledo by getting them to translate from Arabic into Latin the sciences of the ancient world.[5] Nevertheless, so culturally superior was the Spanish Islamic world that bishops complained that their flock spoke in Arabic rather than Latin. This linguistic mix was to lead to the creation of the highly refined Mudejar style of architecture in Andalusia. Europe, cut off from its classical roots by the barbarian invasions, fed off Arabic translations of Greek science and philosophy. Western philosophers and scientists have often ignored the debt they owed to Arab pioneers.

To the east of the Islamic world the *coup de grâce* of the Mughal Empire and its replacement by the British Empire was the Indian Mutiny of 1857. The enlightened Emperor Akbar's eccentric and experimental *Din Illahi* (Religion of God) aroused the hope of Jesuit monks he called to Agra that he was about to become a Christian. Always liberal-minded, he abolished the pilgrim tax at the holy city of Matura as well as the *jizya* tax imposed on People of the Book. After a revolt by the orthodox, he devoted himself to an eclectic cult influenced by Zoroastrianisn and centred on himself. If he was the first Muslim ruler to gain the genuine loyalty of his Hindu subjects, to modern-day Islamic fundamentalists – and many other Muslims, too – he was a pragmatist-apostate who appealed to Christian anti-Islamic sentiment rather than a forward-looking idealist.

The extreme enlightenment of his grandson Dara Shikoh was to frighten many Muslims and thus provoke the usurpation of the throne by his fundamentalist brother Aurangzeb and the ultimate downfall of the Mughal Empire. Hindus had been accepted as *dhimmi*s (people under the protection of the covenant) despite their multitude of deities. Some would even argue that Hinduism is monotheist, given the debate about primal creation in the Rig-Veda, and that gods and goddesses were merely manifestations of the one Brahma, but such arguments found no favour with the fundamentalists. Aurangzeb had his brother humiliated and brutally executed but he understood on his deathbed forty years later that he had sown the seeds of destruction. He realized too late something that Akbar and Dara Shikoh had understood full well, that if the Mughals lost the loyalty of their Hindu subjects they would lose India. A synthesis of the two religions through Sufism, personified by the poet Kabir, and the Bakhti movement in India had preceded Akbar and Dara Shikoh's liberalism but the hard-line fundamentalists would win in the end, and the long-term results of their efforts were the horrors of Partition and the bloody creation of Pakistan in 1948.

FOUR

A Satanic Mess

The death sentence is a necessary and efficacious means for the Church to attain its ends when rebels against it disturb the ecclesiastical unity, especially obstinate heretics who cannot be restrained by any other penalty from continuing to disturb ecclesiastical order.

(Pope Leo XIII, Gioacchino Pecci, *Book of Canon Law*,
Preface, Volume 2, M. de Luca, Society of Jesus, 1901.)

I inform the proud Muslim people of the world that the author of the *Satanic Verses* book which is against Islam, the Prophet and the Qur'an, and all involved in its publication who were aware of its content, are sentenced to death.

(Ayatollah Ruhollah Khomeini, 1989.)

In western eyes today, the issue of censorship in Islamic societies is linked with the *Satanic Verses* saga. Rushdie refuted the accusation of apostasy because, he pointed out, 'I have never in my adult life affirmed any belief, and what one has not affirmed one cannot be said to have apostasized from.' However, his very public celebration in September 1998 of Iran's dissociation from the late Ayatollah Khomeini's *fatwa* calling for his execution stung Iran's hardliners and their followers in Pakistan and Britain. Nothing, they said, could remove the *fatwa*, a legal ruling made by Khomeini in his role of *mujtahid*, a respected Islamic jurist who has the authority to interpret the Qur'an through independent reasoning (*ijtihad*). It seemed, therefore, that Rushdie's safety would always now remain at risk from freelance fanatics.

Even Iran's liberal President Muhammad Khatami during his visit to the Pope in 1999, on hearing that Turin University had awarded Rushdie an honorary doctorate that March, told the Italian newspaper *La Republica* that he was 'profoundly displeased' that such encouragement should be given to 'a man who has offended the sentiments and religious beliefs of more than one billion people of Muslim faith'. Rushdie had, effectively, stepped into a political minefield. The so-called 'Satanic Verses' of the Qur'an were condemned by a later revelation to the Prophet as having been inspired by Satan. There was nothing new in Rushdie's novel published in 1988, apart from the level of mockery he had used against the religion of his birth at a time when, in 1989, the Islamic revolution in Iran was in retreat and vulnerable.

In Bangladesh the 32-year old gynaecologist and writer Taslima Nasrin fell foul of the fundamentalist lobby after the banning in July 1993 of her book *Lajja* (Shame). Apart from the political content of the novel, much of what she wrote was considered too sexually explicit. In one of her poems, for example, a man was depicted as a cockroach invading her vagina. *Lajja* studies Muslim reprisals against Hindus after the 450-year old Babri mosque in Ayodha was destroyed by Hindu fundamentalists in 1992. She became the darling of Hindu militants seeking an excuse to attack India's Muslim minority. She was uncompromising about her attitude to Islamic fundamentalists. 'They demanded my execution by hanging ... They have decreed a *fatwa* against me and set a price on my head ... My crime was that I said the religious scriptures are out of place, out of time ... I am convinced that the only way the fundamentalist forces can be stopped is if all of us who are secular and humanist join and fight their malignant influence. I, for one, will not be silenced.'[2] Although Bangladesh has no specific law against blasphemy, its many self-appointed guardians of the faith were only too eager to respond to her advocacy of sexual freedom and her attacks on male dominance.

Today daily newspapers in the Islamic arena confront an even greater challenge than novelists. Editors of Arab newspapers in London face a dilemma whose solution is usually self-censorship. Indeed, the introduction of this form of censorship has brought great rewards to the censorship departments. It enjoys the sort of advantage that subtle forms of psychological torture have over more traditional forms. When the editor is given the responsibility to censor himself he is inclined to exaggerate his new, undefined responsibility. Commercial considerations, too, are as important to the Islamic world as they are in the West. Jihad al-Khazen, publisher of *al-Hayat* newspaper based in Beirut and London, is open about his own position. 'We cannot afford to lose advertising sponsored by Saudi Arabia', he told me, 'so we have to be careful not to offend the Saudis. With Sudan we can be much freer as Sudan has so little money.' He says that he receives avalanches of letters from literate fundamentalists. He notes the irony that you can watch the film *Basic Instinct* unexpurgated in a Jeddah five-star hotel but that in magazines in Saudi Arabia women's cleavages are painted over by the censor.

Perhaps it is not as simple as that and Arabic translator Peter Clark repudiates such polarization. He believes that the Islamic world and the West are both many-faceted concepts and are intimately entwined; Rushdie, Arab banks in London, British Muslims, US Muslims in Mecca, the Arabic-English translations industry, children growing up with mixed parentage, are all part of a growing cultural merge.

Khazen believes that Islam must be interpreted as intelligently as it was by the Prophet's followers, noting that when Muhammad asked them to organize a doubtful military manoeuvre before the final confrontation with the Meccan merchants, the battle of Badr, they asked 'Is this revelation or your own opinion?' When the Prophet admitted that it was his own opinion they ignored it, convinced that it was the wrong military tactic.

FIVE

Iran's Media Frenzy

In July 1981 Said Soltanpour, an Iranian poet who had been imprisoned many times under the Shah, was executed in Tehran. His books of poems included *Keta-e Avazhe-ye band* (Book of Ballads from Gaol). His last play was called *Koshtargah* (Slaughterhouse). After his arrest the Soltanpour Committee was set up in Paris to campaign for his release. Two years before the Revolution he recited his poems to a huge crowd at the Goethe Institute. He wrote

> I chose defiance
> The way of those poets of the past
> The way of Eshghi, the way of
> Farrokhi.
> So hear my voice
> As it sings in the slaughterhouse.[1]

The Iranian Revolution was eating its children. The atmosphere was no better for ordinary Iranians. In 1984 the London *Sunday Times* published a previously unpublished official report on the *Qissas*, Islamic retributive justice. According to the report at least 1,700 Iranians had their hands cut off between March 1983 and March 1984 and at least 2,000 people were executed. Crimes under the *Qissas* system include 'reading heretical books', 'insulting the leader' and 'thinking evil thoughts'.

The battle between hardliners and pragmatists was being fought in the late 1990s in a journal called *Rah-e No* (New Way). One edition published an article by the late Grand Ayatollah Abolqassem Mousavi Khoei questioning whether Iran's government should have a supreme spiritual leader (*Vale e-faqih* or 'guardian of the Islamic jurist'), at present Ayatollah 'Ali Khamenei, at all. After various other challenges to clerical rule Khamenei had it closed down.

Technically, the Iranian Constitution guarantees freedom of publication and the press, but that freedom is not unconditional. Article 24 states that:

'Publications and the press are free to publish their ideas unless they are injurious to the fundamentals of Islam or public rights. Details will be provided by legislation.' Article 175 goes further: 'Freedom of publicity and propaganda in the Mass Media (radio and television) shall be insured on the basis of Islamic principles. The management of the media shall be under the joint supervision of the Judiciary (High Judiciary Council), Legislature, and Executive. Details of such management are determined by law.'

Iranian cartoonists have suffered considerably under Iranian censorship. In apparent violation of Iran's own press laws, Manouchehr Karimzadeh was sentenced by an Islamic Revolutionary Court to fifty lashes, one year in prison and a fine of 500,000 rials for a cartoon which appeared in *Farad* magazine in 1992. His editor-in-chief Naser Arabha was sentenced to six months in prison. In a cruel twist, after Karimzadeh had served the one-year prison sentence incommunicado in Evin Prison, the Supreme Court ruled that he was to be re-tried and a further arbitrary ten-year sentence was imposed. The cartoon he drew accompanied an article on the poor state of Iranian soccer and depicted a football player which the authorities ruled bore an unacceptably close resemblance to Khomeini. The figure also appeared to have a mutilated right hand and left leg which some saw as a reference to Islamic punishments. Probably through international support, such as an article in Joe Szabo's *Witty World* magazine and a subsequent article in the *New York Times*, Karimzadeh was secretly released in late 1994 after two years in prison. Szabo had reported the case to a UNESCO-sanctioned human rights watch organization.

According to *Index on Censorship* there are some 70 periodicals published by Iranians in exile, representing a wide range of opinion from support for the restoration of the monarchy to a search for a 'true socialist' state. The weekly *Asghar Agha*, published in London by Iranian writer and cartoonist Hadi Khorsandi, so angered the authorities in Tehran that his name appeared on the hit-list of an assassination plot foiled by Britain's Scotland Yard in May 1984. Born in the provincial town of Fariman, Khorsandi became an exile from Iran on 3 April 1979, two days after the official proclamation of the Islamic Republic of Iran.[2]

This is a Khorsandi sketch about a man seeking to acquire a driving-licence.

Official:	Could you sign here, please? And here. Another signature here, please. Could I have your fingerprints here, please? And two photocopies of your identity card, please?
Applicant:	Here you are, two photocopies of my identity card.
Official:	Two passport-size photographs, without glasses?
Applicant:	Here you are.

Official: Certificate of good conduct?

Applicant: Here you are.

Official: Have you got a recommendation from your local revolutionary *komiteh*?

Applicant: Yes sir, here it is.

Official: And you have brought along photocopies of all your family's identity cards?

Applicant: Yes sir, I have.

Official: Do you have a driving licence?

Applicant: No sir, I haven't got a car. I have a moped.

Official: The engine number, frame number, your licence to ride a moped, the insurance cover of the moped, its registration certificate, and road tax receipt!

Applicant: One moment sir, and I'll hand over all of them ... Ah, there you are, I've got all of them ready.

Official: Do you believe in the *Velayat-e faqih* [Iran's spiritual leadership]?

Applicant: Of course I do sir, and how!

Official: Who fought alongside the Imam [Khomeini] in 1963?

Applicant: Tayyeb, sir, Tayyeb Haj-Rezai.

Official: What was the name of the head of the revolutionary *komiteh* based at the American embassy when the American spies were taken hostage?

Applicant: Mashallah the Butcher. (...)

Official: What must one do if a dog licks a plate?

Applicant: One must scrub the plate with earth seven times and then rinse it seven times with water.

Official: What should one do after a call of nature in a desert where there is no water?

Applicant: One should clean one's bottom with stones or dried mud balls until there is no trace of impurity in one's body.

[The interview continues like this until eventually]

Official: Now, say three times: 'I've been a bad boy'.

Applicant: I've been a bad boy. I've been a bad boy. I've been a bad boy.

Official: All right. That's enough. *(Reaches under the desk and brings out two packets of butter)* Here you are, your ration of butter for the month. For your cigarettes, you must come back tomorrow, and we'll see what we can do about it.

But beyond the satire lay much darker realities. In 1999 thirteen Iranians, of whom some were Jews, faced charges of spying for Israel, apparently on account of e-mail contacts with friends in Israel. The trial gave the hard-line head of Iran's judiciary, Ayatollah Yazdi, the opportunity of attacking the USA, whose human rights record he claimed was the 'worst in the world'. He went on bizarrely to say, 'Whether the sentence is hanging, or more lenient or more severe punishment, it will be carried out ... An individual may receive several death sentences. Some are condemned to death twice or more, and some only once.'[3]

By June 1999 students at Tehran's university were launching large protests against the banning of several liberal pro-Khatami newspapers. After violent police crackdowns, apparently supported by units of the Hizbullah (the militant, Shi'i 'Party of God'), had left eight students dead there were hundreds of short-term arrests but the government was clearly frightened of the unrest. Soon the government's supreme security body was ordering the dismissal of two senior Tehran policemen believed to be responsible for the crackdown. The council included Khamenei, Khatami, former President 'Ali Akbar Hashemi Rafsanjani and senior ministers and heads of the security and armed forces. The demonstrations followed what students believed was evidence that hard-line elements within the government and security agencies were getting the upper hand in the conflict between reformist and conservative factions.

This included a demand by the intelligence ministry that the reformist daily newspaper *Salam* be closed after it published a memo allegedly implying the complicity of a senior official in the ministry in the murders in November 1998 of six reformist writers and a nationalist politician and his wife. Another factor had been the passage of the first reading of the press censorship bill by the conservative controlled parliament. Journalists from some 60 newspapers went on strike to show their disapproval of what they said was a campaign by hard-line vested interests to sabotage the government's reform programme. Only four conservative-run newspapers continued publication. Liberalism was becoming fashionable and even members of the establishment were coming out in favour of the reformists. As a sign of the times the former commander of the Revolutionary Guards, Mohsen Rezai, was seen urging university students to stand up for their rights and help develop a fully-fledged civil society in Iran. Tehran's university students had played a seminal role in the Islamic revolution and Friday prayers are still, today, held on the main campus of the university. They could not be ignored. Khamenei addressed a weeping crowd to tell them that he would forgive the students even if they tore up his picture.

But in Iran unpredictability is the name of the game. In a violent snub to the liberals the following September Iran's revolutionary courts sentenced four people to death for taking part in the pro-democracy demonstrations. The decision indicated that the hardliners had no plans to yield to the new judiciary chief, Ayatollah Mahmoud Hashemi Shahroudi, who had taken over in the previous month. Although Shahroudi had been aligned with the conservatives he was now proposing to remove factional politics from the judicial system. The sentences brought the question of the death penalty once again onto the agenda. During the July riots the deputy speaker of parliament, Hasan Rowhand, had told a crowd of 100,000 people 'They shall be punished as corrupt of the earth, *mohareb*s.' To be a *mohareb*, one who declares war on God, is a capital offence in the Islamic republic. During the same month conservatives in the special press court ordered the closure of the liberal *Neshat* newspaper after it questioned, in an article criticizing capital punishment, the concept of the Judaeo–Islamic tradition of 'an eye for an eye'.[4]

The crisis in Iran was exacerbated during that same month when a play published in a small university magazine called *Mouj* (Wave) with a print run of a mere 150, appeared to criticize the Twelfth Imam, the holiest figure in Shi'ism. In the play, called *Resurrection of the Messiah at University Exam Time*, the Imam has a conversation with a university student who has been praying for him to reappear on earth to help him with his exams. The Imam tells him he will return on Friday but the student replies 'I have an exam on Friday. Could you make it on Saturday, instead?' Far from seeing the joke the conservatives responded furiously to this two-page satire, saying that mocking holy figures was beyond the pale. They called for the death penalty for the student authors. Six senior clerics from the Supreme Court acted as advisers to the notorious judge-prosecutor Saeed Mortezavi who pressed the trembling young accused students to confess to premeditation, a prerequisite for the death penalty.

The leading ideologue of the right, Ayatollah Muhammad Taqi Mesbah-Yazdi, made their dreadful position clear, saying quite simply; 'Differences of opinion are not open to all in cases of religious sanctities, only to those theologians who are experts.'[5] The play did not appear to this writer to be anti-Islamic. It is comic, rather charming, reflecting the thinking of young people trying to make their religion human and accessible through gentle humour, just as the great Sufi writers had done. The poet Rumi was known to have lovingly mocked the Prophet Moses in his poetry. But some of Rumi's poetry has been banned even in Kuwait.

The reformers represented by Khatami saw more in this apparently petty incident, believing the play to be a plant written by students but introduced into the public domain by right-wing extremists to provoke a scandal, which in turn would re-ignite the student protest riots. The hard-line conservative plan would be to capitalize on these to clamp down once and for all on Khatami's 'Prague Spring'. From a literary angle the play's natural ending would have had the Imam, disgusted with the student's lack of commitment to his Messianic return, walking away in high dudgeon. In fact it ends with the student clutching a knife, the inference being that he kills the Imam, or as the author claimed in court, the 'false Imam'. One cannot help suspecting, as Khatami's supporters did, that the knife incident has been added by another hand to incriminate the young author further. Interestingly, in October 1999 Khamenei revealed his own sense of fair play when he lashed out at the right-wingers whom he accused of taking the law into their own hands. When far right elements in a Friday prayer congregation began chanting for the death penalty for the playwrights he curled his lip in disgust and told them to shut up. The reformists were jubilant. Their jubilation was well founded as they were to win a landslide victory over the hardliners in the elections of February 2000, although this victory was itself to provoke a further right-wing backlash.

In April 1999 Iran's first women's magazine *Zan* had been banned indefinitely in Iran for running an interview with the widow of the former Shah and publishing a cartoon satirizing Islamic laws on women. *Zan* was edited by Fa'ezeh Hashimi, daughter of former President 'Ali Akbar Hashimi Rafsanjani and a principal supporter of President Muhammad Khatami's liberalizing programme. She is a brave woman. 'I, Fa'ezeh Hashimi, a Muslim, an Iranian and an Iranian woman, with a *chador* over my head, a pen in my hand and a life ready to be offered for sacrifice, wish to see an Iran that is Islamic, free and devoid of tyranny; an Iran for all Iranians. And I will not abandon the torch of freedom.'[6]

Nevertheless, as early as 1991 the US-based Iranian writer 'Ali Ansari was astonished by the reality of the new openness in Iran as reflected in the burgeoning of newspapers.[7] The reformist press, he discovered, outnumbered the right-wing press by at least two to one. If one took into account sales the figure was even more staggering. While newspapers such as *Hamshari* and *Iran* regularly sold 150,000 copies a day, *Keyhan*, regarded as a hard-line newspaper, was difficult to find because it simply did not sell. When Ansari picked up a copy of *Jebheh*, the organ of the hard-line extremist group, Ansar-e Hizbullah, a passer-by gently advised him not to waste his money on such 'rubbish'. To show just how much Iranians value their freedoms, within five days of the court order against *Neshat*, he says, its editorial board had re-formed to produce a new paper, *Akhbar-e Eqtesad* (Economic News). The reformists proclaimed that 'for every paper they close, we will open three'.

At the end of November 1999 Abdullah Nouri was jailed for insulting Islam and Khomeini in his progressive newspaper *Khordad*. At his trial Nouri accused the conservative clerical establishment of being behind the violation of citizens' civil rights, the murder of secular intellectuals and of distorting religious interpretations for political gain. The pro-reform Jalaladdin Taheri told Nouri's parents: 'What Nouri said in court was what everyone knew but would not dare express. It is an honour for you to have such a son.' In an interview the previous week Nouri had said, 'Khomeini did not believe that Islam was a dogmatic ideology. He said we understood people's freedom.'[8]

SIX

Algeria Goes to the Wall

It is in Algeria that the tension between western culture and an Islamic response to it have been most dangerous. Today Algeria has a very young population of 30 million, almost all of whom are Sunni Muslims. After a century of rule by France, Algeria became independent in 1962. The surprising first round success of the fundamentalist Islamic Salvation Front (FIS) party in December 1991 balloting caused the army to intervene, crack down on the FIS and postpone the subsequent elections. There was barely a whisper of disapproval from the West, which dreaded a fundamentalist take-over. The Algerian army's abortion of a democratic process that was favouring Islamic fundamentalists was to lead to an appalling bloodletting by the *eradicateurs* in the army on one side and by self-styled Islamic militants on the other. Violent responses from the FIS and the even more militant Islamic Armed Group (GIA) have resulted in a continuous low-grade civil conflict with the secular state apparatus. The FIS's armed wing, the Islamic Salvation Army, disbanded itself in January 2000 and many armed militants surrendered under an amnesty programme designed to promote national reconciliation. Nevertheless, the killings continue in the *bled* (the countryside).

While civil war was brewing in Algeria after 1991, Algerians could receive pornography from Europe by cable, an experience which divided those who worshipped all things western from those who recoiled from the devilry of the West towards the comfort and security of the purity of Islam. Some 200 newspapers emerged as the National Liberation Front (FLN) infrastructure of state control and state terror collapsed. Islamic fundamentalists (particularly the GIA) were blamed for the violence that was to follow although the perpetrators of savagery were seen to be equally divided between the GIA and the security forces. But was – and is – Algeria's new, so-called free press being manipulated by economic interest groups in Algeria? Can even fundamentalist Muslims justify the butchering of women and children or is the liquidation of villages a macabre method of real estate acquisition by those in power in

Algiers? The targeting of foreigners became official policy among the most hard-line Islamic groups. Rabeh Kebir, the official spokesman of the FIS in Europe, told Radio France International in October 1993:

> It is not the policy of FIS to kill foreigners, but it is very difficult to control actions by the mass of the people ... People are never targeted for their ideas. As long as a journalist's opposition to the Islamist's programme is merely intellectual and his/her criticism is along these lines, there is no problem ... But some journalists have been used to inform on our young men. If a journalist is associated with the process of informing [the authorities], he/she ceases to become a journalist and becomes, in effect, a combatant.[1]

This period of extraordinary barbarity has developed without sanction in Islam. The emergence of thug-militants must be seen against the background of mass education in contrast with the poverty of genuine Islamic teaching. Every Algerian has access to a satellite dish but few can read enough Arabic to interpret the Qur'an. The question of ideological freedoms in Iran, a country undergoing thoughtful revolutionary change, has been entirely overshadowed by what has happened in Algeria. Of all countries belonging culturally to the Islamic world, Algeria is the country to have suffered most severely from a deadly censorship, on the one hand by the *eradicateurs* in the army who wanted to exterminate 'Islamic terrorists' and on the other hand from the militant fundamentalists who had been robbed of their political victory in 1991.

Algeria's first 'Code of Information' adopted in December 1981 by the National Assembly had stated that 'the right of information is a fundamental right of citizens' but such ideals were soon to be drowned out in violence. Both sides committed unbelievable horrors from the end of 1991 when, without a murmur from the democratic West, the army interrupted the electoral process. Algerian women had played a major role in the war of independence and Algeria's first colourful president Ben Bella had rewarded them for it. 'We oppose those who, in the name of religion, wish to leave women outside the construction of our country,' he said in 1963. 'We respect Muslim traditions, but we want a revolutionary Islam and not the Islam left to us by the colonial domination.' The French had understood how to exploit Islam's sensitivities and had encouraged Algerian women to unveil and be photographed in public with their French 'sisters'. Under Boumedienne's dour regime women lost this support. 'Not everyone can be seductive to women,' he told them in a curiously personal reference to Ben Bella, whose whereabouts were then unknown. I knew the war heroine Djamila Bouhired when I lived in Algeria. 'I was sent to China after the war,' she told me. 'I was particularly impressed by the emancipation of Chinese women. As for us women in Algeria – we seem to have lost all the freedom we fought for. Life's getting worse, not better for us. Even I dare not walk in the streets at night.'

From independence in 1962 until the 'October Revolution' in 1988 the Algerian press had been controlled and censored by the one-party government of the FNL. After 1988 it experienced an explosion of freedom and diversity with the introduction of a new constitution that legalized political parties, abolished governmental control of the press and guaranteed journalist's salaries for a transition period of three years. The number of newspapers and journals increased from fewer than a dozen to several hundred although during the Gulf War the government imposed fines, confiscated issues and began libel proceedings against several newspapers. However, it was as early as 10 October 1988 that the head of the Algérie Presse Service, the official news agency, Sid 'Ali Benmechice, became the first victim of the violence. Benmechice was shot dead by an unidentified man in the crowd while covering one of the first great demonstrations of the Islamic Movement during the strikes of October that would open the way to a multi-party system.

Founded in 1990 by journalists from the government daily *El Moudjahid*, the organ of the FLN, *El Watan* defines itself as an independent daily, and it has been the target of attacks from both the government and the Islamists. Its editor Omar Belhouchet was the target of an unsuccessful assassination attack in May 1992. In September 1991 *Le Matin* was founded by journalists from *Alger Republicain*, a daily close to the Algerian Communist party. *Le Matin* identifies itself as pluralist, anti-fundamentalist and independent of political parties and powers. Said Mekbel, its editorial writer, and Dilem, its cartoonist, had made *Le Matin* one of Algeria's foremost newspapers. In December 1994 the 56-year-old Mekbel, who had contributed mainly to *Le Matin* in his satirical column 'Mesmar J'ha' (The Nail of Djeha), was shot dead in a restaurant in Algier's Hussein Dey. They found a note on his desk on the day he died.

Who will kill me? That's what I first want to know because there are other questions; why do they want to kill me, when will they kill me? Although it's the most important question I think that it is the first because I imagine if I know who will kill me – or rather who will order my death – I will know why I am to be killed and even when. ...The victim is alone, the assassins numerous. Many. The victim is alone before dying. Masses gather about him when he is buried, when it is too late.

His burial provoked a wave of anti-terrorist feeling. *El Waqt* is an Arabic-language weekly belonging to the same group as *El Watan*. Created in November 1993 in response to charges that the politically committed Algerian press was exclusively French-language, *El Waqt* adopted an openly modern tone. Its special reports on love, sexuality, culture or terrorism called into question the deeply ingrained taboos of Algerian society. The GIA issued a statement in January 1995 which concluded 'Those who fight us with the pen shall be fought with the sword.'

Tahar Djaout, murdered by Islamists in Algiers in 1993, was the founder and editor of the weekly *Ruptures*, an openly anti-Islamic publication which opposed all dialogue with the fundamentalists. His assassination marked the start of a macabre period in which journalists were targeted not because they got in the way but simply because they were journalists *per se*. Djaout was the author of several novels including *Les chercheurs d'os* (1984), *L'invention du désert* (1987) and *Les vigiles* (1991).

Widespread protests followed the arrest and detention on 4 July 1996 of Chawki Amari, the political cartoonist for the privately owned French-language daily *La Tribune*. He was taken to Serkadji, the top security prison which had become notorious after the deaths of a hundred Islamist prisoners arrested after a riot. His arrest stemmed from the publication in the 1 July edition of *La Tribune* of a satirical drawing which showed Algerian flags strung between houses on a street and a figure asking 'Is this for 5 July?' (Algeria's Independence Day and a cornerstone of the armed forces' claim to legitimacy). The examining Algerian judge said the cartoon was 'an insult to the national emblem', a breach of Article 160 of the Penal Code which stipulates five to ten years for 'anyone who deliberately and publicly tears up, defaces or defiles the national symbol'. Authorities later shut down *La Tribune* and placed legal restrictions on its managing director Kheireddine Ameyar and its managing editor Baya Gacemi, ordering them to report to the police twice a week pending a trial on 29 July.

Algerian journalists held a day-long strike on 15 July, demanding that Amari be released and measures lifted against *La Tribune*. Hundreds of people converged on the Maison de la Presse Tahar Djaout in Algiers (named after the murdered novelist), including representatives from the main opposition parties, women's groups, youth groups, union leaders and university students. The Algerian journalist's union, the Assemblée Générale des Journalistes, issued a statement denouncing the legal proceedings and said that the move would not stop journalists from 'continuing their struggle until their colleague Amari is released and legal action against La Tribune dropped'. According to the International Federation of Journalists' centre in Algiers, the event marked the 'first time that journalists' fight for freedom of expression was so strongly taken up by the politicians and civil society'.

On 16 July 1996 the government censor forced the removal of a drawing in *Le Soir d'Algérie* which was illustrating an article on the previous day's Forum meeting held at the Maison de la Presse Tahar Djaout. This drawing, by Abi, showed uniformed men with padlocks and chains marching on the Maison de la Presse with the caption (written in reference to the sealing of *La Tribune*'s offices) '8ième bataillon des forces de metteurs sous scelles en avant ... marche.' (Eighth battalion of the sealers, forward ... march). In a press release on 15 July the Paris-based *Reporters sans Frontières* asked French political cartoonists Brito, Cambon, Charb, Elho, Honore, Hours, Luz, Chantal Montellier, Nono, Plantu, Slim, Tignous, Trez, and Willem to draw cartoons calling for the release of their Algerian colleague. As of 18 July, several drawings in support of Amari had already appeared in *El Watan*, including two by Slim and Plantu. *El Watan* included two pages of *La Tribune* while it remained under a de facto ban.

Sid 'Ali Malouah, considered the foremost cartoonist and comic artist in Algeria, incurred the wrath of the Islamic fundamentalists. After several attempts on his life starting in 1995 he was forced to go underground. Meanwhile, Guerrovi Brahim, a cartoonist for the *El Moudjahid*, was kidnapped on 2 September 1995, and found executed near his home in a southern suburb of Algiers. In her haunting book *Etre Journaliste en Algérie*, Ghania Mouffok, who worked for *Algérie Actualité*, lists 53 journalists murdered between October 1988 and December 1995.[2]

Many killings of artists and intellectuals followed. On 26 June 1998 the Berber singer Lounés Matoub, who had only recently returned from exile in France, was gunned down at a bogus roadblock on the road to his village in Beni Douala near Tizi Ouzou. On 1 July, the Armed Islamic Group claimed responsibility for the murder, calling Matoub 'among the most stubborn enemies of religion'. The killing occurred hours after another group slit the throats of seventeen people in an isolated village. Matoub had been outspoken in his opposition to both the government and the Islamist groups. His last song not only denounced the regime's alliance with the Islamists, it also openly mocked it by setting its provocative lyrics to Algeria's national anthem.

Born in 1956 in Taourit-Moussa, in the Djurdjura Mountains of Kabylia near Tizi-Ouzou, Matoub was a co-founder of the Berber Algerian Human Rights League in 1976. He made his first album, *Ay Izem* (The Lion) in 1978. It was an instant hit and was quickly followed by *Ayemma a'zizen* (Dear Mother). When anti-government demonstrations swept through Tizi-Ouzou in April 1980, his songs were the anthems of the protesters. Along with the works of an older generation of people such as Lounés Ait Menguellet, whose music had defended Berber culture against forced Arabization, all of Matoub's songs were banned. He defended Berber culture and attacked Islamic fundamentalism in his song 'Kenza' dedicated to the daughter of Tahar Djaout.[3] An armed Islamic group had kidnapped Matoub as a warning in September 1994 but released him after a two-week ordeal, during which they had simulated his execution several times. They had forced him to record his confession and promise never to sing or attack religion again.[4]

The death of Matoub in 1998 led to protests and riots in several cities. According to press reports, nearly a thousand youths in Tizi Ouzou stoned police; police responded with clubs and tear gas, shooting one demonstrator and injuring three others. That October the Government announced the capture of five suspects alleged to be members of the GIA and responsible for Matoub's death. Demonstrators were also reiterating a long-standing demand for official recognition of their Berber Tamasheq language as the government began to enforce a new law providing for fines of up to $170 for officials or business executives who sign any deal or statement not drafted in Arabic. Up to 5 million of Algeria's 30-million population are Berber-speakers. A statement sent to the newspapers *El Watan* and *Le Matin* on 2 July announced the formation of the Armed Berber Movement (ABM), declaring that the movement would 'eliminate' those who 'try to apply the government's Arabization policy'. The ABM also vowed to 'kill all those who contributed directly or indirectly to the killing of our spiritual leader Lounés Matoub'. Thousands of protesters marched through Algiers on 9 July in a protest organized by the Socialist Forces Front, a leading secular Berber opposition party.

An enlightened Civil Concord Act was passed by parliament on 13 July 1999 a few months after Abdelaziz Bouteflika became president. Following the big massacres of 1997–8 the Act laid down a programme to remove or reduce legal sanctions against members of armed groups provided they surrendered within six months. However, the act excluded those who had committed any crime of violence during the seven-year insurrection.

SEVEN

Crackdown in Post-war Lebanon

A free press has traditionally flourished in Lebanon and today several Arabic newspapers are returning to Beirut on the assumption that Lebanon will regain its old media glory, sacrificed in seventeen years of civil war. Of Lebanon's 3.6 million population 70 per cent are Muslim (Shi'a, Sunni, Druze, Ismaili and Alawi) and 30 per cent Christian (including Orthodox, Catholic and Protestant) although a pretence has been retained of an equal Muslim-Christian balance. Lebanon has made progress toward rebuilding its political institutions and regaining its national sovereignty since 1991 and the end of the devastating civil war. Under the Ta'if Accords – the blueprint for national reconciliation – the Lebanese have established a more just political system, particularly by giving Muslims a greater say in the political process while institutionalizing sectarian divisions in the government. Since the end of the war, the Lebanese have conducted several successful elections, most of the militias have been disbanded, and the Lebanese army has extended central government authority over most of the country. The Hizbullah ('Party of God'), the radical Shi'a party, retains its weapons. Syria maintains about 25,000 troops in Lebanon based mainly in Beirut, north Lebanon, and the Beka'a Valley. Syria's troop deployment was legitimized by the Arab League during Lebanon's civil war and by the Ta'if Accords. Israel's withdrawal from its security zone in southern Lebanon in May 2000 encouraged many Lebanese to demand that Syria withdraw its forces as well.

Lebanon has been a catalyst for dramatic media changes, reflecting the social mores of the culturally Islamic world. During an Israeli bombardment of Beirut in the summer of 1982 an Egyptian journalist commented, 'Most Arab rulers enjoy watching this because the sight of an Arab woman reading an uncensored book, printed in Beirut, would upset them far more than the sight of phosphorus-burnt children in a Beirut hospital." Lebanon, prior to its 1976–91 civil war, had over forty publishing houses and 71 newspapers and magazines and Beirut was a safety valve where Arab intellectuals could publish freely but the development of the war undid much of this. Writers like Salim al-Louzi faced kidnapping and death. Syrian control ensured that any criticisms of Syria's President Hafez al-Asad was strictly forbidden. But he was brutally lampooned just the same. The Lebanese exploit the fact that the word for condom in Lebanon is Hafez al-Air (literally The Protector of the Penis and Hafez the Prick!).

So sensitive are the Lebanese now about the ethnic hatreds which sparked off the war that they have been reluctant to speak up about it at all. A comedy film showed two French tourists walking around bombed buildings and asking passers-by which period of the civil war resulted in the damage. Each passer-by would deny any knowledge of the war. One said that it was the result of previous wars, even blaming Greeks and Romans for the damaged concrete buildings.

Randa Shahal Sabbag's *Civilisées* (Civilized People) was hailed by the critics in late 1999 for its frankness. It points to Lebanese responsibility for the violence, no longer placing all the blame on outsiders, and makes the violence and hatred almost mundane with small children tugging at the sleeves of adults, imploring them to kidnap passing foreigners. Foreigners in the film show unfailing kindness in contrast to the cynicism of the Lebanese. The censors refused the film a commercial screening, even after having counted the insults in the film to make sure that Muslims and Christians got an equal share and informed Sabbag that 47 minutes would have to be cut from her 90-minute film. The Government claimed that the offending passages contained inappropriate language and scenes that the censors deemed 'inflammatory' against Jesus, the Virgin Mary, and Islam. It would, the government feared, 'provoke sectarian tensions'.

EIGHT

Islam's Creative Centuries and the Age of the Courtly Poets

One has to look way beyond Islam for the roots of self-expression and its control in the old, sophisticated lands that so suddenly accepted Islam in the seventh century AD. The pre-Islamic people of the Arabian Peninsula were said to wish one another joy for only three things – the birth of a boy, the coming to light of a poet, and the foaling of a new mare. The Pre-Islamic Age is better known as the Jahiliyya or '[Age of] Ignorance'.

In the heyday of classical Arabic literature it was widely believed that the finest poetry was composed during the Jahiliyya period. The best-known examples were the Seven Odes, called the *Mu'allaqat* because they were said to have hung (*mu'allaqa*) in the pagan shrine of the Ka'ba in Mecca. The best-known of these poets were Imr ul-Qais and Labid. Imr ul-Qais's wonderful *Mu'allaqa* begins 'Let us two [warriors] stop and weep in memory of a loved one and a stopping-place'. Labid's references are as lyrical as a poem by Wordsworth, with his description of the huge eyes of the hunted white cow gleaming beneath a tree in the desert storm: 'and she shines bright in the face of the darkness like a pearl from a seashell that has dropped from its string'. The poems are wonderfully onomatopoeic, those of Imr ul-Qais pounding with the rhythm of the sounds of camels' hooves.

If these marvels of the nomadic oral tradition were considered by many Arabs as unsurpassable, its poets were to be condemned by the Prophet as the 'poets of hell-fire' because of their paganism and decadence. But is this really why they were so totally suppressed? The Islamic censorship of them was a tragedy from a cultural point of view as these poems were genuinely Arabian and, in the view of some, they were never to be surpassed. Writers of today, such as the Yemeni poet and historian Abdullah al-Udhari, maintain that Islam is the continuation of the Hanif (monotheist) religion of the Jahiliyya age that Ibrahim (Abraham) and his son Ismail (Ishmael) inherited from Adam and his son Hibatulla (Seth).' Islam, the divine restatement of the biblical cycle, was to be a palimpsest for Byzantine, Persian and Indian culture. Its essential contribution, and that of the region from which it emerged, Arabia, was the divine revelation of the Qur'an, and the Hadith, the sayings of the Prophet. Interestingly, the eminent Egyptian writer Taha Hussein fell foul of the fundamentalist lobby when he claimed in his study *On Pre-Islamic Poetry* that at least some of the poems had been written *after* Islam.

The ancient Arabians regarded the poet as a magician in touch with spirits (*jinn*) or even, some would argue, devils. The poet was more oracle than artist, not unlike the great Celtic bards of Wales and Cornwall, and he or she was seen as a counsellor or even a spiritual leader. When two Bedouin armies faced each other the poets would come forward and attack the enemy with often abusive, satirical verse (*hija'*). The poet with the most deadly verses could force a stronger tribe to flee.

In later 'Abbasid times this poetic power was to intensify with the satirical and often extremely vulgar Abu Nuwas scoring three deadly hits against the blind poet Bashar ibn Burd with the awful line: 'I poked out your eyes with my penis in your mother's womb'. Bashar, incidentally, was to be put to death in 783 for heresy. He had been in close contact with the founder of the Mu'tazilites, Wasil ibn 'Ata. The Mu'tazilites in power were themselves to launch a deadly *mihna* or inquisition against their enemies. They were also to have a strong impact on the Egyptian scholar, Abu Zayd.

At the time of the Prophet the tribal constitution was a democracy guided by its chief men who derived their authority from noble blood, noble character, wealth, wisdom and experience. However, the tribal chief or *sheikh* was a *primus inter pares* and could not impose penalties or commands on fellow-tribesmen. Some regarded it as an early form of democracy. It is a system that has carried over to the modern *majlis*es (audience rooms/council) of Saudi Arabia and the Gulf states although with less and less real significance. Nevertheless, until the assassination of King Faisal in 1975, any man could approach the king (the wives of Gulf rulers have their own *majlis*es for women) with his wish or complaint. Courage, hardship, physical prowess and, above all, *muruwwa* or manly virtue were essential in this bedouin society. Raiders would flee if they had nothing to lose by doing so but would fight to the death for their womenfolk. Essentially they were freebooters.

After the death of the Prophet, when many of the Meccan tribes temporarily withdrew their allegiance or *baya* from the first Caliph Abu Bakr in the wars of the *Ridda* (Wars of Apostasy), some would interpret, with some tongue in cheek, even verses condemning alcohol in a way that allowed them to continue consuming it. According to Jahiz's *Book of the Crown*, the seventh-century Caliph 'Abd al-Malik ibn Marwan used to get drunk once a month to the point where he no longer knew whether he was in the air or in water. 'I seek to clarify my spirit', he would say, 'strengthen my memory and purify the seat of my thought.' He would then purify himself of the forbidden alcohol by throwing up.[2] The exquisite poetry of the Jahiliyya age was sexually explicit in a way that would not be repeated until the great flowering of 'Abbasid poetry. In the *Mu'allaqa* of Imr ul Qais, for example, the protagonist is described making love with his lady companion in her *howdaj* (curtained litter) while the upper part of her body is turned to breast-feed her baby.

Islam condemned this vivid Jahiliyya culture, replacing it with the concepts of obedience, moral behaviour and the unity of mosque and state. Jahiliyya was replaced by Shari'a (law) and the *'asabiyya* (solidarity) of the tribes by an Islamic solidarity that transcended community and race. Islam, the act of submission to the one God of the Old Testament prophets as preached by the Prophet Muhammad in the seventh century AD, sees Abraham as the first Muslim and itself as a reassertion and correction of the Old and New Testaments. No allowances are made in Islam outside of the seminal principle that there is only one God and that Muhammad is the 'seal' of the prophets. Islam's rule is that there is no turning back. Once a Muslim always a Muslim. Apostasy is a capital offence. It is on this hook that Salman Rushdie, Taslima Nasrin and Abu Zayd have been hung.

Within the framework of the urban paganism of the Meccan and Medinan families and of the anarchy of the Arabian tribes the Prophet established a commonwealth based upon a charter offering a limited freedom of conscience. He continued to respect the biblical tradition of the Jewish tribes even when he had come into conflict with them, realizing that they would never accept his own revelations. 'The Jews who attach themselves to our commonwealth', ran the charter, 'shall be protected from all insults and vexations: they shall have an equal right with our own people to our assistance and good offices ... the client allies of the Muslims and the Jews shall be as respected as the patrons.' The late Israeli human rights activist Dr Israel Shahak refers to 'the important fact that expulsion of Jews, being contrary to Islamic law, was virtually unknown there'. Nevertheless, Shahak adds that the Jewish Golden Age in Spain which began after the fall of the Spanish Umayyad Caliphate in 1002 and during the rule of the *'reyes de taifa'* (the petty kings), was 'all based on naked force'.[3]

While Islam protects Jews and Christians as fellow monotheists, People of the Book (*ahl al-Kitab*), paganism is fiercely condemned but as the story of the Satanic Verses implies, Muhammad's confrontation with paganism was cautious to begin with. According to authorities such as the tenth-century Tabari, an important commentator on the Qur'an, one of the Meccan revelations to the Prophet contained positive references to the three Meccan goddesses al-Lat, al-Manat and al-Uzza at a time when he was wearied by opposition from the Meccan merchant confederacy. The revelations were said to have referred to the goddesses as 'the swans exalted whose intercession is expected'. However, he soon received another revelation cancelling the last verses and replacing them with lines such as, 'They are but names you and your fathers have named; God revealed no authority for them.'4 How could this happen? Well, possibly because elsewhere in the Qur'an there is a passage which suggests that Satan may, indeed, at times try to interpose false verses: 'Satan interposed (something) towards his desire; but God abrogates what Satan interposes.'5

In his novel *The Satanic Verses* Salman Rushdie links the verses incident with other episodes in the account of early Muslim analysts which cast doubt on the veracity of the Qur'anic revelations. According to the story related by Tabari, one of Muhammad's scribes, Abdullah ibn Sa'd, temporarily lost his faith in Islam when a mistake he had made in transcription went unnoticed by the Prophet. In Gibreel's dreams in the novel the role of Abdullah goes to Salman the Persian. Such is the reverence of Muslims for the very word of God in the Qur'an that it is little wonder that the book's publication caused such a scandal.

Under the second Caliph, Omar ibn al-Khatab, the Arabian general 'Amr ibn al-'As conquered Egypt and after a fourteenth-month siege ended Byzantine rule and almost 900 years of Graeco–Roman rule of Egypt. By and large his conquest was welcomed. His disciplined followers, who offered good terms to Christians and Jews as *dhimmi*s (protected 'People of the Book'), were a far cry from the Byzantines. Coptic Christianity had been the rebel Christianity of the downtrodden peasant under the pagan Roman rule from which Byzantium emerged. Some Egyptians claim that all Egyptians – Muslims as well as Christians – are Copts, since the word Copt means Egyptian. It is thought that the Christian trinity may have echoes in the triple divinity of ancient Egyptian theology.

In AD 323 Constantine the Great had converted to Christianity. Sadly for Egypt, the country was in time to become polarized between the Coptic Christianity of the shirtless peasantry and the orthodoxy or Melchite Christianity of the Byzantine Roman rulers. The difference was that the Copts believed that Christ had one nature (a divine one 'separate but inseparable') whereas the Melchites said he had a divine as well as a human nature. The Melchites persecuted the Copts ruthlessly. As a last act of cruelty they scourged and cut off the hands of their prisoners and released them as a grotesque procession of welcome to the youthful Muslim idealists who entered the city carrying Qur'ans and mounted on ponies. 'Amr, an extremely cultured man, spared the inhabitants, their homes and their monuments. Some accounts have it that he used the books of Alexandria's great library to heat the city's 4,000 baths but the story is almost certainly invented. Most of the books had already been destroyed at the time of Julius Caesar's naval action in 48 BC. It was rebuilt by Mark Anthony who is said to have given 200,000 manuscripts to Cleopatra. Later, books which smacked of paganism or heresy were destroyed by bishops like Theophilus and Cyril, according to Derek Flower, a writer on Alexandria.[6]

With their inclusivist religion, the Arabs were suddenly exposed to old and elegant cultures. Before them lay the marvellous scientific and cultural treasures of the ancient world. Early Christians such as John of Damascus regarded Islam as a new, albeit heretical, form of Christianity. In his book *From the Holy Mountain* William Dalrymple describes his visit to the Palestinian monastery of Mar Saba whose chapel is built around the tomb and hermitage of St John. John was the grandson of the last Byzantine governor of Damascus who had surrendered Damascus to the Muslim general Khaled ibn al-Walid in 635. Like John himself John's father, says Dalrymple, remained a Christian but also became a senior financial figure in the administration of the early Umayyad Caliphate whose accounts were kept for many decades later in Greek. John became a boon companion of the new Caliph al-Yazid and the drinking bouts of the two young men gave rise to frenzied gossip in the streets of Damascus. John wrote the first ever informed treatise on Islam by a Christian. As Dalrymple points out 'Islam was as much a product of the intellectual ferment of Late Antiquity as Gnosticism, Arianism, and Monophysitism, and like those heresies it had great success in areas disgruntled with Byzantine rule.'[7]

After the murder of the third Caliph 'Othman (d.656) his cousin Mu'awiya ibn Abi Sufyan led a rebellion against the Prophet's nephew and son-in-law, 'Ali ibn Abu Talib, who would become the fourth Caliph, demanding vengeance for 'Othman. This was to be the first great battle between Muslims and, as such, was utterly repugnant to both sides. 'Ali was forced by his followers, horrified to see Muslims preparing to slaughter Muslims, to accept an arbitration on the matter. To add to the confusion some of his diehard supporters objected after the terms of the arbitration were announced, crying 'La hukma ila lillah' (Power belongs only to God). Only God could judge on these matters. They withdrew from the community and were called Kharijites (those who *kharaj*, leave), maintaining that in countenancing arbitration their colleagues had ceased to be genuine Muslims.

No one had been closer to Muhammad than 'Ali. His father, Abu Talib, had brought up Muhammad in his home. Abdullah, Muhammad's father, had died before his birth and Amina, his mother, when he was still a child. 'Ali was one of the first three male Muslims and was married to Fatima, Muhammad's daughter by Khadijah. Fatima bore him two sons, Hasan and Hussein. 'Ali represented the ideal Arab. He was eloquent, generous and heroic. In Iran today the *javanmard*, the perfect man of integrity, is based mostly on the character of 'Ali. 'Ali's election to the Caliphate had been passed over in favour of the rough Bedouin consensus of the Muslim community which had chosen Abu Bakr, Omar and 'Othman in that order. When in 656 'Ali was eventually elected as Caliph the dreams of those who hoped that a member of the Prophet's family might restore the framework of early Muslim society were to be bitterly dashed.

The Shi'is (of the Shi'a, or sect of 'Ali) believed that 'Ali's knowledge of God was passed like a holy flame from imam ('spiritual guide') to imam. When an imam died he would choose a relative to inherit this knowledge. Each was a *hujjah* or proof of God's presence and as Karen Armstrong notes in *A History of God* 'in some mysterious sense, made the divine incarnate in a human bring. As Christians had seen Jesus as the Way, the Truth and the Light that would lead men to God, Shi'is revered their imams as the gateway (*bab*) to God, the road (*sabil*) and the guide of each generation.'[8] The 'twelver' Shi'is venerated twelve imams – descendants of 'Ali through Hussein – until in 939 the last imam went into hiding. Since he had no descendants the line died out. They believed that the Twelfth Imam would return to inaugurate a Golden Age.

Civil war ended with 'Ali's murder in 661. His death saw the accession to power of the Umayyad dynasty under Mu'awiya ibn Abi Sufyan, a dynasty which would flourish until extirpated in a bloodbath by the 'Abbasids in 750. Under the Umayyads in Damascus the Caliphs saw themselves as God's deputies on earth. From an early stage the Kharijites had established themselves as hard-core puritan opponents of government control in contrast with the Shi'a who sought egalitarian principles but argued not that government was wrong in itself but that it was in the wrong hands.

For 'Ali's followers his mantle was inherited by his son Hasan, the second of the Shi'i imams. Mu'awiya was succeeded by the venal and arguably secular Yazid, a man who loved wine and courtly life and showed little interest in the changes that Islam had brought. Discontent centred on Hussein who followed Hasan as the Shi'i imam. He moved from Medina to Mecca to escape swearing allegiance to Yazid and in Mecca received messages from Kufan merchants to set up a government to rival the Umayyads there. Hussein set out but by the time he had reached the plain of Karbala in present-day Iraq the Kufans had been neutralized by Yazid and Hussein and his 72 followers faced Yazid's 4,000 troops. Hussein and all his fighting men were killed and Hussein's surviving son 'Ali (better known as Zein al-Abedin) became the fourth Shi'i Imam.

This tragic story is regularly enacted in Iran and among all Shiʻi communities during Moharram in passion plays knows as *taʻzieh*. On the day of Ashura the focus of the drama is usually on the actual battle at Karbala and the massacre of Hussein and his followers, the courage of Hussein and the cruelty and corruption of his enemies. On other occasions the story follows Hussein's sister Zeinab's journey into captivity and her brave and noble conduct in the court of Yazid.[9] Daryush Shayegan traces the manner in which Hussein's martyrdom developed from being an apolitical cult motivated by tears of mourning and passion to a human and historical drama, 'in the same way that Christ was crucified to absolve our sins, so Hussein allowed himself to be killed at Karbala to purify the Muslim community of its sins'.[10] In this historical context Shayegan quotes Khomeini: 'It was to prevent the formation of a monarchy and the adoption of hereditary succession that Hussein revolted and became a martyr. It was because he refused to acquiesce to Yazid's succession and acknowledge his royal status that Hussein revolted and called on all the Muslims to rebel.'[11]

After exterminating the Umayyads in 750 the ʻAbbasid Caliphate based in Baghdad lasted until the sack of Baghdad by the Mongols in 1258. The ʻAbbasids had created a highly centralized administration in Baghdad in contrast with the Umayyads who had wielded power from provincial centres. Under the ʻAbbasids earlier laws re-emerged in Islamic guise, now authenticated as Prophetic Hadiths rooted in Arabia. During the ninth century a huge corpus of Hadiths appeared which would serve as the basis for Shariʻa law for future *ʻulama* (religious scholars).

In addition there was a tension between two different concepts of governance: the Sunni concept of a community living under a law which emanated from the will of God and the ancient Persian concept of a Shah designated by God to regulate the life of society by statecraft. This duality provided the foundation for the classical Islamic combination of a temporal power which was in the hands of the ruler and a religious authority which resided with the *ʻulama*. It was under the son of Harun ar-Rashid, the ʻAbbasid Caliph al-Ma'mun (813–33), and his successors that the Muʻtazilites used their power to compel Muslims in public office to accept the doctrine of the 'created' nature of the Qur'an.

In Islamic history the control of free expression may have become stronger commensurate with increasing contact with non-Islamic societies. The Muʻtazilites, for example, developed their discourse from discussions between Jewish and Christian scholars at a time when in the eighth century AD Greek works were translated into Arabic. Al-Ma'mun promulgated a decree binding all Muslims to accept the Muʻtazilite dogma on pain of losing their civil rights.

He established a *mihna* or inquisition in order to win the agreement of the judges and *'ulama*. Those who refused to take the test were flogged and threatened with execution. The most prominent figure in the orthodox camp opposed to the new dogma was the Imam Ahmad ibn Hanbal, patron of the most conservative of the four legal schools.

With the rapid decline of the 'Abbasid Empire which set in towards the middle of the ninth century, small dynasties emerged and provincial courts challenged the magnificence of Baghdad. These petty rulers were often patrons of the arts and literature but none more elegantly than the Hamdanid Sayf ud-Dawla who became ruler of Aleppo in 944 AD. The great panegyrist poet Mutanabbi visited his court and spent nine years there praising Sayf ud-Dawla until he fell out with his patron and left for Egypt in 957. There he attached himself to the black ruler, Kafur, a eunuch and former slave, for whom he wrote panegyrics first and, when their relationship soured, insults such as 'do not buy a slave without buying a stick with him, for slaves are filthy and of scant good'.[12] Praising rulers was unavoidable and always a problem. Kafur 'picked my brain', wrote Mutanabbi, 'forbade me to depart, postured abroad as patron of the arts'. In the eleventh century al-Ghazali, considered by many Islam's greatest theological analyst, was to warn writers against becoming involved in this patronage: 'Do not mix with princes and sultans. Do not see them … If circumstances necessitate such contacts, then leave their praise and their flattery.'

The proselytizing Fatimid movement began in Ifriqiyya in modern-day Tunisia in the early tenth century. The Fatimid version of Ismaili Shi'ism was a dynastic cause which established the right of the descendants of the children of Fatima – the Prophet's eldest daughter, married to his nephew 'Ali – to the leadership of the Islamic community over that of the ruling Baghdad Caliphs. In 969 the Fatimids founded Cairo and established al-Azhar University and mosque as a propaganda bureau for the propagation of Fatimid ideas. There was little pressure on the Sunnis and Copts to convert and Sunni Muslims, Christians and Jews were able to hold the highest office. The *da'wa* of Ismaili preachers spread revolutionary ideas throughout Syria and Arabia. Fatimid influence spread until 1059 when they briefly controlled Baghdad. But as Fatimid power and its revolutionary zeal declined other movements emerged such as the Druze in the 1020s and the Ismailis in Syria and Iran in the 1090s.

With the arrival from the east of Turkish tribes who soon took northern Iraq and Anatolia, Sunnis began to dominate Shi'i populations but as anti-Shi'i propaganda intensified so the distinction between the Sunnis and Shi'is increased. The Sunnism of most of the eleventh-century Turkish elite developed a conscious Sunni identity. In 1055 the first Seljuk Sultan Toghril took control of Baghdad. Like the Buyids they replaced, the Seljuks claimed to act in the name of the Caliph. Nizam al-Mulk, the chief minister of the Seljuk Sultan Malik Shah (1072–92) produced the *Siyasat Name* (Book of Politics) in which he elaborated court protocol and administrative structures based on Sasanian and 'Abbasid precedents. Sunnism was developed and controlled through the Seljuk system of *madrasah*s (schools). The Seljuks governed partly through the *atabeg* system of tutorship to the princes which was open to corruption when the tutors usurped their wards' inheritance and partly by the *iqta* system where the *muqti* collected revenue, a system clearly open to abuse.

If censorship by assassination is pre-eminent in Algeria, Turkey and various other Islamic countries today, it may have its roots in the sweet gardens of Alamut where the young *fida'een* ('those who sacrifice themselves') would drink sherbet drinks among lovely maidens, lulled into sensual pleasure by the effects of hashish. They were known as the Assassins (*hashishin* from the Arabic word *hashish*, 'grass' although certain recent researchers believe that the etymology of the word assassin is really *asasi*, Arabic for 'basic' or fundamentalist). These *fida'een* were also called Nizaris and were an offshoot of the Ismailis, the 'sevener' Shi'is who recognized the seventh imam as being Ismail, the son of Ja'afar al-Sadiq. The mainstream 'twelvers' passed over Ismail in favour of his brother Musa Kadhim who died in 799. The Ismailis became a radical, militant movement and developed esoteric doctrines around the imam. Among their offshoots were the Qarmatians of the ninth–twelfth centuries, the Fatimids of Egypt and North Africa (969–1171) and the Nizaris.

The Assassins were led by the 'old man of the mountain', Hasan ibn al-Sabbah with their base at Alamut in Iran's Elburz Mountains. Like the modern Shi'is and like Khomeini, he preached the glory of martyrdom in the conduct of a war. Ibn al-Sabbah spent a year and a half in Egypt studying the *batinid* (*batin*, secret) system of the Fatimids. He then returned to his native Rayy as a Fatimid missionary. In 1090 he gained possession of the strong mountain fortress of Alamut north-west of Qazwin. Here he created a secret organization based on Ismaili antecedents. The organization, says Philip Hitti, 'developed an agnosticism which aimed to emancipate the initiate from the trammels of doctrine, enlightened him as to the superfluity of prophets and encouraged him to believe nothing and dare all'.[13]

Marco Polo describes the wonderful gardens surrounding the elegant pavilions and palaces built by Ibn al-Sabbah. Nobody was allowed to enter the garden except for the young *fida'een*. The only entrance was via a well-guarded fortress. The youths were put to sleep with some wonderful potion, presumably hashish, and carried inside. When they awoke they thought they were in paradise. Beautiful women ministered to them to their hearts' delight. Back in the drudgery of the real world they would be ordered by Ibn al-Sabbah to assassinate a man he had targeted. When the mission was completed, they believed, his angels would bear them into paradise. If they died they would be likewise taken to paradise. The assassination in 1092 of the famous wazir of the Seljuk sultanate, Nizam al-Mulk, by a *fida'i* disguised as a Sufi was the first of a series of notorious murders that set off a chain reaction of terror throughout the Muslim world. Attempts by rulers to defeat Ibn al-Sabbah failed and it was not until the Mongol Hulagu arrived that the fortress and subsidiary castles were destroyed in 1256. The descendants of the Assassins are scattered through northern Syria, Iran, Oman, Zanzibar and India. Nevertheless, this traditional story of the Assassins has been strongly challenged by more modern scholarship.

In 1099 the Norman knight Tancred, having already helped to slaughter much of the population of Jerusalem in the bloody First Crusade, handed his banner to the Muslims who had held out inside the Citadel as a pledge of his protection. The following day the Crusaders slaughtered all 70,000 of them and waded up the winding streets of Old Jerusalem knee-deep in Muslim and Jewish blood. Shi'i preachers were at first in the lead in urging a united front against the hated Crusader states that developed but in the long term this *jihad* against Christendom was to be led by a Sunni-dominated movement under the banner of Salah ad-Din (Saladin). Like the Zengids before him this chivalrous Kurdish warrior led the most effective resistance at any time and defeated the army of the Kingdom of Jerusalem at the Battle of Hattin in 1187.

In 1258 Hulagu went on to capture Baghdad and put the Caliph to death but the Mamluks (the 'slave' dynasty) of Egypt were soon to halt the Mongol terror. Once they had attained power the Mongols were curiously tolerant and cultured. The eastern part of the 'Abbasid Empire was to be ruled by Mongol or Turkish dynasties until 1500. In literature the period between the end of the Middle Ages and 1800, when almost no Arabic literature of outstanding merit was written, is called *asr al-inhitat* (The Age of Depression).

Islamic culture was to reach its high point in Spain where small dynasties prevailed. The greatest was the al-Muwahidun, known in the West as the Almohads, who ruled from Tunisia to Senegal at the height of their power and flourished in Andalusia. The Christian Reconquest that dated from the Christian victory at Las Navas de Tolosa in 1212 entirely altered the balance of power although the splendid Moorish kingdom of Granada continued until 1492.

Egypt was ruled by the Fatimids from 969 to 1169, the Ayyubid dynasty of Salah ad-Din ruled until 1250 and the Mamluks from then until the Ottoman conquest in 1517. The Mamluks with their vast, solemn mosques such as Cairo's

Ibn Tulun and vast gates such as Cairo's Bab Zuweila, left behind them a splendid culture. Meanwhile, Islam was spreading into West Africa, the Indian sub-continent and South-East Asia. Although India had been penetrated under the Umayyads, the spread of Islam was largely thanks to Mahmoud of Ghazna (ruled 998–1030).

The centuries from 1500 to 1800 were dominated by the Ottoman Empire – perhaps the best example of decentralized liberalism – the Persian Safavid Empire and the Mughal Empire in India. The Ottomans finally took Constantinople from the Byzantine in 1453 and in the sixteenth century took Syria, the northern African coastline from Algeria to Egypt and, a century later, Iraq. The Safavid Empire was created by Shah Ismail (1502–24) who made Imamite Shi'ism the state religion at a time when Shi'is were considered fifth columnists. By the end of the First World War only Asia Minor and a small portion of European territory survived and that thanks to Mustafa Kemal (Atatürk).

The Ottomans tried as hard as possible to emulate the West and thus protect themselves from western encroachments in the nineteenth century. Sultan Mahmoud II used the Janissaries to bring local warlords to heel, then in 1826 exterminated this fractious militia. The Ottomans then started to build on western structures. As Francis Robinson notes,[14] 'The Ottoman state which once existed to spread Islam now regarded Islamic knowledge as irrelevant to its purposes.' The important edicts of the period, the Noble Rescript of the Rose Chamber (1839) and the Imperial Rescript (1856) declared that all the Sultan's subjects, irrespective of religion, were equal. The state rejected its former Islamic basis, offering justice and equality to all. Although at the end of the Ottoman era Abd ul-Hamid II was to try to appeal to the *'ulama* by restoring the old Islamic identity, in 1908 the Young Turks brought an end to this Islamic option once and for all. In any case, although throughout the period of Ottoman rule Christians and Jews had to pay the poll tax and show allegiance to the Sultan, on balance they were left to their own devices and ran their own affairs.

In 1526 Babar, ruler of Afghanistan, had occupied the Kingdom of Delhi and became founder of the great Mughal Empire. Under the tolerant and syncretist Akbar (1556–1605) the Mughal Empire covered most of the Indian sub-continent. However, by the eighteenth century it was in decline and British influence had greatly increased from its commercial ports. The *coup de grâce* of the Mughal Empire and its replacement by the British Empire was the Indian Mutiny of 1857 (many Indians and Pakistanis refer to it as the War of Independence).

Between 1500 and 1800 Islam came to influence most of the peoples of present-day Indonesia and its island neighbourhood. In northern Sumatra, so long exposed to Arab and Indian Muslim trade and culture, Islamic orthodoxy took root. On the other hand in Java where Hinduism and Buddhism had flourished, the new religion took root more cautiously. While sculpture of the human form was abandoned the Hindi epics were still valued and the intercession of certain goddesses sought. The traditional cycle of plays based on the Hindi Ramayana or Mahabharata contributed to the development of a new style, the *wayang golek* in which the most popular cycle of plays was based on stories about Amir Hamza, the uncle of the Prophet Muhammad. Meanwhile, the words of the *wayang* or shadow theatre continued to feed the Hindu pantheon alongside the spreading culture of Islam.

Meanwhile, in the Arab Near East, in Syria, 'Abd al-Rahman al-Kawakibi (1854–1902) was to be the key figure in the rise of pan-Arab nationalism. An Aleppo-born idealist and writer, his two books, *Umm al-Qura* (Mecca) and *Taba'i al-Istibdad* (The Nature of Tyranny), attacked Ottoman tyranny and called for an Arab revival. He enumerated 86 causes for the weaknesses of the Islamic world, among them fatalism, religious dissension, intolerance, lack of freedom of speech, inequality and injustice, uncritical acceptance of the written word, hostility towards the sciences, inefficient use of time, and neglect of women's education.

The nineteenth century saw the penetration by the West into the decaying lands of the Ottoman Empire. In a series of bilateral treaties with the Sublime Porte ('the Sublime Gate', i.e. to the government of the Ottoman Sultan) known as the Capitulations, the European powers established extra-territorial rights within the empire which meant that European nationals who committed crimes could not by tried by Ottoman courts without the approval of the consul of the European country in question. In 1839 the Hatt-i Sherif decree reflected the French Declaration of the Rights of Man but came up against Christian and Muslim opposition. In February 1856 the Sublime Porte introduced the Khatt-i Humayun which declared all Ottoman subjects equal, but in theory only. The revolution of the Young Turks in 1908 gave the Arab nationalists a genuine measure of renewed hope. The Young Turks reintroduced the 1876 constitution, freedom of the press and the Ottoman parliament and for a moment Arabs rejoiced in the streets of Damascus, Beirut, Jerusalem and Haifa. However, anti-Arab feeling among the Turks resurfaced and Arab hopes for a new golden age soon fizzled out. The Young Turks carried out a campaign of Turkification with as much zest as Sultan Abd ul-Hamid. In 1913 the Arab nationalists organized the First Arab Congress in Paris. They called for political rights for the Arabs, decentralized administrations in the Arab provinces and the official use of Arabic in the Ottoman parliament. But Turkish promises to recognize these agreements came to nothing.

In Mecca in June 1917 the Arab Revolt, based on British promises to the Sharif Hussein of Mecca of an Arab kingdom liberated from Ottoman Turkish rule, was led by his son Faisal and involved T.E. Lawrence ('Lawrence of Arabia') as his military strategist. Faisal's forces defeated the Turks at Aqaba in a campaign made famous by Lawrence's classic *Seven Pillars of Wisdom.* Jerusalem fell to General Allenby in December 1917 and in October 1918 Faisal and Lawrence took Damascus. Faisal's rule in Syria was popular but brief because the French forced him out of their mandated territory in 1920 and he was given Iraq as a British lackey instead. The Bolsheviks exposed the Anglo-French Sykes Picot Agreement which had deviously divided up the region (with an area west of Homs and Aleppo set aside; as it turned out for a 'Jewish homeland' based on the Balfour Declaration of 1917).

The inter-war years saw the alarming increase in Jewish immigration into Palestine. The British fiercely put down a Palestinian Arab revolt provoked by fears of Jewish domination. This weakened the Palestinians and strengthened the Jews, although with the bombing by Jewish terrorist groups of the British administration in the King David Hotel in 1948 and other atrocities the British were to suffer more from the Jews than from the Arabs. After the Second World War the influx of Jewish immigrants became a stampede despite British attempts to stem it. On 14 May 1948 the British pulled out of Palestine, handing their responsibility over to the United Nations. The creation of the state of Israel on the following day and the expulsion of 700,000 Palestinians became for the latter the *Nakba* (the Catastrophe). Massacres by Jewish terrorists of villages such as that of the friendly village of Deir Yassin had succeeded in ethnically cleansing the majority of Palestinians from their homeland. Most of Palestine's 500 Arab villages were razed to the ground.

Four Arab-Israeli wars followed in 1948, 1956, 1967 and 1973. The Camp David Agreement of 1979 brought Egypt out of the conflict and saw a bitter division between those Arab countries willing to recognize Israel and those who were not. The Iraqi invasion of Kuwait in 1990 and Iraq's catastrophic defeat at the hands of the USA and its allies the following year widened these rifts. The Palestinians, seen by their Arab neighbours as supporters of Saddam Hussein, were the first to suffer. Saddam had won Palestinian support by calling for a *jihad* against Israel and by dropping a few ineffective Scud missiles on the Jewish state. The Intifada (uprising) against Israeli occupation lasted from 1987 to 1991 when the secret Oslo Peace Accords began. The Palestinians felt compelled to sue for peace after losing the support of the Arab Gulf countries during the Gulf War. The Oslo peace process, however, came to an abrupt and violent halt with the so-called 'al-Aqsa' Intifada (Palestinians call it the Independence Intifada) which was sparked off, in the view of most Arabs, by Ariel Sharon's visit to Jerusalem's Dome on the Rock in September 2000. The new Intifada helped to liberate the Palestinian media, suppressed by Arafat and his corrupt coteries, because Palestinian society was beginning to control the political and social environment over the Tunis cabal that had misruled for seven years from Arafat's lair in Gaza.

NINE

Turning Midgets into Heroes: the Power of the Arab Poet

Modern Islamic literature has emerged from political resistance to the colonial powers, essentially Britain and France, since the Ottoman yoke was lifted from much of the Arabic world after the First World War. Unfortunately, many Muslim scholars believe, the new order had little cultural legitimacy. Dogma and nostalgia have tended to dominate in the form of semi-military states.[1] Despite the emergence of the Internet and satellite technology, most media and communications continue to be controlled and owned by the state. In an article in *Index on Censorship* Haifaa Khalafallah notes that Arabic literature has followed three different directions: 'first, literature of exile, which does not reach those who can comprehend it; second, literature which receives the sanction of the state as being acceptable and not in conflict with the basic ideologies of the state; third, literature of the underground, which deals boldly with the true aspects of its time.' To underline his distressing argument, Khalafallah quotes the Syrian poet Nizar al-Qabbani:

In that Arab homeland I travel...
Guards shove me to the hands of other guards,
Police stations hand me to other police stations,
All I carry across the border is a notebook
The words in my country need passports to go through.

Born in Syria in 1923 Qabbani is probably the best-selling poet in the Arab world. His poem 'Footnotes to the Book of the Setback' is one of the most genuine *samizdat* poems distributed in the Arab world. Published shortly after the catastrophic Arab defeat at the end of the 1967 June war (known by many, disparagingly, as the 'Six Day War'), it was widely banned in Arab countries who did not wish to confront this profound humiliation. His poems are an important example of the *Adab al-Huzairan* literature (June literature) inspired by the defeat which had an immense influence on the Arabic and the wider

Islamic world. This poem is also an indictment of the braggadocio, the cowardice and the cruelty of any tyranny. Nevertheless, as Peter Clark points out, in Syria, whose regime was a main target of his poetry, the official attitude was ambiguous. Qabbani returned to Syria to give a reading in the early 1990s which was attended by Asad's eldest son, Basil. When Qabbani died Mustafa Tlas, the Minister for Defence, led the mourners at his funeral. This was, says Clark, another case of the regime co-opting the dissident. Qabbani often generalized his attacks. Listeners knew whom he was targeting but it was convenient for regimes to pretend that the target was elsewhere. He wrote:

> Friends,
> The ancient word is dead
> The ancient books are dead
> Our speech with holes like worn-out shoes is dead.
> Dead is the mind that led to defeat.

Humiliation and self-mockery show clearly through his verses:

> Stirred by Oriental bombast,
> By Antaric swaggering that never killed
> By the fiddler and the drum,
> We went to war
> And lost.

And by dark judgements of the Arab world:

> In short
> We wear the cape of civilization
> But our souls live in the stone age.
>
> You don't win a war
> With a reed and a flute.

Qabbani recognizes Israel's genius at testing the weakness of its enemies:

> Our enemies did not cross our borders
> They crept through our weaknesses like ants.
>
> We are a thick-skinned people
> with empty souls.

We spend our days practising witchcraft,
Playing chess and sleeping.
Are we the Nation by which God
Blessed Mankind?

Our desert oil could have become
Daggers of flame and fire.
We're a disgrace to our noble ancestors:
We let our oil flow through the toes of whoredom.

We run wildly through the streets
Dragging people with ropes
…
Turn midgets into heroes
And heroes into scum
…
And beg God for victory
Over our enemy.

However, he acknowledges that it is fear that prevents men under tyrannies from demanding justice, recognizing that the Arabs have themselves to blame for many of their troubles:

If I knew I'd come to no harm,
And could see the Sultan,
I'd tell him:
'Sultan,
Your wild dogs have torn my clothes
Your spies hound me
Their eyes hound me
Their noses hound me
Their feet hound me
They hound me like fate
Interrogate my wife
And take down the names of my friends.'

But he ends on a note of hope amid despair:

We are a nation of crooks and jugglers
Arab children

Spring rain
Corn ears of the future,
You are the generation
That will overcome defeat.[2]

The other beacon of poetic light is Adonis ('Ali Ahmad Sa'id). He was born in
Syria in 1930. In 1956, following imprisonment, he was exiled to Beirut. In 1957
he and the Lebanese poet Yusef al-Khal launched their hugely important and
influential poetry magazine *Shi'r* (Poetry) which, says the writer and translator
Abdullah al-Udhari, led to the break-up of classical Arabic poetic conventions.
In 1968 Adonis founded *Mawaqif,* a platform for avant-garde poetry. During
the Lebanese civil war he went to live in Paris where he secretly joined the
Syrian Writers' Union, which is thought to be run by the Syrian security
services. He was later banned for having read poetry with an Israeli poet at an
international conference. Today his incredibly loved works are often banned
in Arab countries. His poetry was banned in Kuwait when Kuwait launched
what was meant to be one of the region's most prestigious book fairs, in
November 2000. The government denied that Islamic fundamentalists were
putting pressure on them to ban books that offended them, but few believed
the denial.

'In Arab society', Adonis told a London meeting in 1981, 'most poets are
part of a cultural system which is controlled by a political structure. The system
has to accommodate pressure from every angle. Today, the new oil wealth
intensifies this tyranny by presenting a distorted picture of the Arab poet who
to the outside world looks as if he is tied with silk when in reality he is bound
by ropes of blood.'[3] In 'The Pearl' Adonis's view is bleak and beautiful:

Obsessed
I
Hold the earth like a woman
And sleep
...
How can I walk towards myself,
Towards my people?
My blood is fire,
My history a heap of ruins
...
I hear voices singing in my ashes,
I see them walking like the children of
My country.

And in 'A Mirror for Beirut' he is sardonic:

A cemetery
A gold purse tucked in a belt.
A babbling woman sleeps
With a prince or a dagger in her arms.[4]

TEN

The Eternal Problem of Palestine

I would have liked to tell you
The story of a nightingale that died
I would have liked to tell you
The story...
Had they not slit my lips.

(Samih al-Qasim, translated by Abdullah al-Udhari
in *Index on Censorship*, No.5, 1997, p.31.)

The Palestinian Israeli poet Samih al-Qasim was imprisoned many times by the Israelis for his political activities but spurned PLO overtures to move to Beirut on the grounds that if people like him left their homeland there would be no Palestine. Born in 1939, his first collection of poems appeared in 1958. His second book, *Songs of the Alleys* (1965), was, he said, 'full of empty pages'. The censors cut whole poems, parts of poems, or individual lines. He regards freedom and democracy in Israel as 'pure hypocrisy', telling the translator Abdullah al-Udhari in 1983, 'I can write and read a poem against Menachem Begin according to Israeli law, but according to the same law, Menachem Begin can confiscate the land on which I stand to read my poems. And he does that. Personally I prefer the worst regime in the world to the *beautiful* Israeli law.'[1]

The leading poet of the Palestinian resistance today is Mahmoud Darwish who returned to Palestine after the 1993 Oslo Peace Accords and edits the cultural journal *Karmal*. Darwish was born in al-Barwa, a village east of Acre, in 1941. When fighting broke out in Palestine in 1948 Darwish, then seven years old, fled his village with his grandfather to southern Lebanon where they retained the hope of returning to their village once the war was over. Finding their stay in Lebanon longer than expected Darwish made his way back into Israel secretly with one of his relatives in 1950 and rejoined his family. As a pupil of Deir al-Adad school he remembers being hidden by the Palestinian headmaster whenever an Israeli inspector visited the school. His poems are understandably bleak. In 'The Earth is Narrowing on Us' he writes

> We will cut off the hand of the song to be finished by our flesh
> We will die here, here in the last passage. Here and here our
> Blood will plant its olive tree.[2]

In the eyes of most Arabs and many Muslims the new colonial power in the region is Israel and until the Oslo Accords Israel was barely to be found on most Arab maps at all. In fact, this attitude of utter rejection seemed to be ready to return with the so-called 'al-Aqsa' Intifada which began in September 2000 at a time when Palestinians felt that they had been duped by the Israelis and now had nothing more to lose by a new and bloody uprising aimed at restoring freedom and honour. However, protests against the occupation throughout the Arab world were sometimes suppressed brutally, even in apparently benign countries like Jordan.

Nevertheless, censorship is a much greater problem for Palestinians in the West Bank and Gaza. When I visited the Palestinian Minister of Information, Yasser Abed Rabbo, in May 2001, several months into the 'al-Aqsa' Intifada, he assured me that there were no 'red lines' in Area A (areas of full Palestinian control according to the Oslo Accords). But Palestinian censorship is ad hoc. If the Palestinian National Authority (the effective government) does not like something it will act, but media organs do not know in advance what will bring trouble for them.

A more dangerous and more real censorship is Israeli army rockets and settler missiles. In February March 2001 the Brussels-based International Federation of Journalists noted that at least three main media, including the PBC building in Gaza and *al-Hayat al-Jadida* and al-Salam Television in Ramallah, had been recently shelled by Israeli forces. There had been systematic destruction of journalists' equipment, including cars with press markings and cameras, the Israeli authorities had prevented the circulation of Palestinian newspapers from the West Bank to Gaza for at least three days, and they had restricted the free movement of Palestinian journalists. According to leaders of the Palestine Journalists' Association, more than forty journalists, mostly cameramen and press photographers, had been injured between September 2000 and May 2001. The numbers included eight foreign journalists of different nationalities. The International Federation of Journalists said that there was a strong suspicion that the media were being singled out by the Israelis for special treatment.

Palestine's thirty or so private television stations are independent. Rabbo assured me that he does not interfere at all with them. He even told me that his ministry runs workshops and training programmes for them with the aid of the universities. Nevertheless, according to a Bir Zeit University's Media Institute (BZMI) survey nearly 60 per cent of journalists feel that they have red lines which they cannot cross in their coverage. This is especially so with issues related to security, politics, corruption, the PA, VIPs and sex. According to the survey, 53.5 per cent have had material censored by their editor for political or security reasons and 62.6 per cent feel that they must adopt self-censorship when writing.

The majority of Palestinian journalists believe that they have a direct political role to play while they are active as journalists. The BZMI believe that this relates to how Palestinians understand the role of the media in general under direct Israeli occupation. It believes that it demonstrates that much needs to be done to help journalists develop a more sophisticated understanding of the role of media and to realize that it is not within their remit to attempt directly to manipulate the reading public. Sixty per cent of journalists questioned believed that there was a contradiction between being 'nationalist–patriotic' and being 'professional' in the media. They would prefer to give priority to the nationalist–patriotic side. At the same time 71.3 per cent of them thought that journalists should play a direct role in political manipulation through their work.

The General Manager of *al-Quds* newspaper, Maher el Sheikh, told me that Israeli censorship is still a bigger problem than Palestinian censorship. The 'red line' is Arafat. The Palestinian press tends to be soft on powerful people in the PA. Fatah people once tried to attack *al-Quds* for criticizing the PA but it could not call the Israeli police; this would be considered by the PA to be treason. The Israeli press used to be more sympathetic to newspapers such as *al-Quds* but since the Intifada began things deteriorated. Such newspapers must always keep in mind the Israeli censor while the Palestinian censor, in contrast, is often lazy. All Israeli security people want a say in checking *al-Quds* stories from the adviser to the police chief to the adviser to the minister for Arab affairs. Sheikh told me that Israeli censorship is as bad as in any third world country. Nevertheless, because they are close to the PA the Palestinian newspapers *al-Ayyam* and *al-Hayat al-Jadida* can publish things that *al-Quds* cannot. Others must be more careful. The prominent Palestinian media figure Daoud Kuttab was jailed by the PA for seven days when al-Quds Educational TV, which he runs, aired sessions of the Palestinian Legislative Council dealing with Palestinian corruption.

Today there are eleven radio stations in Palestine. Most of them are in the West Bank. All are on FM. They function under a temporary licence from the Palestinian Ministry of Information and without Israeli approval. Most of them broadcast music or phone-in programmes. The PA has so far refused to give any private radio station in Gaza a licence. However, if enough trained people were to be made available, this would put more pressure on the PA to give licences.

In Palestine censorship comes like the wrath of the Greek gods from the sky. It was a helicopter over the sea before my window at midnight that started the shelling of Gaza in May 2001. Wave after wave of rockets came over us to hit Palestinian military and police targets. I joined the crowds in the street to watch and was treated with usual Gazan courtesy as the helicopter used its clinical targeting technology and the shells slammed into their targets for over half an hour.

Earlier that day the deputy-head of the radio station of the Palestine Broadcasting Corporation (PBC) had driven me through miles of bustling city – Gaza is a huge town of a million people – pointing out the various buildings the Israelis had targeted with rockets over the previous few weeks in tit-for-tat revenge for ineffective Palestinian mortar attacks on Jewish settlements. Near Gaza's two universities we saw walls covered with carefully painted graffiti of Hamas heroes, exploding hand-grenades, and crimson buses blowing up or snapping in two with pin-men and pin-women scattering out of them into the air. Eventually we climbed a hill in the old quarter of Shuja'iyya and reached the PBC headquarters. Its transmission room had been targeted several weeks before – the rocket missed the vital equipment – and had just been rebuilt. A huge aerial, also hit by the rocket, lay abandoned outside. We glanced up to check for spotter-planes and listen for the sound of helicopters, but the evening was quiet despite several Palestinian mortar attacks on settlements earlier in the day. The PBC's strongly nationalist tone and the films of Palestinian victims of rocket attacks and attacks by settlers constantly broadcast are considered by the Israelis an incitement to terror. Even the private television stations that I had been visiting in the West Bank towns of Ramallah, Bethlehem and Nablus were frightened of being targeted. 'They may shell us again', the station's head told me 'but usually we see a spotter plane first and have time to evacuate our staff.'

The following day I was sitting in the office of the director of the PBC's satellite station when news came through that Sharon had suggested targeting Palestinian television stations again. We were quite eager to leave the building and a worried director drove us to our hotel. He lived in Khan Younis, a Palestinian town near the Egyptian border hemmed in by Jewish settlements.

It was constantly fired on by the Israeli army. Khan Younis turned its lights out after 10.30 so as not to attract fire. Whenever a door slammed Yousef's three-year-old started screaming 'They're shooting, Daddy. They're shooting.' One night his ten-year-old asked him as they stood outside their flat what the shiny red spot was on his father's chest. He looked down. It was an infrared ray trained on him by an Israeli army sniper a few hundred yards away. He rushed his son into the apartment before the soldier could fire.

The myth that Palestinians are by their nature terrorists is sustained in much of the Israeli media. However, in April 1998 Patrick Cockburn wrote in the *Independent on Sunday*: 'By the time the tourist had made the quick trip from Jerusalem to Bethlehem, the Israeli guide had used the word "terrorist" and "terrorism" no fewer than 32 times. He informed the passengers that he would take no responsibility for their safety if they strayed far into the town of Bethlehem, a placid warren of ancient streets made to sound like a cross between Belfast and Beirut in the civil war.'[3]

But the Palestinian leadership has also shown little respect for the truth. When the Palestinian uprising known as the (first) Intifada broke out in December 1987 Arafat and the PLO in Tunis felt challenged by this extraordinary grassroots response to occupation and tried to ignore it. Through the painstaking labours of Arafat's most loyal friend Abu Jihad they then took the other tack by capitalizing on it and eventually leading it, but when Abu Jihad was murdered by the Israelis in 1988 Arafat may have been relieved to be free of so popular and effective a rival and to be able to surround himself with the sycophants and mediocrities with whom he felt safe and at ease.

Again and again local initiatives have been either suppressed or hijacked by Arafat. When the people of Beit Sahur rebelled and the Israelis imprisoned them and uprooted their vital olive trees, liberals worldwide were appalled but Arafat neutralized the rebellion because he did not control it. He sidelined and humiliated highly charismatic and dignified figures like Hanan Ashrawi and Faisal Husseini. Crude language is his norm. He stomped out of a Legislative Council meeting in 1996 shouting 'Dogs and sons of bitches'. In 1997 Arafat ordered Faisal Husseini to stop acting as spokesman against Israeli plans to build a settlement at Abu Ghneim (the Israeli Har Homa) because he felt that Husseini was stealing his thunder. He will not abide criticism. The books of that very symbol of Palestine, Professor Edward Said, are banned because they criticize Arafat.

Arafat's vanity may be his underlying weakness. His asides to journalists such as 'When I ran Lebanon' are dangerous, says his biographer Said Aburish,[4] for the vulnerable Palestinian refugees in Lebanon. When Rabin called him '*Rayees*' (President) he was delighted. The Israeli Labour Party understood that they could roll on with settlements and manipulate the Palestinians as long as they massaged Arafat's ego. Netanyahu, on the other hand, put prejudice before wisdom and went out of his way to humiliate Arafat. He would not allow him even the pretence of dignity, says Aburish.

A Palestinian human rights leader in Jerusalem once admitted that Arafat's human rights record was even worse than that of the Israelis, then suddenly added 'But I love him because he *is* Palestine.' Aburish describes Arafat calling a prisoner up from his cell to his office merely to remind him why he was being incarcerated. I was a close friend of Iyad al-Sarraj, a prominent psychiatrist and a budding critic of Palestinian human rights abuses. Sarraj was imprisoned and treated so violently that when I took him for lunch in London he was contemplating taking a long sabbatical in the Oxfordshire countryside to rest and write his memoirs.

According to Aburish, Arafat's strength and weakness is his mastery of double-talk. When asked about corruption he replied absurdly that this was impossible since the Palestinians had no money. Aburish, who grew up near Jerusalem in the biblical village of Bethany – the grandson of a renowned Muslim judge – believes that the only loyal Palestinian is one who is capable of making judgements that demystify Arafat. Contradictions in Arafat's personality abound. He claimed that left alone the Palestinians would have won the 1948 war. He later resorted to convenience after being imprisoned by Nasser by trying to find common ground with the Egyptian leader. Arafat sought money but did not compromise his principles to acquire it. When in 1961 the Iraqi dictator Kassem pronounced Kuwait part of Iraq Arafat's Fatah movement refused to consider the potential rewards of siding with Iraq and supported the independence of Kuwait, in contrast with his disastrous siding with Saddam Hussein in 1991. He is a tidy man who lives frugally – he doesn't drink or smoke – but is surrounded by lavish corruption. Aburish speaks of the will of a Palestinian construction magnate which left $70 million to the PLO but not even the dead man's family knows what happened to this money. Although there is no suggestion that Arafat uses money for personal gain, according to Edward Said, of $18.5 million the International Monetary Fund (IMF) gave the Palestine National Authority (PNA) in April 1995, $18 million was deposited in Arafat's name. Aburish says that when a Palestinian businessman approached the PNA for a licence to build a cement factory the PNA treacherously passed the contract to a Tunis loyalist.

Arafat always fought bravely and after the 1967 war with Israel the Israelis played into his hands by responding too violently and confirming the soundness of his judgement to fight. Interviewed by journals like *Time*, he liked to pose as a general, half Saladin, half General Douglas MacArthur, says

Aburish. Although he was not behind the hijackings of the Popular Front for the Liberation of Palestine in the 1970s, he capitalized on them, recognizing that they introduced Palestine to the world, albeit gruesomely. The same was true of the massacre of Israeli athletes at Munich in 1972. Terrorist politics started without his support but the strength of Palestinian feeling cornered him into accepting the idea of a terror organization. He allowed things to happen.

In contrast, after the 1973 war he sent peace feelers to Kissinger which Kissinger ignored contemptuously. Arafat insisted on carrying a gun to the UN when he gave his famous 'gun and olive-branch' speech. Mossad put it about that he was homosexual but Aburish records several relationships with women. From the early 1970s he had implicitly accepted UN Security Council Resolution 242 and Israel's right to exist and after Sadat's visit to Jerusalem in 1977 he ordered his followers to refrain from any calls to murder Sadat and to stop referring to him as a traitor. But there was always that martial spark. After Israel invaded Lebanon in 1982 he said that Beirut would be 'the Hanoi and the Stalingrad of the Israeli army'. During the fighting in Lebanon he had no fixed abode and gave orders from the street or travelling in cars. He also had a sense of humour. When forced to beat a retreat from Lebanon and the adjutant came to tell him that envoys had come to say goodbye, he replied promptly, 'Where are they going?'

In Palestine many regret that there is no Mandela-figure. Aburish's solution for the replacement of Arafat was to create a triumvirate of Heidar Abdel Shafi, the grand old man of Gaza, Faisal Husseini and Hanan Ashrawi as an interim administration (Husseini died suddenly in mid-2001). This group he said, would address itself to negotiating a better deal with Israel, while technocrats would replace Arafat's entourage of corrupt men to run the internal affairs of the entity under Palestinian control. This would be in the interest of the Palestinian but not in Arafat's, not in the Israelis and possibly not in the West's. Third world dictators are easy to manipulate and – sad to say – the West has often supported them as long as they toe the line.

Since the 1993 Oslo Accords key newspapers in the West Bank have been brought to heel. For a while the Palestine Broadcasting Corporation headed by the charismatic Radwan abu Ayyash in Ramallah was forbidden to broadcast, all its output being sent for broadcast to the local television station in Gaza run from Arafat's beach villa. The enlightened Ramallah newspaper *al-Hayat al-Jadida*, which had challenged taboo social problems such as wife battering and child abuse, had to seek Arafat's financial backing and is now the voice of Arafat and only a shadow of its former, campaigning self.

One of the martyrs to Palestinian censorship was Naji el-'Ali who developed a stark and symbolic style during his thirty-year campaign on behalf of the Palestinians. Unaligned with any political party he strove to speak to and for ordinary Arab people. Because of invasion, censorship and threats he lived in exile most of his life, much of the time between Beirut and Kuwait. He spent the last two years of his life in London. Born in Galilee, he fled Palestine with his family in 1948 to live in exile in the south of Lebanon in the Ein al-Helwe Palestinian refugee camp. In the late 1950s the late Palestinian poet Ghasan Kanafani discovered Naji's talent in drawing while on a visit to this camp.

> I started to use drawing as a form of political expression while in Lebanese jails. I was detained by the Deuxième Bureau (the Lebanese intelligence service) as a result of the measures the Bureau were undertaking to contain political activities in the Palestinian camps during the sixties. I drew on the prison walls and subsequently Ghasan Kanafani, a journalist and publisher of al-Huria magazine (assassinated in Beirut in 1971) saw some of those drawings and encouraged me to continue, and eventually published some of my cartoons.[5]

In the early 1960s he joined an Art Institute in Lebanon but discontinued his studies to work in Kuwait on *al-Tali'a* magazine. 'Later I fled to Kuwait. The margin of freedom and democracy that exists in Kuwait enabled me to grow. There my cartoons concentrated on the dangers surrounding us as people.' In the early 1970s he returned to Beirut from Kuwait and was on the editorial board of the prominent Lebanese newspaper *al-Safir.*

> Working for al-Safir newspaper in Beirut in 1971 was the best part of my life, and the most productive. There, surrounded by the violence of many an army, and finally by the Israeli invasion, I stood facing it all with my pen every day. I never felt fear, failure or despair, and I didn't surrender. I faced armies with cartoons and drawings of flowers, hope and bullets. Yes, hope is essential, always. My work in Beirut made me once again closer to the refugees in the camps, the poor, and the harassed.

During this period he also contributed drawings to *al-Khalij* newspaper in the United Arab Emirates. The Israelis invaded Lebanon in 1982. Fearing Phalangist threats on his life Naji el-'Ali returned to Kuwait in 1983 and worked in *al-Qabas* (The Light) newspaper. In October 1985 he was expelled from Kuwait by pressure from the PLO but continued to work for *al-Qabas* in London and continued to contribute his work to *al-Khalij*. He is thought to have been the highest paid cartoonist in the Arab world.

He was opposed to terrorism and the absence of democracy and, not belonging to any political group, tried to be a true representative of Arab public opinion.

> As soon as I was aware of what was going on, all the havoc in our region, I felt I had to do something, to contribute somehow. First I tried politics, to join a party, I marched in demonstrations, but that was not really me. The sharp cries I felt within me needed a different medium to express what I was going through. It was some time in the fifties that I started drawing on the walls of our camp. During that period, the refugees had begun to develop some political awareness as a reaction to what had been taking place in the region: a revolution in Egypt, a war of independence in Algeria, things were brewing all around the Arab world. My job, I felt, was to speak up for those people, my people who are in the camps, in Egypt, in Algeria, the simple Arabs all over the region who have very few outlets to express their points of view. I felt my job was to incite them. For the function of a political cartoonist, as I see it, is to provide a new vision. He is a missionary, in a sense, because it is just a little bit harder to censor a cartoon than an article.

Few regimes or political groups in the region escaped his satirical drawings. His cartoons portrayed the bitter struggle and plight of the Palestinian people against Israeli occupation and oppression. He also campaigned against the absence of democracy, widespread corruption and gross inequality in the Arab world. He was said to have antagonized virtually everyone in the Middle East; Arab, Jew, conservative and radical alike. He believed his period of work in Beirut was the best part of his career and that his periods of exile in Kuwait and the UK restricted his creativeness in ways he could not understand and counter. He missed the inspiration of the reality of the refugee camps in southern Lebanon. Naji el-'Ali's philosophy can perhaps be best encapsulated in his explanation about Hanzala, the little boy who appears as a spectator in each of his cartoons:

> This child, as you can see, is neither beautiful, spoilt, nor even well-fed. He is barefoot like many children in refugee camps. He is actually ugly and no woman would wish to have a child like him. However, those who came to know 'Hanzala', as I discovered, later adopted him because he is affectionate, honest, outspoken, and a bum. He is an icon that stands to

watch me from slipping. And his hands behind his back are a symbol of rejection of all the present negative tides in our region.

Hanzala is now the official logo of the Commission for Freedom and Justice Through Humour and an affiliate of UNESCO.

Between 1958 and 1963 Naji el-'Ali was frequently detained by police and continually censored. He received many death threats during his life. Because of his work he was said to be one of the most wanted men in the Middle East and this forced him to leave Lebanon and work in Kuwait and London. He emphatically refused to speak about his oppressors and those who might censor his work; he drew them instead.

On Wednesday 22 July 1987 he was shot in the head by a lone gunman as he was going to work at the *al-Qabas* offices in Ives Street, Chelsea. After five weeks in a coma on a life support machine in St Stephen's and Charing Cross hospitals in London, he died at 1am on Saturday 30 August at the age of 51. Apparently he had been warned by a telephone call from a friend, a senior member of the PLO in Tunisia, that his life was in danger. The call, about two weeks before his death, came after the publication of a cartoon attacking a female friend of Yasser Arafat, but his prophetic cartoon 'Achilles Heel' was drawn after the warning. He had once said:

> When I was younger I thought I would actually be able to help achieve all our aspirations for independence, unity, justice. Many died for those aspirations and things are only getting worse. That, certainly, can make one despair. But more than ever, I feel a sense of duty to go on doing what I have to and can do.[6]

He was posthumously awarded the annual Golden Pen award of the International Federation of Newspaper Publishers (FIEJ) in 1988. This award is given to recognize outstanding actions in favour of freedom of expression and the jury was composed of publishers from twenty-eight member countries.[7] His cartoons remain as relevant today as they were then.

In 1996 Palestinian cartoonist Bahaa al-Boukhari, who worked for the largest Palestinian newspaper *al-Quds*, depicted Palestinian police chief Brigadier Ghazi Jabbali sitting at his desk with a bookshelf behind him holding scissors and handcuffs. A sign on his desk read 'Ruler by Order of God'. After publication, the powerful Jabbali let it be known that Boukhari had overstepped his limits, and that he would retaliate at a time of his choice. The absence of democracy makes cartooning a dangerous profession in Arab East Jerusalem and Boukhari is also immensely frustrated by the Israeli authorities. The *Japan Times* reported in May 1996, that about 20 per cent of the cartoonist's work was still being banned by Israeli censors 'for security reasons'.[8]

Confusion surrounded an application of the Palestinian press law in August 1999. Hani Masri, manager of publications for the information ministry, reported the rescinding of press licences for a number of news venues in the West Bank and Gaza Strip due to their sporadic appearance. 'There is no political reason for closing these papers. These are all rumours,' said Masri. While WAFA, the official Palestinian news agency, listed forty-two newspapers and magazines that were allegedly closed down by the order, none of those contacted had been informed of their closure. One of the publications, *Sawt al-Watan*, was once connected with the Authority but split, a possible reason for the rescinding of its press licence. Other publications have been out of print for years or originally obtained their licences from the Israeli authorities. Since the outbreak of the 'al-Aqsa' Intifada, journalists and reporters of local and international press agencies have been threatened or even killed by Israeli forces.

The visit of Israel's hard-line Likud leader Ariel Sharon to the Haram as-Sharrif on 28 September 2000 was a catalyst for this new Intifada which both Arabs and Israelis recognize as a low-level guerrilla war of liberation. It had started on fertile ground because the Palestinians had begun to see themselves as the victims of a double swindle. They had lost 78 per cent of Mandate Palestine in 1948 (including Katamun, Talbieh and other smart districts of mainly Christian West Jerusalem). Oslo involved their unqualified recognition of the state of Israel and their formal acceptance of their 1948 loss in exchange – they believed – for a state. What they could not possibly agree to was to turn the 22 per cent that remained of Mandate Palestine – the West Bank and Gaza – into a honeycomb of Biblical slave states.

ELEVEN

Democracy and the Shari'a: Torment or Justice?

The Fulani tribesman in northern Nigeria must have imagined that he had one last chance before he suffered the most odious punishment demanded by the Shari'a. He was wrong. As he attempted to steal from a house the mob grabbed him, a long knife was produced and his right hand was cut right off. This took place in October 1999 at a time when the Nigerian state of Zamfara prepared to introduce the Shari'a. 'We are following the Saudi Arabian role model,' the governor of the state told the *Guardian* newspaper. 'Go to Saudi Arabia. People just leave their houses open when they go to pray. They do not live in fear of robbers ... But Shari'a is not limited to the laws. It is a comprehensive way of life; what you do from the moment you wake up. When you go to the toilet you walk in with your left leg first and leave with your right leg first. That is Shari'a.' As such quotations demonstrate the Shari'a can be interpreted in many ways – from enlightened to brutal – in many different cultures.

In October 1998 six people were executed by stoning in Iran. According to *Salam* newspaper and international news agencies, Kheirollah Javanmard, 'Ali Mokhtarpour, Parviz Hasanzadeh, Fataneh Danesh, Massumeh Einy and Marziyeh Falah were stoned in public in Khazar Abad, near the Caspian Sea, after a court found them guilty of adultery and prostitution. This followed the stoning of a twenty-year old woman the previous August, in the western town of Bukan, after she was convicted of similar charges. In that incident, reported by *Kayhan* newspaper, the woman survived after she was mistakenly assumed to be dead and left at a morgue.

As one appalled reader noted in a letter of protest to *The Iranian* journal, Article 119 of the Law of Hudud and Qissas, passed by the Majlis, states 'In the punishment of stoning to death, the stones should not be too large so that the person dies on being hit by one or two of them; they should not be so small either that they could not be defined as stones.' The reader noted that no matter how one interpreted Article 5 of the Universal Declaration of Human Rights (UDHR) ['No one shall be subjected to torture or to cruel, inhuman or degrading treatment or punishment.'], to which Iran is a signatory, there is absolutely no way to argue that stoning people to a slow and painful death does not constitute 'cruel, inhuman or degrading punishment'. She added that such a practice was contrary to any of the cultural and moral values that were taught to her by the Iranian family, school system and society in which she was born and bred.

Do such punishments really come within the remit of the Qur'an and the Hadith? Commanding good and forbidding evil ('al-amr bi'l-ma'ruf wa'l-nahy 'an al-munkar') is the Islamic foundation stone of the freedom to express opinions. The concept lies at the heart of the Shari'a, is incumbent on rulers and is commonly known as *hisba* in Arabic. The authority for *hisba* is the Qur'anic injunction: 'Let there be among you a group that calls others to good, commanding good and forbidding evil.' (Qur'an III:104). In one Hadith the Prophet says: 'If any of you sees something evil, he should set it right with his hand; if he is unable to do so, then with his tongue, and if he is unable to do even that, then (let him denounce it) in his heart. But this is the weakest form of faith." Since the Umayyads the office of Muhtasib (Inspector of the Markets, from the root *hisba*) was responsible for enforcing Islamic morals. As Fauzi Najjar notes 'He assumed great powers, such as flogging the drunk or amputating the hands of thieves.'[2]

Hisba involves Man's right and Man's duty at the same time. The Universal Islamic Declaration of Human Rights (UIDHR) published by the Islamic Council of Europe sees *hisba* as involving 'the right and duty of every person' to speak for and defend the rights of others and those of the community when these are threatened or violated. Muslims see *hisba* as conferring on those who are capable of forming an opinion the liberty to express that opinion or even to criticize others. Nevertheless, as we have seen, Muslims also believe that whoever witnesses an evil action which violates the Shari'a should prevent the action or denounce the culprit. The Qur'an allows freedom of religion and does not compel non-Muslims to convert to Islam. Both Muslims and non-Muslims may defend their religion from seditious provocation (*fitna*). An important Qur'anic *aya* reads, 'Had thy Lord willed, everyone on earth would have believed. Do you then force people to become believers.' (X:99). In principle the UIDHR reflects this: 'Every person has the right to freedom of conscience and worship in accordance with his religious beliefs' (Article 13).

Another concept in the Qur'an, 'sincere advice' (*nasiha*), is a show of brotherhood that can be proffered to anyone including the religious jurists or *'ulama*. But it is above all the Qur'anic principle of consultation (*shura*) which entitles ordinary Muslims to be consulted on public affairs. According to Islamic fundamentalists those who may sit on a *shura* council are called *ahl al-hall w'al-aqd* ('those who have the power to bind and unbind'). According to

Olivier Roy three groups compete for this function, the clergy, the entire community – implying western democracy, reviled by many Islamists – and Islamic intellectuals.[3]

The Egyptian writer 'Abd al-Rahman al-Sharqawi regards Islam as by its nature democratic on the basis of the Hadith, 'Consult your companions on communal matters.' As Daryush Shayegan notes, another Egyptian, Youssef Idris, goes even further, arguing:

> When we examine the context of our cultural heritage we find, intimately mingled with this rich and complex whole, notions and values which are indissoluble Islamic; so it may be said that notions and ideals such as socialism, for example, or democracy, have been known here for a very long time, much longer than they have been known in the West.[4]

In Saudi Arabia, as we will see, any man may, in principle, approach the king on allotted days and seek redress. In addition the key concept of *ijtihad* (individual judgement to establish a legal ruling by creative interpretation of the Shari'a) together with the citizen's right to criticize government leaders (*haqq al-mu'aradah*) are often cited by Muslims as recognition by the Qur'an and the Shari'a of a Muslim's right to freedom of expression. The Qur'an divides Man's choice in life into that which is recommendable (*mandub*), that which is permissible (*mubah*) and that which is reprehensible (*makruh*).

According to Muhammad Hashim Kamali[5] there are four degrees of *hisba*. The first is informing (*ta'rif*) the person who is committing a wrong of the enormity of his or her conduct. The second is kindly admonition (*wa'z*) to invoke the fear of God in him and appeal to his reason. The third authorizes the use of harsh words such as 'Oh tyrant', 'Oh Ignorant One' or 'Do you not fear God?' The fourth and final one involves using anger or even force. Only the first two can be applied to one's father or husband or to a head of state. From these examples it is clear that violence is only condoned in the very last resort.

There is no priesthood in Islam but an Islamic jurist who has undergone rigorous spiritual training might interpret the laws for the benefit (*maslaha*) of society. He is a *mujtahid*, one who used *ijtihad* to interpret the law. The *mujtahid* is an expert in the most important of Islamic sciences, the principles of jurisprudence (*usul al-fiqh*). It is the duty of Muslims to follow (*taqlid*) the laws laid down by the *mujtahids*. In Islam the *umma*, the collectivity of Muslims, takes precedence over the individual who is bound to the *umma* within the framework of *al-fara'id* (religious obligations). One of the greatest sins in Islam is *shirk* or 'associationism' with other deities, thus compromising God's majesty.

Although analogy was the early method of establishing legal criteria in Islam, *ijtihad* became increasingly popular, particularly with the nineteenth-century modernists. After Muhammad's death various schools of law emerged of which there are now four principal schools: the Hanafi, the Maliki, the Shafi'i and the Hanbali. The Hanafi, which tends to use *ijtihad*, is the prevailing school among the Sunnis in Iraq, Syria, Turkey, central Asia and India. The Maliki school lays emphasis on the practice of Medina as a guarantee of the interpretation of the Prophet's practice and is widespread in North, Central and West Africa. The Shafi'is take their name from Muhammad ibn Idris ash-Shafi'i. They are found mainly in northern Egypt, the Hejaz, South Arabia, East Africa and South-East Asia. The Hanbalis, who follow Ahmad ibn Hanbal, adhere to the Hadith above all else. They are the official school of Saudi Arabia and are by far the most conservative of the four schools. As Malise Ruthven points out,[6] the FIS leader in Algeria, 'Ali Ben Hadj, far from operating within the regional Maliki school which allows for considerable latitude of interpretation 'in the public interest', has tried to impose the rigid tenets of the Hanbali school on the leadership of the FIS.

The Shari'a embraces every aspect of life in Islam, including *jihad* (struggle), the treatment of non-Muslims, marriage, divorce, inheritance, the status of women, penal and commercial law, slavery, food taboos and ritual slaughter. Jurists divided the world into the area of Islam (*dar al-Islam*) and the area of war (*dar al-harb*). *Dar al-Islam* is territory where the Shari'a applies in its entirety. In theory its rulers cannot legislate because the law has been revealed by the Prophet Muhammad in its perfection. Their duty is confined to 'commanding good and forbidding evil' as we have seen. In a famous phrase quoted by the fourteenth-century Hanbali fundamentalist Taqiyyu'l-Din ibn Taymiyya, 'the Sultan is the shadow of God on earth. Sixty years with an unjust imam is better than one night of anarchy.' This makes it difficult to sanction revolt against authority, as so-called Islamic regimes are aware. *Jihad* was the duty of every Muslim to preserve Islam from threat, either through war or through other forms of struggle. Some adherents of political Islam regard Ayatollah Khomeini's *fatwa* against Salman Rushdie as *jihad* because they feel that he genuinely believed that *The Satanic Verses* threatened the corpus and status of Islam.

In the Shari'a *hadd* (limit, plural *hudud*) punishments are definitely fixed by the Qur'an or the Hadith, although there are mitigating circumstances, for example if the accused is in need or if the property to which he lays claim is public property. Generally speaking, the *hadd* penalty for theft is amputation of the hand, for armed robbery amputation of the foot, thirty whippings or the death penalty. For rape or *zina* (unlawful penetration) by adult married Muslims the *hadd* punishment is stoning to death; for adult non-Muslims and adult single Muslims it is 100 lashes. The *hadd* punishment for false accusation of unlawful intercourse is 100 lashes.

Ta'zir (discretionary punishment, literally 'prevention', 'reformation') is a fall-back for *hadd* where no revelation can be identified to support it. If *hadd* does not apply, the accused usually is still liable to *ta'zir*. Western scholars tend to regard *hadd* punishments as disproportionate to the crimes committed. A Muslim who steals $100 from an enclosed place, for example, may have his hand amputated if the theft is witnessed by two adult Muslim men but if he steals an expensive car in front of thirty women or non-Muslim men he only suffers *ta'zir*. Astonishingly, in rape a victim's own evidence counts for little if she is a woman.

Among the Sunnis, by the tenth century the gates of *ijtihad* were considered more or less closed. This was because the four main Islamic legal schools or *madhabs* had now created a system where precedents apparently existed for every legal eventuality. New attempts at *ijtihad*, therefore, were to be condemned as *bid'a* or innovation. In Shi'ism, however, the gates of *ijtihad* are generally considered to have remained open, giving *mujtahids* considerable freedom to make judgements on the basis of the Qur'an and the Hadith. As we will see, the Wahhabi Ikhwan in Saudi Arabia, Muslim die-hard extremists, rejected any deviation from the model of the Prophet's life based on the Qur'an and the Hadith and opposed cars, telephones and the radio, all of which they considered *bid'a*.

A key word in Islam, *fitna* (sedition, temptation, trial) appears in 60 places in the Qur'an. Among the legal meanings of *fitna* is seditious speech when this challenges the legitimacy of a lawful government. The debate over the word led to contradictions. When Abu Bakr became Islam's first Caliph after the death of the Prophet he urged the people to correct him if he went astray. 'Yes', they replied promptly. 'If you err we will correct it with the sword.' Abu Bakr reflected the simplicity of the early Arabians, casually going to the souk to sell goods after he became Caliph. This attitude only changed a little when his friends insisted he be paid a stipend for the job. Abu Bakr died in his bed but the three Caliphs after him, Omar, 'Othman and 'Ali, were all murdered when they attracted serious criticism.

Fitna also has the meaning of 'enticement', as in the Qur'anic lines 'Know that your possessions and your offspring are but a trial (*fitna*) and that with God lies an immense reward' (Qur'an VIII:28; LXIV:15). According to Kamali,[7] the most usual meaning of *fitna* in the Qur'an is one denoting verbal or actual aggression leading to the denial of the right of Muslims to practise Islam. Note the Qur'anic verse, 'And expel them from where they have expelled you. For oppression (*fitna*) is worse than killing' (II:191).

The ubiquitous slogan for contemporary Islamists is 'The Qur'an is our constitution'. They seek sources within the text of the Qur'an to defend modern ideologies. They use Qur'anic phrases such as *B'ism illahi* (In the name of God) to introduce even scientific facts, seeking to give these the imprimatur of divine sanction. According to Fariba Adelkhah's *Being Modern in Iran*, the wide distribution of Qur'ans has altered people's relationship with the Holy Book, which is now transmitted through the written press. Some newspapers have chosen Qur'anic verses as mottoes, other punctuate socio-political statements with Qur'anic *aya*s. While the Qur'an was handled with immense care and delicacy in private homes before the Revolution, she says, it is now much more difficult to ensure this with mass production and distribution. It is also difficult to ensure that newspapers with Qur'anic motifs do not end up as wrapping for meat and vegetables.

Jokes around what Adelkhah calls '*B'ism illahi* mania' circulate in Iran. When a reporter asks a peasant what he places around the roots of his fruit trees he replies 'In the name of God, the Merciful, shit!' Religion has been dumbed down. The 'believer-consumer' can hear the *sura* of his or her choice by dialling 114 (the number recalling 114 *sura*s in the Qur'an). The Ministry of Justice has since 1995 played *sura*s for waiting callers. Adelkhah notes that religion has also entered the world of computer games with disks named Touba, Rezvan and Taha, helping people to familiarize themselves with the Qur'an in Persian, English and French.[8]

The Muslim Brotherhood and similar groups use the Qur'an between two swords as their emblem. As Olivier Roy points out[9] Abu'l 'Ala Maududi and Hasan al-Turabi classify concepts of political Islam as functions of areas of law and of western political conscience as if they were universal. The ideologues of revolutionary Iran also attempt to make Qur'anic concepts meaningful in a modern context. The former Iranian Prime Minister Bani Sadr, for example, equates the Qur'anic concept of *tawhid* (oneness) with a classless society and the *mustadafin* (wretched of the earth) with the proletariat while in 'Ali Shariati's works Shi'i concepts take on a modern revolutionary hue. Qur'anic ideas like *shura* (advisory council), made up of *ahl al-hall w'al-aqd*, were and are used by Sayyid al-Qutb and other thinkers to claim democratic principles in Saudi Arabia while *jahiliyya* today describes Islamic societies that have moved away wickedly from behaviour conducive to the divine truth of Islam. The Iranian revolutionary term *taghuti* (from the name of a pre-Qur'anic god) is today used to refer to someone who denies the Qur'anic order of things.

Da'wa (missionary activity) plays an important role in Islam and was behind the Saudi-sponsored creation in 1962 of the Rabita, the World Muslim League, which prints Qur'ans and subsidizes Islamic institutes throughout the world. Many states use the Qur'an as the theoretical bedrock of their constitution. Article 2 of the Egyptian Constitution of 1971 specifies that the Shari'a is 'the main source of legislation' while the Afghan constitution of 1987 specifies that Islam is the state religion. Meanwhile, as Roy points out,[10] the Algerian Family Code of 1984 reintroduced into divorce and child custody the Qur'anic asymmetry between men and women.

Moderates such as Sadiq al-Mahdi in the Sudan seek to draw from the Qur'an and the Hadith a Shari'a adapted to the needs of the modern world. Similarly, the Pakistani scholar Fazlur Rahman (1919–88) tried to produce an antidote to the spiritual despair of Muslims by suggesting a Qur'anic exegesis which would be in line with the spirit of Islam but provide for the needs of modern life. In Iran Ayatollah Shariatmadari was ousted by Khomeini because of his moderation and his softness towards the Shah. Shariatmadari had argued that the drastic penalties called for by the Shari'a, such as the chopping off of hands, should only be applied when a perfect society has been constructed in which no temptation other than 'the inner whisperings of Satan' could be held to have misled the criminal.

The Shi'a use of *taqiyya* or dissimulation stems from living as a minority in hostile Sunni territory until the rise of the Safavids in the late sixteenth century. The Shi'is justify this concept – which would be considered cowardice or treachery by other religions – from the Qur'anic verse 'Anyone who, after accepting faith in God, utters unbelief – except under compulsion, his heart remaining in faith'.[11]

TWELVE

Women: Conundrum or Contradiction?

One who believes in God and in the Judgement Day ought not to stay with a woman in private while no *mahram* [near relative with whom marriage is not permitted, e.g. brother, father, uncle] is with her, because in such cases the third is Satan.

(The Hadith.)[1]

Tell the believing women to lower their gaze and be modest, and to display of their adornment only that which is apparent, and to draw their veils over their bosoms.

(Qur'an, *Sura an-Nur* (The Sura of Light).)

An Egyptian friend of mine who lived near the Pyramids of Giza heard the terrible screams of a young woman across the orchard. He ran to her house and found his foster daughter bleeding horribly from her vagina. It was several hours into her wedding night. Her simple-minded, peasant husband stood beside her, paralysed with fear. A bloody knife lay on the earthen floor. The man had been told by his mother to take a knife to the matrimonial bed and cut away the bonding of her clitoris because it narrowed her opening down to a tiny aperture too small for him to penetrate. My friend raced her to the hospital along dirt tracks in his Jeep where her life was saved with minutes to spare. Nothing, however, was reported in the Egyptian press. Was it not done to write about such delicate issues?

In a short story called 'She used to be the weaker', the feminist writer Nawal El-Saadawi describes the disgusting scene of a young Egyptian woman's wedding night.[2] Two big women sit on her spread-eagled legs so that the husband can penetrate her with his finger and break her hymen before waving the bloodied sheet at the vigilante crowds outside. Saadawi's most famous book, *The Hidden Face of Eve,* caused a great storm throughout the Islamic world. After her first work of non-fiction *Women and Sex* appeared in 1972 it caused a furore among political and theological circles and she was dismissed from her post at the Ministry of Health. Saadawi was one of the 1,500 people arrested during the former President Sadat's purge of opponents in September 1981. In 2001 she was accused of apostasy by Egyptian fundamentalists who sought to force her to divorce her husband on grounds similar to those directed at Abu Zayd that she was no longer a Muslim.

But these are really just the headline-making stories so popular with western jingoists and Islamophobes. Female circumcision apparently originated in Pharaonic times and probably owes nothing to Islamic tradition. Islam, we are told in the West – and the Taliban, the GIA and hardliners elsewhere are, of course, all there to prove it – insists on veiling women from head to toe. Everywhere women are utterly suppressed. And yet we forget that women in Britain only had the vote, and then with various property caveats, in 1918. The veil, meanwhile, was already worn by the free Roman women. The Prophet not only emphasized the obligation of parents to provide education to both their daughters and their sons but also the necessity of encouraging both to learn how to ride horses and swim and take exercise. Some argue that even women in the West until the turn of the last century were discouraged from doing different sports in the name of protecting their reproductive functions.

The Prophet is said to have remarked of his eighteen-year-old and charismatic wife 'Aisha: 'Draw half of your religion from this ruddy-faced woman.' According to the commentator Ibn Sa'd, when a verse allowed the Prophet to marry as many women as he wished on condition that they were not more than four at any time she commented hotly, 'God always responds immediately to your needs.'[3] But it was to be in her arms that the Prophet would die. It is worth noting that the very first Muslim was Muhammad's first wife Khadija. Today, women are a majority of Muslims globally and it has been shown that more British women convert to Islam than men.

The veil, it seems, was meant only for the Prophet's wives at a time when they were threatened by the Meccan merchants opposed to the new message of Islam. A verse asking believers to speak to the Prophet's wives from behind a screen may account for the development of the veil but the Qur'an merely enjoins women not to display their charms, to draw their head-coverings over their bosoms and not to swing their legs so as to draw attention to their hidden charms.[4] In the West these considerations have created serious mis-understandings, with veiled women occasionally forced off London buses because they refuse to identify themselves by showing their faces. On the other hand Muslim Iranian women have been drawn into the educational system since they feel comfort in segregation and as a result are demanding more rights from their menfolk. When her book *The Map of Love* was published in 1999 Ahdaf Soueif told the *Guardian*, 'But if by moving forwards what you mean is that you are more free to make your own decisions and to implement them, then women are much better off than they were 100 years ago. Taking the veil is a decision.'[5]

Traditionally, to adopt the veil has been a sign of upward mobility. Some of the later Roman sculptures at Palmyra show veiled women. Veiling was prevalent among the urban upper classes in the non-Muslims areas of Syria and Greece at the time of the Prophet and was certainly not introduced into Arabia by Islam or prescribed in the Qu'ran. 'It was, if you like,' Jordan's Princess Sarvath told a meeting in London in October 1988, 'an affectation of the privileged, similar to foot binding in China, and was an indication that their women could enjoy the luxury of remaining in seclusion since they were not obliged to take a share in agriculture or any task that would make such a restricted lifestyle virtually impossible for a rural woman or for one from a less pampered background.' We know that during the Hajj women are, in fact, strictly forbidden to veil their faces. Modern women don the veil with a sigh, slipping into more comfortable attire at the slightest opportunity. The sociologist Shayegan finds little excuse for the veil, noting in Iran

> a sovereign disdain for what is beautiful. The ruthless extirpation or concealment of any attractive feature liable to stimulate the imagination, the moribund insistence on dark, muddy colours, entomb the variegated charms of life behind a sad, funereal veil ... Music, elegance, beauty, anything along those lines, is assumed to mask impropriety, indecency; to represent the seductive face of hidden perversion.[6]

In Afghanistan the Taliban promptly put the Tomb of Rabia Balkhi out of bounds. A beautiful medieval princess, Rabia was the first woman of her time to write love poetry in Persian. She died tragically when her brother slashed her wrists as punishment for sleeping with a slave lover. She wrote her last poem in her own blood as she lay dying. For centuries young Uzbek girls would pray at her tomb for successful love affairs.[7]

But it is not only the Islamists who see Islam today as it must have been viewed in the seventh century, a forward-looking reform movement. Ordinary devout Muslims will argue that men and women are treated equally in Islam in principle. They remind us that before Islam women's rights were limited and they were often the victims of temporary *mot'a* and *ba'al* marriages. According to the first, which still exists among the Shi'is, a traveller could marry a woman for a brief period and divorce her before moving on. Young seminarians would have sex with menopausal women within the framework of these *mot'a* marriages. Here they would marry a woman for an hour and divorce and pay her according to the *mot'a* tradition. The young men believed that they killed an infidel each time they made love in this way and would go to pray in the shrine to 'Ali afterwards.[8] To a non-Muslim such behaviour may appear cynical and hypocritical.

After the Battle of Uhud, when 70 Muslims were killed, a verse was revealed to the Prophet allowing polygamy under certain conditions: 'If you fear that you cannot treat orphans with fairness, then you may marry such women (widowed) as seem good to you: two, three or four of them. But if you fear that you cannot do justice, marry one only.'[9] However, it is widely believed that the verse referred to a state of emergency when widows needed protection and is thus restricted to one specific period of history. The *ba'al* marriage was one where the woman had been captured or bought. She and her children became the property of her husband. Seen at the time as a reformer, Muhammad was influenced by the Jews and Christians of the Hejaz region in limiting the number of a man's wives to four on condition that their husbands treated them equally, and in ensuring their property rights. Islam did not go as far as Christianity in insisting on monogamy but it did greatly improve women's lot at a time when widowhood could mean starvation. The groom pays a nuptial gift or *mahr* to the bride or her guardian. The Shari'a recognizes the property rights of married women. Divorce is through a threefold declaration of repudiation by the husband. Normally a woman must have her husband's consent for a divorce although she can sometimes ask a *qadi* (religious judge) to dissolve the marriage. The sons stay with the mother until they are seven or nine while the daughters stay with her until they come of age. A daughter inherits half as much as a son and the testimony of a woman in a court of law has only half the value of that of a man. However, women enjoy the same property rights as men.

Women have played a powerful role throughout Islamic history. In the Qur'an the *Sura Miriam* (*Sura of Mary*) is one of the most moving of the *sura*s. She is considered the most perfect example of *'ubudiyya* or 'service' to God. Significantly, women played an exalted role in Islam during its early centuries. Sukaina, for example, the daughter of the martyred Husain and the granddaughter of the Prophet's nephew and son-in-law 'Ali, was the most accomplished and virtuous woman of her time. In the twelfth century the Sheikha Shuhda, called by her admirers the *Fakhr un-Nisa* ('the Glory of

Women'), lectured publicly at the great mosque in Baghdad. As Amir 'Ali points out in his book *The Spirit of Islam*, had she belonged to the world of Christendom she would have been burnt to death as a witch.[10] In 1236 Raziyya was initially brought to power over the (Turkish) Delhi Sultanate as a figurehead. However, she became increasingly self-confident, wearing men's clothing and riding about on an elephant. Her rule reflected the greater freedom women of the Turkish steppes enjoyed. Raziyya's reign and downfall are described in a book on the Delhi Sultanate by Peter Jackson.[11]

During one of Muhammad's campaigns 'Aisha walked off into the desert in search of a missing necklace. Not realizing that she had left her *howdaj* the camel-train moved on and she was left alone. A handsome young soldier called Safwan found her and carried her back to the city on his camel. Gossip raged because when a man and a woman spent a night in each other's company seduction was more or less assumed. But after a month the Prophet received a revelation clearing her name. It was since this incident that the Shari'a insisted on four adult male witnesses or eight female witnesses to the act of copulation. Sexual relations could only be proven if a cord could be passed between the man and the woman during coition. In other words, proof was only possible on the basis of voluntary confession without which the threat of punishment had to be considered as merely symbolic.

However, sensitivities among Muslims may run deeper today than in former years. In November 2001 one of the Netherlands' best independent theatre companies Het Onafhankelijk Toneel cancelled the production of an opera telling the story of the necklace incident, based on Assia Djebar's novel *Far from Medina*, two weeks before the start of rehearsals. According to *Index on Censorship*[12] the Moroccan actors, singers, the composer and even some of the musicians refused to participate when a fax was sent to a Moroccan newspaper and the Ministry of the Interior denouncing the participants for being involved in a work that would offend the Prophet Muhammad and 'degrade him as a pederast'. According to the fax the physical representation of 'Aisha, whom the Prophet married when she was nine, is also forbidden.

The Saudi regime was bitterly offended by the showing on British commercial television of the film *Death of a Princess* in 1980. At the end of July 1977 Princess Misha'il bint Fahd ibn Muhammad, the granddaughter of King 'Abd al-Aziz's eldest surviving son, and her lover Khaled Muhalhal, a nephew of General 'Ali Shaeir, the Saudi ambassador in Lebanon, were executed. They were executed for adultery although the story was not to be known abroad until January 1978. There was nothing remotely Islamic in their executions, which took place in a parking lot off Jeddah's King 'Abd al-Aziz Street instead of in the Midan Bab al-Sharif where executions are usually carried out. It also broke convention by being carried out on a Saturday rather than a Friday. The princess was shot in the head six times while Khaled Muhalhal was clumsily decapitated with a sword. It seemed clear that the execution had not been carried out according to due process of the law but was ordered by her uncle Muhammad as his tribal right. On 9 April 1980 relations between Britain and Saudi Arabia deteriorated after the screening of the programme. A scene in which Saudi princesses made 'trysts' with young men from their cars in the desert had particularly upset the Saudis. On 5 April 1980 the British Foreign Minister, Lord Carrington, expressed his 'deep regret' at the television programme. Despite this, on 23 April the Saudi authorities asked the British ambassador James Craig to leave the kingdom.

Today Islamic control is increasing in countries like Malaysia where in early 1997 Muslim couples were wrongfully detained by the religious police under the Shari'a law governing *khalwa* or close proximity. Film producer Julie Dahlan was accused of committing *khalwa* with her production manager Rudy Rasiman (a non-Muslim) in a hotel in October 1996. In the following month pornographic films and publications were destroyed in an open burning session at the Malaysian Civil Defence Headquarters. In September 1999 police broke into a flat where a tell-tale had reported an immoral liaison only to find the woman had leapt to her death from the window.

When Muhammad received his early revelations from God he appealed to the well-established Jewish communities whose monotheism he respected and whose biblical revelations form the spiritual core of the Qur'an. However, the Jews were clearly unwilling to exchange their ancient scriptures and beliefs for the new compact of Islam and in time relations became bitter. The break seems to have become formalized when Muhammad changed the *qibla* (the direction of prayer) from Jerusalem to Mecca. After the Battle of the Ditch Muhammad eliminated opposition from the Jewish tribes whom he believed had betrayed him. When the Jewish Banu Qurayza accepted the arbitration of their own leading ally, Sa'd ibn Mu'ath, as he was dying of his wounds, Mu'ath himself ordered that their 600 adult menfolk be killed and women and children sold into slavery. This was *realpolitik*. Mu'ath may have realized that nothing must hinder the new allegiance to Islam that must now be seen to triumph.

Muhammad's death in 632 saw the wars of the 'apostasy' where tribes who refused to submit to the Prophet's heirs were suppressed by the first Caliph Abu Bakr. The Islamic conquests of Syria, Iraq, northern Mesopotamia and Egypt followed. By the time of the Caliphate of 'Othman Arab armies were campaigning as far east as Afghanistan. At the age of forty-two the Prophet's widow 'Aisha led an army that challenged the legitimacy of 'Ali. The battle, called the Battle of the Camel, took place in Basra in 656. Her stand, which she is said to have regretted, was an early example of *bid'a* (innovation). For many misogynist commentators it was a prime example of the threat of *fitna* or 'strife' posed by women in Islam. Her example set a dangerous pattern, her critics maintained. Her biographer Sa'id al-Afghani, believes that had she not intervened in politics 'Muslim history would have taken the path of peace, progress and prosperity'. As well as the petulance of her response to the *sura* allowing four wives mentioned earlier[13] she displayed jealousy of Khadija, Muhammad's first wife, a rich and devoted widow to whom he remained faithful until her death. According to 'Aisha, Muhammad would not leave home with praising Khadija.

Under the 'Islamic' military regime of Zia ul-Haq, which took power in Pakistan in 1977, women were to suffer the most. The report of a government commission submitted in 1982 recommended that women should be barred from holding the office of head of state or government, that the age limit for women candidates to parliament be fifty and that the value of a murdered woman should be half that of a murdered man when settling a murder case financially. There were proposals to ban women from radio and television and to prohibit them from driving, to withdraw their right to vote and to keep them from most jobs. Inhuman and unjust punishment became common by the mid-1980s.

Under Pakistan's *Zina* Ordinance laws rape had to be substantiated by four male witnesses and the victim had to identify the perpetrator of the rape. A blind girl called Safia was raped by a father and a son who had employed her as a maid. Obviously unable to identify them and having born a child out of wedlock, she was sentenced to a public flogging and three years in jail. After six months of protest by Pakistani women and lawyers she was quietly acquitted by the federal Shari'a court, the highest Islamic court in Pakistan. Despite the public outcry, the perpetrators retained their freedom.[14] According to one story in Karachi a new-born baby was stoned to death at a mullah's behest. According to this somewhat doubtful story published by *Index on Censorship* the baby had been left on the doorstep of a mosque and the mullah had inferred that it was illegitimate and decreed that it be 'executed'.[15]

The history of women in Iran since the Islamic revolution has been different. Despite the *chador* and other encumbrances, in some ways women across the classes have become more rather than less evolved. *The hejab-e zaher* (exposed covering) as an article of clothing is only important for women through respect for *hejab-e baten* (the secret covering), the whole range of values to which they must adhere to be fully women. According to Adelkhah, in the 1996 parliamentary elections women candidates dominated events. Key women such as Faezeh Hashemi often scored higher than male candidates. In Mashhad

Mrs Alavi was elected but her husband Mr Fattah was defeated.[16] The religious field has given women opportunities for access to the urban public space in an entirely legitimate social and even political way. At present many of them manage Islamic institutions or associations, especially in the charity field. Some women open body-building halls, which conform to Islamic norms although they must be segregated. It is worth noting that charity work in Victorian Britain gave way to the militant feminism of the suffragettes. Islamic feminists write in the quarterly magazine *Farzaneh*.

THIRTEEN

Afghanistan: the Heart of the Matter

Afghanistan's Taliban regime, which collapsed in early November 2001, has played a depressing role in influencing western attitudes to Islam. Almost all Afghans are Muslim, the vast majority Sunnis. In the nineteenth century Afghanistan was a buffer state between Russia and British India. Of its population 40 per cent are Pashtun. The first of two Anglo-Afghan wars (1839–42 and 1879–80) led to appalling British losses. Britain installed the Durranis as amirs (rulers), a dynasty which continued until 1973 when Prince Muhammad Daud staged a military coup and abolished the monarchy.

Soviet involvement with Afghanistan goes back to the 1920s. In 1921, as a means of reducing British influence in the region, Afghanistan signed a treaty of friendship with the Soviet Union. The treaty also called for the Amir Amanullah to close his northern border. However, Afghanistan has usually followed in foreign policy the principle of a balanced relationship with the Great Powers. In 1978, Daud was overthrown and executed. The new president, Nur Muhammad Taraki, signed a twenty-year treaty of friendship and cooperation with the Soviet Union but in 1979 Taraki was ousted by Amin. Finding their position in Afghanistan imperilled, the Soviet leadership decided to invade the country in December 1979. Soviet troops or guards allegedly killed Amin and brought in Babrak Karmal. The invasion resulted in worldwide condemnation of the Soviet Union. In 1986, in an attempt to win Afghan support for the Soviet-installed regime, Karmal was replaced by Sayid Muhammad Najibullah and a campaign was intensified calling for national reconciliation between the Soviet-supported regime and the Islamic resistance, the Mujahidin (those who undertake jihad (struggle, by extension holy war).

According to a US Department of State estimate in 1987, almost 1 million Afghans had been killed and more than 5 million had fled the country since the 1979 Soviet invasion. In 1988 Afghanistan and Pakistan signed accords, with the USA and the Soviet Union acting as guarantors, calling for the withdrawal of Soviet military forces from Afghanistan over a nine-month period beginning on 15 May 1988. The withdrawal was completed in early 1989. Once the Soviets had withdrawn and the Cold War had been won, the Afghans felt bitterly that Washington had lost interest in their country.

The USA insisted that the widely respected Communist president Najibullah step down. In his place it installed the seven squabbling factions of the Mujahidin. Pakistan was unhappy with the choice of a Tajik, Burhanuddin Rabbani, as president rather than a Pashtun. It encouraged its own protégé Gulbuddin Hekmatyar to oppose him. Hekmatyar was one of the most extreme figures in the Mujahidin. Women who refused to wear *burqa*s (the all-enveloping tent-like veil) had acid thrown in their eyes by his followers. When Hekmatyar's forces failed to defeat Rabbani, Pakistan supported the newly emerging Taliban and the USA gave it at least indirect support. In 1992 Afghanistan had been declared an Islamic state. No sooner had the Mujahidin won, however, than severe splits occurred. The two key movements were the Jamaat-i-Islami (Islamic Society), headed since 1971 by the al-Azhar University-educated Rabbani, and the Hezb-i Islami (Islamic Party) of the more radical Pashtun Hekmatyar.

An agreement to cooperate was reached between the forces of Ahmad Shah Masoud, a Tajik Mujahidin commander (who was killed two days before the World Trade Centre attack on 11 September 2001) and 'Abd al-Rashid Dustam, an Uzbek leader who had brought about the collapse of Dr Najibullah's Marxist government in Kabul. However, they failed to create from this a credible Islamic government because of widespread mistrust, encouraged by foreign patrons, among the factions.

In 1996 a new group emerged, the Taliban (The Students), Pashtun theological 'students' of the rural *madrasah*s (Qur'anic schools) whose power-base was Kandahar and who represented the Pashtun 40 per cent majority. Supported by Pakistan (and indirectly by the USA) who saw in them a stable power-base which would ensure the security of the vital trade routes from Pakistan through to the newly opened-up Central Asian Republics, the Taliban were soon to control 90 per cent of the country under their remote leader Mullah Omar. Nevertheless, real military power and the regime's financial backbone lay with Arab Mujahidin and their leader, Osama bin Laden. The Taliban, passionately Sunni, were responsible for the massacre of between 2,000 and 5,000 members of the Shi'i Hazara community after the capture of Mazar-e-Shari in August 1998. At the same time they brought Iran to the brink of intervention by murdering nine of its diplomats in Mazar.

When the Taliban seized Kabul they were determined to purge what they saw as a satanic den of iniquity and set about imposing their fanatical rule. The Taliban victory was a visible symbol of the revenge of the countryside on the city. The Pakistani authorities found it impossible to seal the 1,200-mile mountainous border. Meanwhile, there were many in Pakistan's Inter Services Intelligence (ISI) agency who were long-term supporters of Osama bin Laden. The ISI was the principal conduit for western aid to the Afghan Mujahidin during the war against the Soviet Union. The then ruler of Pakistan, General Zia ul-Haq, encouraged hard-line Islamists in the army and the intelligence services as a counter to the more secular opposition to his dictatorship. Ten years later, they have risen to the senior ranks. Pakistani police say they believe they failed to capture Osama bin Laden in 2000 after he was warned of their raid by sympathetic ISI elements. Western security sources blame Osama bin Laden's sudden decision to leave a meeting of al-Qaida commanders in the hours before it was hit by US cruise missiles in 1998, following the East African embassy bombings, on a tip-off from the same source.

The destruction of the Bamiyan Buddhas in 2001 was a turning point, creating splits between Taliban hardliners and moderates. Nationalist members of the Taliban realized that they had destroyed the greatest symbol of their heritage. The order to destroy the statues had almost certainly come from bin Laden and his Arab coterie who were already resented as foreigners indifferent to Afghanistan's heritage by other members of the Taliban.

The situation for women in Afghanistan had become so bad that western journalists began comparing it the treatment of Jews in pre-Holocaust Poland. Saira Shah, an Afghan brought up in Britain, made an apparently secret film highlighting Taliban oppression in Afghanistan for Britain's Channel 4 Television in June 2001. The destruction of the huge, rock-hewn Buddhist statues some months earlier had prepared a huge viewership for this programme. In the village of Mawmaii Shah came across three little girls hunched up 'in a row like broken birds'. The twelve-year-old told her that the Taliban had shot their mother in front of them. While their mother's body lay in the courtyard of their home, the soldiers remained alone with the girls for two days. When she asked what the Taliban did in that time 'Fairuza's fifteen-year-old sister wept silently'.

Taliban recruits, often orphans from Pakistani refugee camps, had been brought up in a totally male society. Simi Wali, the head of an Afghan non-governmental organization said:

This conflict against women is rooted in political beliefs and ideologies, not in Islam or the cultural norms. The Taliban are a new generation of Muslim males who are products of a war culture, who have spent much of their adult lives in complete segregation from their own communities. In Afghan society, women have traditionally been used as instruments to regulate social behaviour, and as such are powerful symbols in Afghan culture.[1]

The Taliban banned women from school, work and light entertainment and from wearing white socks. Women who did not wear the *burqa* were publicly beaten. In 1998 the Taliban even forbade parents from giving children such 'non-Muslim' names as Rita, Parkash and Guita, all of which had featured in the Indian films popular before they came to power. Television was fiercely banned in what had been a country of passionate film-goers. Singing and dancing at weddings were banned. 'Through their fossilized policies the Taliban stop girls from attending school, stop women working out of their homes and all that in the name of Islam. What could be worse than committing violence, narrow-mindedness and limiting women's rights and defaming Islam.' These are the words of Iran's Ayatollah Ahmad Jannati in 1996.[2] Nevertheless, even in the anti-Taliban Northern Alliance city of Faizabad, the fiefdom of Burhanuddin Rabbani, women may not appear on screen and amorous scenes are edited from films.

Husbands had the power of life and death over their women relatives, especially their wives, but an angry mob had just as much right to stone or beat a woman, often to death, for offending them in the slightest way. According to reports circulating in 1999 one woman was reported to have been beaten to death by a mob of fundamentalists for accidentally exposing her arm while she was driving. Another was stoned to death for trying to leave the country with a man who was not a relative. According to these reports women were not allowed to work or even go out in public without a male relative, while professional women such as professors, translators, doctors, lawyers, artists and writers had been forced to quit their jobs and idle away their time at home. Homes where a woman was present had to have their windows painted over so that she could never be seen by outsiders. Women had to wear silent shoes so that they were never heard. Relief workers estimated that the suicide rate among women, who could not find proper medication and treatment for severe depression and would rather take their lives than live in such conditions, had increased significantly.

Because they could not work, those without male relatives or husbands were either starving to death or begging on the street, even if they held PhDs, said the reports. There were almost no medical facilities available for women. At one of the rare hospitals for women a reporter found nearly lifeless bodies lying motionless on top of beds, wrapped in their *burqas*, unwilling to speak, eat, or do anything, but slowly wasting away. Others had gone mad and were seen crouched in corners, rocking or crying, most of them in fear. One doctor was said to have considered, when what little medication that was left finally ran out, leaving these women in front of the president's residence as a form of peaceful protest.

As Ahmed Rashid points out,[3] Kandahar's Pashtuns were notorious for their affairs with young boys and it was the rape of young boys by warlords that had been one of the key motives for Mullah Omar to mobilize the Taliban. In February 1998 three men sentenced to death for sodomy in Kandahar were taken to the base of a high mud and brick wall which was then toppled over them by a tank. 'His Eminence the Amir al-Mu'mineen [Mullah Omar] attended the function to give Shari'a punishment to the three buggerers in Kandahar', reported *Anis*, the Taliban newspaper.[4]

The emergence of the Taliban must be blamed principally on support offered to marginalized young Afghans by *madrasah*s in Pakistani refugee camps. Pakistan is a country where tolerance and intolerance make strange bedfellows. In late 1999 Islamic hardliners took issue over scenes in a film about Jinnah starring Christopher Lee as Jinnah. They were angry over a scene that showed his wife collapsed on a bed wearing a skirt. Although she was dying of cancer and morphine had left her unconscious, the scene was still criticized as indecent. One Pakistani newspaper, the daily *Khabrain*, ran a sustained attack on the film, calling the actresses 'prostitutes'.

Music under the Taliban was entirely condemned but even before the Taliban it was often considered a trivial pursuit, or even downright sinful.[5] However, for many music has strongly positive connotations, being connected with Sufism. Traditionally music has always been considered indispensable in the celebration of weddings, circumcision and birth. The *adhan* (call to prayer) is in Arabic but other kinds of religious singing are in Pashto, Dari and other languages of Afghanistan.

Afghanistan's Shi'as have their own special kinds of singing connected with the commemoration of the martyrdom of their saints, Hussein and Hasan. The principal Sufi ritual is the *dhikr*, the 'recollection of God', in which the Sufis form a circle and recite together a sequence of religious formulae such as *Allah Hu*, 'God is He'. The recitation is performed with forced breathing and complex rhythmic movements of the body and head, and participants may go into a trance-like state which is experienced as union with God.

FOURTEEN

Trouble with the Mystics

It was under the 'Abbasids that the Orthodox became increasingly troubled by those who sought a more intimate union with God, one that involved *fana* (annihilation) of the self in order to attain subsistence (*baqa*) in the Divinity as well as an elaborate system of stations (*maqamat*) and states (*ahwal*). Orthodox unease reached its apogee when the mystic al-Hallaj declared after a state of ecstasy '*Ana l-Haqq*' (I am the Truth), suggesting an intimate association with the Divine. For this dangerous claim he was brutally executed in Baghdad in 922. Rather in the manner of Christ, Hallaj went into the Mosque of Mansur and gathered his disciples around him. 'You ought to know this,' he told them, 'God has made me your outlaw. Kill me.' Those in the crowd began to weep but the Sufi 'Abd al-Wahid came closer to him and said: 'Sheikh, how could we kill a man who prays and fasts and recites the Word?' When 'Abd al-Wahid followed Hallaj home, Hallaj said to him: 'Dear son, no task is more urgent for the Muslims at this moment than my execution. Realize this, that my death will preserve the sanctions of the Law: he who has offended must undergo them.' Finally the scholar-jurist Ibn Dawud gave his opinion which was that what Hallaj said was false. 'He may be lawfully put to death.'

After his arrest Hallaj was accused of claiming divinity and of asserting that the Deity took up his abode in members of the 'Alid house. When his followers were accused of claiming that he was a god, he denied it. 'God forbid that I should pretend to divinity, or to prophecy – I am merely a man who worships God and practises prayer and fasting and good works: that is all.' Studying the evidence the judge decided that Hallaj's crime was atheism, a crime punishable by immediate death since the atheist is given no choice of repentance in Islam. Hallaj was given 1,000 stripes, then had a hand and a foot amputated. He was then left hanging on a gibbet for a day and night before he was beheaded. His corpse was rolled up a strip of reed matting, soaked in naphtha and burnt. His head was set up on the bridge for two days, then sent to Khorasan to be exhibited in the various districts. All booksellers were summoned to appear and forced to swear an oath that they would neither sell nor buy any of his works.[1]

Other mystics, some of whom influenced Ayatollah Khomeini, suffered accusations of heresy. In his biography of Khomeini,[2] Baqer Moin quotes Khomeini as reminding his critics that when he taught philosophy at the Faizieh academy the conservative clerics were so outraged that the jar from which his son Mustapha had drunk had to be ritually washed afterwards. Moin quotes him as saying as a young cleric: 'Keep the door of the tavern open for me night and day. Farewell seminary, farewell mosque, let me go my way.'[3]

Khomeini studied *erfan*, the Shi'i version of the Greek *gnosis* as well as *hekmat*, intellectual wisdom, from teachers soon after he arrived at Qom as a young seminarian. *Hekmat*, says Moin, provides the main intellectual stream of *erfan*, the mystical knowledge of the inner world of Man seeking intimacy with God. According to Moin, the mystical love poetry he wrote at a time when his enemies were being rounded up and executed was inspired by Hafez and by Mansur Hallaj. In the words of Mehdi Ha'eri-Yazdi, Khomeini was a man who saw himself as the truth and believed, like Hallaj, that he had completed the fourth journey which meant being with God among the people. Ha'eri argued 'had the Orthodox clergy been in charge, Khomeini would have been sent to the gallows as Hallaj was'.

Khomeini was following a philosophical tradition which traces its lineage back to Ibn Sina (Avicenna, 980–1037). Ibn Sina tried to articulate the truths of Islam in terms drawn from Aristotelian logic and later Greek metaphysics. As Albert Hourani points out in *Arab Thought in the Liberal Age*, the basic problem posed by Islamic revelation was the apparent contradiction between the absolute goodness of God and the apparent evil of the world. Ibn Sina followed a Greek school of thought which believed that God was the first cause from whom ten intelligences emanated. It was from the active intelligence that ideas were communicated to the human body by a radiation of the divine light, and thus the human soul was created. This implied that prophecy was not an exclusive gift to prophets and that a man of high spiritual gifts could also attain it by way of spiritual transcendence. Such a scheme seemed to run against the content of divine revelation in the Qur'an.

The orthodox philosopher and one-time Sufi, Abu Hamid Muhammad al-Ghazali, attacked Ibn Sina on this point in his book *Tahafut al-falasifa* (Incoherence of the Philosophers). A century later Ibn Rushd (Averroes, 1126–98) was to rebut al-Ghazali's refutation arguing that demonstrative study did not conflict with scripture, although Hourani notes that his views appear to have more impact on Latin Christian philosophy than Islamic thought.

An attempt to formulate Ibn Sina's philosophy of *ishraq*, the radiation of divine light, was made by al-Suhrawardi, which led to his execution by the Ayubbid ruler of Aleppo in 1191. The central idea of the mysticism of Ibn Arabi of Andalusia (1165–1240) was a transcendent state, which he called 'opening', through which direct knowledge of God and the unseen is achieved. As Moin says he suffered a great deal and was imprisoned for a while. 'He claimed' writes Moin, 'that he had met the beatified Muhammad, that he knew God's greatest name and that he had acquired his knowledge not through his own labour but through direct inspiration.'[4]

Numerous *fatwas* were issued against Ibn Arabi but his orthodoxy was vindicated by the Ottoman Sultan Selim 1 (1512–20) who restored Ibn Arabi's tomb in Damascus when a *fatwa* was issued in his favour. Khomeini was strongly influenced by Ibn Arabi and his neoplatonic idea of the *logos* or perfect man. 'Whoever knows the perfect man has known god,' wrote Khomeini. Khomeini's writings are certainly a far cry from the image of him as a narrow-minded bigot developed in the West. Another mystic, says Moin, Ain al-Qozat of Hamdan, was hanged in 1131 and his body burnt with oil and marsh reed, while Mullah Sadra, the last great philosopher of Islam and the founder of Transcendent Theosophy, a tradition that was followed by Khomeini, was driven out of his home town Shiraz.[5]

Fear of persecution, says Moin, forced mystics and philosophers to hide behind a secret language. One such was Mir-Damad, who died in 1631 and whose work Khomeini came to know. 'Legend has it', says Moin, 'that when at the moment of his death the angels Nakir and Monkar descended to interrogate him and in the Muslim tradition asked: "Who is your creator?" the philosopher replied in a mixture of Arabic and Greek: "Ostoqoson fawq al-ostoqossat" (an element above all elements). The angels of death reported their conversation back to God, adding: "We cannot understand this creature of yours, this Mir-Damad fellow." The Almighty responded: "Don't worry. Nobody in the world understands him."' This, adds Moin, was how Mir-Damad remained safe from the zealot's wrath. In fact Khomeini was himself considered heretically Sufi by many.

There is nothing in the Qur'an explicitly condemning music; it has been closely associated with Sufism and evidence in the Hadith shows that Muhammad sometimes listened to music with pleasure. The recitation of the Qur'an and the *adhan* (call to prayer) are central to Islam, but generic terms for music have never been applied to them, according to *The New Grove Dictionary of Music and Musicians*.[6] From an early period, the *'ulama* debated the perceived dangers of music and the word *sama'* is used to distinguish between licit (*halal*) and illicit (*haram*) music as understood by the four legal schools and in discussions between representatives of these schools and the Sufi orders. The chanting of the Qur'an and the *adhan* is universally allowed while certain types of devotional singing have been variously tolerated within the different Islamic schools of law, according to Grove.

A rejection of music was expressed immediately after the Prophet's death, and the *'ulama*'s condemnation extended to court musicians of the Umayyad dynasty. Concern about inadmissible music increased in the ninth century, when Sufi communities introduced dance and spiritual audition (*sama'*) into their ecstatic rituals. In Islamic thought, the basis of hostility to music lies in its power to stimulate the 'lower passions' (*nafs*). Individuals such as Ibn Abi al-Dunya (*d.* 894) theoretically condemned almost all instrumental and vocal music, yet Majd al-Din Ahmad al-Ghazali (d. 1126) and Abu Hamid Muhammad al-Ghazali (1058–1111) defended the practice of listening to music, including its usage by the Sufi orders. Arguments in favour of music have stressed the individual's ability to listen (*sama'*), drawing close to the Divine. An extensive literature in Arabic, Turkish and Persian discusses admissible and inadmissible music with constant reference to verses of the Qur'an and the Hadith. The most exhaustive collection of learned opinions is contained in the *Kitab al-imta' bil-ahkam* (Guide to the application of the rules for listening to music), *c.*1300, by Kamal al-Din al-Adfuwi.[7]

Abu Hamid Muhammad al-Ghazali taught at the Nizamiyya University in Baghdad from 1091 to 1095, and from 1106 in Neyshabur. He wrote his principal work, *Ihya' 'ulum al-din* (Revival of the religious sciences) in an attempt to reconcile Islamic orthodox tradition and Sufi experience. In the first part he deals with Qur'anic recitation (*tilawa*) and the call to prayer. The second part, on morals and customs, includes a detailed chapter on the extent to which performing and listening to music should be permitted. Noting that nowhere in the Qur'an is music expressly forbidden, al-Ghazali demonstrates with numerous examples that the issue is not one of condemning specific musical forms or instruments, but depends on whether the intention is to arouse or strengthen good or bad qualities through music. His views culminate in the remarkable statement that 'singing (*ghina'*) is more powerful than the Qur'an in arousing to ecstasy (*wajd*)'.[8] His liberal attitude to the dervish dance ('allowable, unless ecstasy is shown off') and religiously motivated music ('desirable') has influenced the theory and practice of mosque and monastery music, especially in Turkey. The chapter on music in the *Miftah al-sa'ada* by the Turk Tashkupri-zadah (Tashköprüzade) *(d.* 1561), for example, is wholly indebted to al-Ghazali.[9]

No universally acceptable agreement about the legal status of music in the Islamic world was ever reached, leaving interpretation open. This has led to ambiguities. In Iran at the beginning of the 1979 Revolution, the broadcasting and public performance of music was banned. Yet, shortly before his death in 1989, Ayatollah Khomeini pronounced that music was admissible, except in the case of women singing to men and as long as it did not incite sensual feelings.[10]

FIFTEEN

Who Thinks for Islam?

The failure after independence of nationalist movements to live up to the expectations of their people stimulated Islamic fundamentalism in the 1970s and 1980s. The fundamentalists argued that modernity must appear in an Islamic guise. Since then regimes have manipulated Islamic slogans. The most positive result for the future of Islam would be a lessening of the culture-gap between traditionalist Muslim societies and those which have become more westernized. Iran's complex Islamic experiment may, in the long run, be the answer to Islam's search for a reasonably democratic, modern Islamic state.

The appearance in Iran in 1979 of a radical Islamic political movement has its roots in the nineteenth century when leading Muslim intellectuals first began to counter European domination. The catalyst for their exposure to the West had been Napoleon's brief venture into Egypt in 1798–1801. The failure of successive *jihad*s against the colonial powers, in particular Britain and France, had convinced the more urbane Muslims that 'Christian' power would remain undefeated until Islam was thoroughly reformed from within.

When in 1798 Napoleon invaded Egypt it was the first time since the Crusades that Egyptians had been exposed to the culture and military muscle of the West. The latter caused panic but, as the Islamic historian 'Abd al-Rahman al-Jabarti noted, Egyptians were beguiled by the scholars and scientists who accompanied Napoleon. The three-year sojourn of the French was a complete failure militarily but was to be the catalyst for the frantic modernization programme of Muhammad 'Ali (1805–48) that ensued and for the intellectual struggle of the nineteenth century. Napoleon's hundred savants led by Monge and Denon were to produce the greatest work ever compiled on Egypt, *La Description d'Egypte*.

Napoleon's visit had been short. Nelson sank his fleet, the Egyptians derided his interest in Islam and he himself scuttled to Paris to take over the Directory, leaving General Kleber to extricate himself from the mess. Kleber was brutally murdered and the French army made an ignominious escape under an arrangement of British safe passage. However, the French episode was to be the beginning of a long period of profound French cultural influence. In the century ahead, the latter part of it a period of effective British colonization, French schools, cultural centres and hospitals proliferated. It was France's 'Civilizing Mission'. Many modern Egyptians have had French schooling and French is the lingua franca today in many a Cairene or Alexandrian drawing-room. This charged contact with France made Egypt's enlightenment possible.

The nineteenth-century Islamic reformers wanted to rationalize Islam with the technical and scientific developments that had made Europe unassailable. In this context they called for a return to *ijtihad*, the creative interpretation of the Qur'an. Legally speaking, *ijtihad* was the principal means by which Islam has for centuries achieved its social expression. It involved reforming the superstructure of *fiqh* (jurisprudence) created by generations of *'ulama* according to *taqlid* (imitation) of the earliest authorities and applying it to modern society. In Egypt, which remained a nominal part of the Ottoman Empire until the First World War, the modernizers were seen as reformers who wanted both to benefit from western advances and challenge the political ambitions of the West.

The first modernist thinker to have an impact was Sir Sayyid Ahmad Khan (1817–98) whose goal was to create an educated Muslim elite in India able to compete with Hindus in Britain's Indian Civil Service. He founded the Muhammadan Anglo-Oriental College at Aligarh in India. His greatest critic was Jamal al-Din Afghani (1839–97), an important champion of Pan-Islamism. Afghani's foremost disciple was Muhammad 'Abduh (1849–1905) who collaborated with the British in Egypt in order to achieve his far-reaching reforms. 'Abdu believed that the truths of science must be harnessed to religion. After 'Abdu came men such as Sheikh 'Ali 'Abd al-Raziq, a graduate of al-Azhar. He reasoned that the original *umma* (nation) of the Prophet Muhammad had no essential relationship with any particular state or form of government. 'Abdu's closest disciple was Rashid Rida, who was to become the most important advocate of a modernized Islamic state.

In 1928 in Egypt Hasan al-Banna founded the Muslim Brotherhood, the Ikhwan, first as a moral rather than political movement. It sought reform by purging Islam of both western influence and decadent medievalism. However, it became radicalized in the mounting crisis over Palestine during and after the Second World War and some of its members took to terrorism. In 1948 they murdered the Egyptian Prime Minister Nuqrashi Pasha and in 1949 Banna was killed by Egypt's security forces. The movement came into conflict with the Egyptian President Gamal Abd al-Nasser's secular nationalism and, after an attempt on Nasser's life in 1954, found refuge in 'Wahhabi' Saudi Arabia where

King Faisal used it against Nasser during the increasing conflict between secular socialist Egypt and monarchical, religious Saudi Arabia. The Ikhwan gave a sense of identity to a new 'thinking' class of school-teachers, junior officials and small-time merchants.

Ikhwan also refers to the fundamentalists spearheaded by Ibn Saud in what is now Saudi Arabia at the turn of the century. A conflict of identity was to ensue between Ibn Saud who remained a 'Wahhabi' (follower of the strict beliefs of Muhammad ibn 'Abd al-Wahhab) but sought to absorb the best of the modern world and the Ikhwan, Muslim die-hard extremists who rejected any deviation from the model of the Prophet's life based on the Qur'an and the Hadith and opposed innovations such as cars, telephones and the radio which were considered *bid'a*. This conflict reached its nadir in the rebellion of three Ikhwan leaders whom Ibn Saud defeated at the crucial battle of Sibilla in 1929 when their women sought shelter in the Saudi camp, a traditional Bedouin gesture of submission. An Ikhwan massacre of the people of the hill-town of Ta'if had acted as a morbid prelude to Ibn Saud's conquest of the Hejaz and its holy cities, Mecca and Medina, in 1926. His Ikhwan committed serious massacres at Buraydah and al-Huda and then went on to try to destroy the Tomb of the Prophet Muhammad at Medina when their iconoclastic zeal went unchecked.

The seminal thinker of Indian Islam in the twentieth century was the poet and mystic Muhammad Iqbal who argued that political activity must not be directed at the restoration of an idealized past, but towards a future in which the Caliphate would be equated with the service of mankind. Despite his liberal outlook he was succeeded by the ultra-conservative but extremely influential Sayyid Abu'l-'Ala Maududi (1903–79), the most important intellectual force among modern Sunni radicals. Maududi believed that *jihad* was not merely a defensive war for the protection of *Dar al-Islam* (the Abode of Islam) but must be waged aggressively against the forces which threatened to destroy it (i.e. the West). This is the argument used today by Osama bin Laden's al-Qaida movement in Afghanistan.

The leading heir of Maududi's doctrines in the Arab world was Sayyid Qutb, the Muslim Brotherhood theorist and militant who was executed in 1966 for allegedly plotting against Nasser. Qutb's ideas set the agenda for radicalism in Egypt. After 11 September 2001 Qutb was increasingly cited as the figure who had most influenced Osama bin Laden's al-Qaida movement. In modern times, notes Robert Irwin,[1] Qutb has been the most influential advocate of *jihad*. In the 1960s and 1970s, when Afghan religious scholars came under the influence of the Muslim Brotherhood, his ideas had had an important impact on the faculty of religious law in Kabul. In 1948 he had been sent to the USA to study education. On board ship he decided that salvation depended on an unswerving allegiance to Islam. When a drunken American woman tried to seduce him his resolve was put to the test. When he reached America he described the churches he saw as 'entertainment centres and sexual playgrounds'. On his return to Egypt in 1952 he joined the Ikhwan. After ten years in an Egyptian prison he was briefly released, then re-arrested after an assassination attempt on Nasser and hanged.

From his study of the Qur'an Qutb deduced that Christians were destined for hell and in later works he attacked Christians, Jews and the western way of life. As with bin Laden, however, his strongest criticism was aimed at Arab regimes which had strayed from Islam. These corrupt regimes had to be resisted and overthrown. To legitimize such resistance he went back to the writings of ibn Taymiyya (1268–1328). When the Mamluk sultans of Egypt found themselves at war with the Muslim Mongol Ilkhans of Iran he obliged them by sanctioning their war. He argued that as they had not fulfilled their Islam obligations they could be fought as pagans. Irwin notes that Islamic resistance movements from the 1950s onwards have been supported by this argument. Osama bin Laden's al-Qaida movement like Qutb sees corrupt regimes such as that of Saudi Arabia as the primary target rather than America or Israel.

One of the groups influenced by Qutb was dubbed *Takfir wa Hijra* (declaration of 'Infidelity and *Hijra'**). They have been responsible for many assassinations and acts of terror. Another Sunni group who followed Qutb's line were the Muslim Brotherhood in northern Syria. Its rebellion in Hama was suppressed by Syria's then President Hafez al-Asad at the cost of some 10,000 lives.

Throughout the Arab world and in Iran the secular nationalism and Marxism of the 1960s and 1970s have given way to Islamic fundamentalism with its deep and popular roots. Beyond the call for a return to the Shari'a lies a popular need for a cultural identity challenged by the inroads of the West. Among many modern Muslims there exists a common desire to use the instruments of the West without necessarily adopting the lifestyle of the West. Qur'anic punishments, the veiling of women and the segregation of the sexes have all become symbols of this new cultural thinking. Ironically, the Islamic movement has often been spear-headed not by illiterate fanatics but by westernized elitists such as Hasan al-Turabi, the Svengali of the past decades of Islamic rule in Sudan. Islamic scientists and engineers have, in particular, felt that their studies have forced them away from the Islamic heritage in which they seek their roots.

---

* Hijra, Emigration of the Prophet Muhammed from Mecca to Medina in 622 AD.

Of Sudan's 36 million people 75 per cent are Muslim. Southerners are Animist/Christian although the Christian population may be as little as 5 per cent. Military dictatorships have mostly run the country since independence from the UK in 1956. From 1969 the country was headed by Colonel Ja'afar Nimairi, a left-wing secularist. However, in 1983 he introduced Shari'a law which was applied rigorously; during 1983–5 it is estimated that at least two hundred victims had limbs amputated. His execution of Mahmoud Muhammad Taha, the elderly leader of the Republican Brothers, shocked many Sudanese. He also badly mismanaged Sudan's frail economy. In 1985 he was removed by the army. Over the past two decades, a civil war pitting black Christians and animists in the south against the Arab-Muslims of the north has cost at least 1.5 million lives in war- and famine-related deaths, as well as the displacement of millions of others. A coup in 1989 brought an Islamic regime to power, formally headed by General Omar Bashar but supported by the Islamist leader Hasan al-Turabi. Sudan soon became a pariah state. US missiles flattened a pharmaceutical factory in Khartoum in 1998, two weeks after 240 people were killed in bomb blasts at the US embassies in Nairobi and Dar es Salaam. The Americans claimed that the factory was partly owned by Osama bin Laden who had spent five years in Khartoum building bridges, roads and farms and developing his al-Qaida terrorist group. But bin Laden was forced to leave Sudan two years earlier in 1996. In September 2001 the USA agreed to a UN lifting of sanctions against Sudan on the grounds that it had agreed to support their war against international terror.

The 1980s and 1990s witnessed a dramatic growth in the influence of political Islam both through its civil and military factions in Arab and other Muslim countries. At times it has become the equivalent of a shadow government, while in Sudan it became for a period the actual government and in Iran it has remained so.

In Egypt political Islam has become the primary censor of intellectual and literary activity. Despite the fact that the law traditionally limited the role of al-Azhar University to the supervision of books concerning the Qur'an and the Sunna only, with the growth of the Islamic political movement the unlegislated role of al-Azhar began to increase. Religious taboos were no longer restricted to scepticism about God, the Prophets and the Qur'an. The sphere of al-Azhar's censorship extended to include anything related to Islam, whether intellectual, historical, analytical, political or fiction. Today its rector enjoys pre-eminence among the Sunni *'ulama* although his opinions are not binding on his peers.

The Cyprus-based *Middle East Times* notes that the following issues are off-limits in Egypt today: to report on human rights abuses, to criticize the President or his family, to criticize the military, to point out the ill-treatment of Egyptians in 'friendly' Arab countries, especially in Saudi Arabia, to discuss modern, unorthodox interpretations of Islam, or to report on discrimination against Coptic Christians. The Egyptian government censor reviews all issues of newspapers and magazines before allowing them to be distributed. The *Middle East Times* had to censor itself for some years but sometimes found itself pushing to the limits and losing three to four issues every year. This was disastrous for sales and advertising revenue. A new system evolved whereby it submitted a proof of each issue to the censor in advance. If the censor did not like an article or a paragraph, the newspaper would remove it and leave a blank space in its place. It was not allowed, however, to mention in this new space the reason why it was there.

Writing in *Le Monde Diplomatique* its diplomatic editor Alain Gresh[2] describes a film on the Saudi religious dissident Sheikh Salman al-Awdah in 1994. The film shows al-Awdah at a mosque addressing a tightly packed gathering of men. The sheikh recites the words of a Saudi poet:

They have forbidden the word, writing and speech!
Be silent! And if injustice remains
When the tongue is mute, it will burn like a moth in the flame.
For opinion now is trash, secreted away and thrown in the bin.
The word is a crime,
Beware he who would start a debate.

At dawn the following day, the police arrested and imprisoned the sheikh along with dozens of his followers.

Gresh explains how in September 1992, 107 prominent members of the community addressed a private memorandum of forty-five pages to Sheikh 'Abd al-Aziz ibn Baz, the Kingdom's highest religious official. Though they were careful not to attack the king personally, the signatories put forward some revolutionary demands: equality for all before the law, official accountability, an end to corruption and usury, the redistribution of wealth, the strengthening of the army and national independence, the curtailing of police powers. These demands were combined with others of a more militant Islamist nature: more religious courses in the universities, a ban on the teaching of 'western doctrines', censorship of television and foreign programmes and so forth. It was the origins of the signatories, more than their demands, that worried the authorities, says Gresh: 72 per cent were from the Najd region; half of them were clerics. Since its foundation, the stability of the Kingdom has been underpinned by the alliance between the Al Saud – whose tribal base is in Najd – and the *'ulama,* chiefly those descended from Muhammad Ibn 'Abd al-

Wahhab, founder of Saudi Arabia's puritanical interpretation of Islam, known in the West as Wahhabism.

In the 1950s opposition movements based on socialism or Arab nationalism gathered support mainly among the Shi'a minority in the Eastern Province or in the outlying areas of the country. Relying on the loyalty of the Najd and armed with the banner of Islam endorsed by the *'ulama*, the monarchy was able to defeat them, notes Gresh. Today, it is from the heartlands of the Najd and from the *'ulama* itself, speaking in the name of a 'purified' Islam, that the most serious threat comes.

In 1993 six prominent religious and intellectual figures launched an unprecedented challenge to King Fahd by announcing the formation of the Committee for the Defence of Legitimate Rights (CDLR). It proposed to 'abolish injustice, support the oppressed and defend the rights which have been given to Man by the Shari'a'. Their action, they went on to explain, was dictated by the desire to 'stop the accelerating deterioration pushing society towards chaos. The only alternative to violence is a balanced and moderate reform movement.'

Their professed moderation did nothing to mitigate royal outrage, says Gresh. In the days that followed, organizers were dismissed from their jobs in the public sector, interrogated and arrested. Some months later, CDLR spokesman Muhammad al-al-Mas'ari secretly crossed into Yemen en route for London from where he bombards the Kingdom by fax and Internet.[3] Al-Mas'ari puts the case for reform:

> The level of education in Arabia has risen, illiteracy has fallen below 35 per cent, lower than in Egypt. In every home there is someone who knows how to read; everyone has a radio and listens to foreign stations; they can even distinguish between the BBC which they consider biased, and the more objective broadcasts of Dutch radio. The law prohibiting satellite dishes is not being applied and there are between 100,000 and 600,000. Who can stem the tide of information?

For Saudi society, says Gresh, the Gulf War was an irreparable trauma. The presence of 500,000 foreign troops on the 'Holy Land of Islam', the inability of the Kingdom to defend itself despite the billions spent on sophisticated weaponry and the systematic destruction of Iraq by the allied armies, provoked questions from a highly nationalistic – not to say xenophobic – and religious population. 'Wherever one raised questions or debated the issue,' Gresh quotes al-Mas'ari as saying, 'one had the impression of an awakening. But people were afraid of Saddam and rallied round the king, even the Islamists. Personally, I wasn't part of that.'

Society was run in an archaic, though from a government perspective effective, manner. The all-powerful, non-elective Council of Princes, representing the most powerful members of the royal family and the major tribes, became the means of communicating to the public only that information the council chose to divulge and of filtering out information deemed too sensitive for public consumption.

For a long time, recalls another dissident, Khalid al-Fawwaz, director of the Advice and Reformation Committee (ARC), a more radical opposition group than the CDLR, people who wanted to change their situation were thrown back on their own resources. 'In the 70s it was difficult to organize collectively,' says al-Fawwaz. 'Officials, even the king, held their weekly public meetings at which they listened to individual grievances – and made promises.' Osama bin Laden, another director of the ARC, was stripped of his citizenship in February 1994 for his financial support of militant Islamic groups in Egypt and elsewhere.

Dissent, says Gresh, was by no means limited to the Islamists. Early February 1991 saw the publication of an open letter to King Fahd from forty-three liberal businessmen and intellectuals. Their demands, formulated with great deference, were moderate in the extreme: without questioning the Shari'a-based constitution or the monarchy, they called for the creation of consultative councils at the national, provincial and local level, a 'basic law of government' and control over the Mutawwi'in, the 'morals police'. These demands, including one reference to human rights, were considerably milder than those made by the same liberal opposition in the early 1980s and represented no challenge to the monarchy.

However, in March 1992, the liberals got some satisfaction when the king issued a Basic Law and announced the formation of a Consultative Council and the role to be played by the regions. In August 1993, the king appointed the 60 members of the Majlis. They were largely made up of 'modern' elites with only nominal representation of the traditional *'ulama*. In practical terms, the Consultative Council did nothing to curb the power of the royal family or increase representation in government. Gresh believes that it was more a matter of the king co-opting western-educated Saudis, including certain opponents, who represented little threat to the status quo and could be enlisted against the more dangerous Islamist opposition.

In 1960, only 2 per cent of girls attended school, but by 1981 this had risen to 41 per cent and, by 1991, to over 80 per cent. Women now make up the majority of graduates – though they are excluded from certain fields such as engineering, journalism and architecture – but the regular labour market remains virtually closed to them. Young people, more urbanized, better educated and with higher expectations than their parents and less subject to tribal relationships, have also been cut off from their roots. Meanwhile, the development of Islamic universities in the 1970s led to the entry of thousands of new *'ulama* onto the market for religious experts, and left them exposed to new currents in a highly charged Muslim world.

Gresh points out that the international media seldom lifts a corner of the veil of secrecy that cloaks scandals involving Saudi business. Any efforts to do so are swiftly stifled by western governments, as was the case, for instance, with a British official commission created in 1989 to investigate the backhanders paid by British representatives to the Saudi royal family for the multi-billion armaments deal signed by the Thatcher government in September 1985. The UK press reckoned that handouts were up to 30 per cent of the total deal; the commission decided not to publish its report.

Given a potentially explosive situation, says Gresh, King Fahd developed a two-pronged strategy. With western governments he has invoked the spectre of the 'Islamic menace' and presented himself as the one and only bulwark of civilization. In September 1994, after the arrest of Sheikh al-Awdah, a communiqué of the Battalions of the Faithful threatened western institutions and officials of the regime. On 10 April 1995, another unknown organization, the Islamic Movement for Change, warned western forces to leave the region by 25 June. Neither of these communiqués resulted in any action by the King; on 13 November 1995, a car bomb exploded in the centre of Riyadh.

Internally, the King has strengthened political control over the clerics. In November 1992, he reorganized the council of senior *'ulama*, seven members of which were expelled for refusing to condemn the dissidents' communiqué that September. In October 1994, he followed up with the creation of a Supreme Council for Islamic Affairs, presided over by Prince Sultan. He has also instigated approaches to certain dissidents. In Autumn 1993, the regime reached a compromise with the moderate Shi'a opposition. One such group, based in London, from where it published the newspaper *al-Jazira al-Arabiyya*, suspended its activities and returned home. But the Shi'a, around 10 per cent of the population, are still profoundly alienated from the regime. Even if material conditions in the Eastern Province, where they mainly live, were improved, they would remain second-class citizens. Numerous posts, especially in the army, are closed to them; they cannot worship in freedom; there is only one Shi'i in the consultative council. The only response to all those who refuse to fall into line, says Gresh, is repression.

The battle for freedom of expression in Iran is arguably a more interesting and subtle one than the clumsy goings-on in Riyadh and Jeddah. It is clear that the attacks on Tehran student dormitories that led to riots against the ruling mullahs in Iran in July 1999 were initiated by conservative-led militias aiming to expose and liquidate liberals demanding a more open society. After two decades of clerical rule and two years after the elections making Muhammad Khatami president, ordinary Iranians supported the students' sentiment for reform. They were sickened by interference in their lives by the regime as well as by its inefficiency and corruption. Ironically, the clergy had allowed some room for popular expression and encouraged education for men and women. Even traditionally Muslim women have responded to the call to learn in Iran and demanded more say in running the country. Iran is a young country with 19 million students and pupils, including one million in higher educational institutions who are increasingly politically aware and have high expectations. However, their desire to improve their lot and participate in the political scene is constantly blocked by the clerics. They crave for what the West has to offer, anathema to right-wing militants to whom 'Death to America' has remained their principal mantra since 1979.

Young reformers have little in common with their parents who brought the Shah down and the Ayatollah Khomeini to power in a massive Islamic revolution in 1979. But contrary to the image one has of him in the West as an obscurantist mullah, Khomeini always saw himself as a religious reformer or *mujaddid* (renewer) and a political activist, even a rebel. The great irony is that today it is the religious conservatives, represented by Khomeini's heir as *Vale-e faqih* or spiritual leader 'Ali Khamenei, who have adopted his political radicalism and the reformers, represented by the popular but entrenched president Muhammad Khatami, who are furthering what Khomeini initiated in reforming religious traditions. This is what the conservatives do not like. This conflict between clerical hardliners and secular pragmatists has dominated the Iranian political scene since Khomeini's death in 1989.

It was the debate over the freedom of the press, in particular the forced closure of the opposition newspaper *Salam*, that led to the riots in 1999. *Salam* had investigated the death of Saeed Emami, an intelligence ministry official, publishing a secret memo in which Emami had detailed a planned crackdown on the press. Emami, who was said to have committed suicide in jail the previous June, had also been the leading suspect in the murders of Iranian dissident writers and activists the previous winter. Reformers believe that he was murdered to prevent him giving evidence about the killings, which they believe to have been engineered by extremists in the intelligence ministry controlled by Ayatollah Khamenei. *Salam* had enthusiastically backed the presidential campaign of Khatami.

At the heart of the present confrontation lies the legacy of Khomeini, whose childhood in the town of Khomein in central Iran coincided with the period of Iran's constitutional revolution of 1905–6. This so-called revolution led to the emergence of a constitutional monarchy. From Khomein, Khomeini followed Sheikh Abdolkarim Ha'eri, a spiritual teacher who profoundly influenced him, to a nearby seminary. Khomeini then followed his teacher to Iran's holy city of Qom. After completing his studies he was pronounced by his fellow mullahs a *mujtahid*, one who could interpret the Qur'an as a *faqih* (jurisconsult), and was soon considered a *marja-e taqlid* (a cleric 'worthy of emulation'). Meanwhile, in 1929 he married a woman to whom he remained faithful for 60 years to the day he died.

Khomeini grew up during a period in which the mosque was almost constantly on the defensive. In 1921 a Persian Cossack officer, Reza Khan, marched on Tehran and became the country's effective ruler. He was crowned Shah in 1925. He pursued modernizing reforms, including the creation of a model army, pioneered in Turkey by the Turkish leader Kemal Atatürk. The crunch came in 1928 when the Iranian Queen dramatically took off her veil in the shrine of Fatima in Qom. The clergy were horrified but intimidated. When Ayatollah Bafqi reprimanded the Shah he marched on Qom, entered the shrine without taking off his boots and horse-whipped Bafqi. He forbade women to wear the veil in public. However, these harsh ordinances were to be reversed when in 1941 Shah Reza was sent into exile by the British for his pro-Axis sympathies and replaced by his effete, Swiss-educated son Muhammad Reza. The young Shah was at first popular and his liberalization allowed the clergy to regain the activism that his father had crushed. Newspapers proliferated and veiled women re-emerged.[4]

In 1951 Dr Muhammad Mosaddeq became prime minister. Honest and passionately nationalistic, he provoked the West by nationalizing the Anglo-Iranian Oil Company and was overthrown in a coup sponsored by the CIA and the British in 1953. This coup was led by an extraordinary march through Tehran of wrestlers and prostitutes with dollars, it was said, tucked by CIA employees into their bras. Nevertheless, the period following Musaddeq's downfall was a honeymoon between the new Shah and the clergy who had been repelled by Mosaddeq's anti-clericalism. The honeymoon, however, came to a sudden end after 1961 when the Shah decided, with backing from President Kennedy's administration, on a land reform programme which threatened the lands of religious endowments and challenged Islam's belief in the sanctity of private property. Khomeini did not attack the land reforms at first and it was only when local councils were opened to non-Muslims and women were offered enfranchisement that he broke his silence, saying chillingly 'The son of Reza

Khan has embarked on the destruction of Islam in Iran. I will oppose this as long as the blood circulates in my veins.'

The Shah reviled his enemies in clumsy language, calling the communists 'the red reaction' and clerical opposition 'the black reaction'. In January 1963 he gave an extraordinarily insensitive speech in the shrine of Fatima to celebrate his reforms, saying of the clergy 'They were always a stupid and reactionary bunch whose brains have not moved ... Black reaction understands nothing ... its brain has not moved for a thousand years ... The Red subversives have clear decisions and, incidentally, I have less hatred towards them.' He responded to Khomeini's criticisms by sending him into exile in Turkey. From there Khomeini moved to Shi'i Islam's holiest city, Najaf, in Iraq, where he became a magnet for opposition to the Shah. After the OPEC oil price hikes of 1973 the Iranian economy overheated. Huge wealth was amassed by the few while most Iranians groaned in poverty. By the late 1970s the Shah was claiming that Iran would become another Japan but electricity cuts all over Tehran during the hot summer of 1978 belied these claims as absurd. In 1977 the Shah had made the fatal mistake of having Khomeini expelled from Iraq. From Najaf he went to a village near Paris where he was to be in the media spotlight until he returned to Iran in glory to massive, hysterical crowds in February 1979. The Islamic revolution that followed was Khomeini's, not Islam's. Nowhere else in the Islamic world have clerics gained power in this way. Without Khomeini Islam might well have remained merely an early partner in revolution.

When I stood amid a million-strong crowd in central Tehran and watched buildings burn and tanks mutiny during a day of anarchy in November 1978, everybody I spoke to hoped for a social democratic revolution with the support of the clerics, the bazaars, the students and the army. Early the next morning I ran into a middle-class Iranian girl whom I had previously met at a Tehran publishing company. 'What are you doing here, Farida?', I asked her. 'It is a dangerous'. She smiled. 'I know', she said, 'but I wanted to be with the people. Many of my friends are here.'

Nobody expected clerical government. Indeed, on his return, Khomeini accepted the mantle of spiritual leadership, initially eschewing a political role, and supported a series of sophisticated prime ministers. However, his protégés were ousted one by one when they found his interference intolerable. The first, Bani Sadr, fled to France. The last, Montazeri, his heir apparent whom he loved like a son, was utterly humiliated by him. The eight-year war with Iraq was devastating for Iran, ending in a compromising armistice when Khomeini had to 'drink from the poisoned cup'.

It was a year after this humiliation that he was able to reinforce his authority by issuing his *fatwa* or 'legal opinion' condemning Salman Rushdie to death as an apostate for writing *The Satanic Verses*. Ironically, it was in that same year that he reminded his critics how he had once been a pariah among fellow clerics in Qom when he had taught philosophy.

Nevertheless, Khomeini would turn a blind eye to appalling human rights abuses, including the torture and rape of women in prison. He claimed to respect legal systems and democracy but firmly supported the students who seized American hostages inside the US embassy on 4 November 1979. When he was first shown a digest of *The Satanic Verses* in February 1989 he dismissed it, saying 'The world has always been full of lunatics who have talked nonsense. It is not worth replying to this sort of thing.' However, some weeks later he changed his mind. 'I call on all zealous Muslims to execute them [the author and publishers] quickly.'

On a personal level he had an enlightened attitude towards women; when he married in 1929 he assured his young wife that he was not an obscurantist and that his only request was that she observe the rules of Islam. He even encouraged her and other women in his family to wear pretty and colourful clothing. He is unlikely before his marriage to have frequented the houses of menopausal women that served the needs of his fellow seminarians although he must have known about them.[5]

By the time of his death many of the ideals that characterized the very early part of the revolution had been eclipsed by human greed. Shayegan portrays the increasing corruption in Iran with an anecdote:

> It is said that a young man returning to Iran after several years abroad took a taxi from Tehran airport. On the way he asked the driver to stop at a tobacconist. 'What for, sir?' the man asked.
> 'What do you think? To buy some cigarettes.'
> 'If you want cigarettes the mosque is the place to go to.'
> 'But that's the house of God. People go there to pray.'
> 'You're wrong there, mister. If you want to pray, you go to the university.'
> 'So where do people go to get educated?'
> 'People do most of their studying in jail, nowadays, don't they?'
> 'Jail! I thought that was where they kept criminals.'
> 'Listen, friend! Got the villains all locked up in the government, haven't they?'[6]

SIXTEEN

Western Misperceptions of Islam: Islamophobia

Peace be upon me [Jesus, Son of Mary]
The day I was born
The day that I die
And the day that I shall be raised up to life.

(Qur'an XIX:33.)

Disperse, thou heavenly light, and save
The souls by that impostor led.
The Arab thief, as Saturn bold,
Who quite destroyed the Asian fold.
Assert thy glorious deity
Stretch out thine arm, thou triune God,
The Unitarian fiend expel,
And chase his doctrine back to hell.

(Hymn No 443 in the *Collection of hymns for the use of people called Methodists*, 1830.)

In October 1999, a senior Kuwaiti Sunni figure 'Abd al-Razzak al-Shayije told the weekly Arabic magazine *al-Wasat*: 'There is a global campaign against Islam, and not only in Kuwait. Those who attack Islam say nothing useful, have no credibility and do it to attract the West's attention, like Salman Rushdie and Abu Zayd.' al-Shayije may be right but if the Islamophobia of the western media is profoundly unjust it does also reflect an iconoclastic trend in the Islamic world that would shock the heroes of Islam's early period. Many modern Muslims recognize that Islam has to confront its own heart of darkness before it can develop.

The modern Muslim is placed in a peculiar dilemma. In many Islamic countries today there is a tendency for intellectuals to show caution in condemning the behaviour of governments for killing and torture, for fear of giving unintended support to militant fundamentalists with even less sense of human rights than the governments they are fighting. On the other hand, human rights advocates are discouraged from supporting minorities or intellectuals condemned for apostasy on the grounds that they would be propagating the interests of the *kafir* (infidel) West. There is also the sad question of intimidation. When the great Arab poet Adonis fell out with the clergy over his attendance of a conference in Granada attended by Israelis, for example, some fellow Arab writers were afraid to defend him.

Where Article 18 of the Universal Declaration of Human Rights declares that 'Everyone has the right to freedom of thought, conscience and religion: this right includes freedom to change religion' this freedom encompasses for Muslims one of the worst ills, *shirk* (associationism) by which God's majesty is compromised by being polluted by alien gods. Once a Muslim, there is no turning back. For apostasy the punishment is, in principle at least, death.

Western human rights movements are lavish in their coverage of abuses and censorship routinely attributable to Islamic centres of government or control. On the British cocktail circuit Saddam Hussein becomes the symbol of Arab tyranny. The Islamic refrain 'Allahu Akbar', which Saddam has cunningly embroidered across the Iraqi flag, is prominently but inadvertently displayed on western news channels every time Iraq becomes the West's whipping boy.

Meanwhile, in Afghanistan the Taliban were seen by the casual westerner absurdly as the exemplars of the Shari'a at a time when even their claim to represent Pashtun nationalism is in doubt. Their understanding of the reality of Islam is as dubious as that of the Wahhabis of Saudi Arabia who, despite the honoured status of Jews and Christians in the Qur'an, until the 1980s insisted on a religious certificate from visa applicants, forbidding Jews to enter, and still forbid Christians to perform mass or any other service. Of course, the Saudis might argue that Jews were Israeli fifth-columnists but this argument holds little water on balance. Even during the Gulf War these taboos were not abandoned. One of the few Christmas carols allowed in Saudi Arabia was 'Jingle-Bells' because there was absolutely nothing religious about it.

The writer Olivier Roy highlights the distinct nationalist make-up of the Islamic movements of the 1990s, the Taliban in Afghanistan, Refah in Turkey, Hamas in Gaza, Hizbullah in Lebanon and the FIS in Algeria. Roy points out that even revolutionary Iran has failed to spread its message beyond its own

Shi'i community despite the efforts of Khomeini to transcend the Sunni–Shi'a sectarian divide.[1] The war in Afghanistan was provoked by the emergence of an Islamic movement inspired by Pakistan's Jamaat-i-Islami and Saudi Wahhabi activists. It spoke the language of revolution, says Roy, and aimed at the establishment of an Islamic State by way of a political party that shared its ideology.[2] Gulbuddin Hekmatyar's hard-line Hezb-i Islami (Islamic Party) received Pakistan-administered US aid and, with the logistical help of the Muslim Brotherhood, the Saudis helped finance Pakistan's Jamaat to create a network of Islamic groups based in Peshawar. Nevertheless, the Hezb-i Islami remained basically Pashtun and Masoud's Jamaat remained essentially Tajik. Even after the withdrawal of the Soviets Najibullah's Communist government played on these ethnic differences.

Once Kabul fell in 1992, says Roy, the gathering of the northern coalition of Tajiks, Uzbeks and Hazaras against the Pashtun Hezb-i Islami became all the more apparent. When the Taliban took Kabul in 1996 they were conservative, Sunni, close to the Saudi Wahhabi 'wee free', and anti-Iranian and anti-Shi'a. Their only goal was the strict implementation of the Shari'a and the seclusion of women. However, they were also vengefully Pashtun and opposed to the other ethnic groups. Support for the Taliban's version of Islam was nurtured in the religious schools of neighbouring Pakistan but, as the British militant Tariq 'Ali notes, during the Islamic-oriented era of General Zia it was state patronage rather than popular support from which political Islam derived its strength. The ascendance of religious groups, wrote 'Ali, 'is the work of General Zia, who received political, military and financial support from the USA and Britain throughout his eleven years as dictator. The West needed Zia to fight the Afghan war against the former Soviet Union. Nothing else mattered. The CIA, for example, turned a blind eye to the sale of heroin to fund the Mujahidin, and the number of officially registered heroin addicts in Pakistan rose from 139 in 1977 to 30,000 in 1988.'[3]

The western media revels in revealing such chilling inconsistencies but it also severely distorts the image of the purer aspects of the Islamic world. Article XIX (the Global Campaign for Free Expression) and *Index on Censorship* publish excellent reports on the tribulations of Salman Rushdie, Abu Zayd and Taslima Nasrin, and on human rights abuses in Algeria, Sudan and Iran, while the cruelties of the Islamic armed groups in Algiers are daily fodder for the press. We see films on television of babies' heads flung yards from their torsos on the roofs of Kabylie villages. During the 1980s we watched with fascination interviews when the urbane, highly articulate Sorbonne-educated Hasan al-Turabi – the *éminence grise* of the Islamic government in Sudan – defended crucifixions or cross-amputations for murderers, rapists and certain thieves.

Even Israel's grossly imbalanced war against the Palestinians – who have long since renounced claim to 78 per cent of Palestine and are struggling to claw back the 22 per cent that remains – has tended in the western media to be between nice 'white' Israelis who make 'tragic mistakes' and pathetic Arabs who commit 'terrorist' atrocities and who are nameless when they die before the bullet of an Israeli sniper, tank or gunship. In common parlance anti-Semitism refers to the sufferings of the Jews, never to the far wider family of Semites which includes, above all, the Palestinians.

The murder of a pregnant Muslim girl by her family in London provokes western revulsion of the Islamic world's apparent barbaric 'otherness' but does not such obsession with family honour still exist in southern Italy and Greece? Targets of Edward Said's book Orientalism, we no longer read the great classical writers of the Arab world, Charles Doughty, Gertrude Bell, T.E. Lawrence and Freya Stark. We are less likely to pick up the searching novels of Naguib Mahfouz, Egypt's answer to Dickens and Zola, than Betty Mahmoudy's lurid book *Not Without My Daughter* or Jean Sasson's *Princess* which describes itself as 'A shocking, true story of life behind the veil [in Saudi Arabia]'. When Israelis bomb a Lebanese village we tend only to hear that Arab villagers have died, but if an Israeli is murdered by an Arab terrorist we are fed intimate details about his or her background. The Palestinian spokeswoman Hanan Ashrawi notes that Palestinian victims of Israeli live fire are daily given as 'x' numbers killed and 'y' numbers wounded. 'Their names, identities, dashed hopes, and shattered dreams are nowhere mentioned. Absent too are the grief and anguish of their mothers, fathers, sisters, brothers, and other loved ones who will have to live with that tragic loss.'[4]

Has the romantic orientalist of yesterday become the Islamophobe of today, obsessed with Huntington's trendy philosophy of a 'Clash of Civilizations'? Commenting on the American political scientist Samuel Huntington's famous claim in the summer of 1993 that 'The paramount axis of world politics will be "The West and the Rest" and a focus of conflict for the immediate future will be between the West and several Islamic-Confucian states', the Egyptian thinker Saad Eddin Ibrahim noted sadly that when a respected political scientist like Huntington 'speaks in a manner not so different from that of the mass media, the matter becomes a cause for serious alarm'. Juan Goytisolo is equally dismissive of Huntington's trendy theory. 'It is not the struggle among different but non-opposing civilizations that required a final conclusion, but rather, the struggle of all these civilizations against an uncontrolled modernity', he says.[5]

It is enough to glance at America's provincial press to understand how the average American sees the Islamic world. In an article provoked by the start of the 'al-Aqsa' Intifada in Palestine of November 2000 Dick Yarbrough, who describes himself as a retired vice-president of Bell South Corporation and active in the civic and business community in Atlanta, wrote an article entitled 'Arab terrorists are big cowards' for the Atlanta newspaper *The Neighbor*. Mr Yarbrough writes:

> I'm ready to solve the problem of Arab terrorism. Enough is enough. When a bunch of weirdoes crash a boat into the side of an American destroyer and kill 17 US sailors, kids who were simply doing their duty, we need to employ the Reagan doctrine – bomb the terrorists into the Middle Ages where their lifestyle would be much more appropriate. People who plant bombs in order to kill bystanders are cowards, pure and simple. And don't give me this crap about oppression. Arabs sit on most of the oil in the world, but they are too busy burning flags, chanting gibberish and throwing rocks to really care. They are always mad at somebody – usually the United States – about something. They ought to be thanking us. ... The screwballs think blowing themselves and others to smithereens gets them some kind of attaboy from Allah. You'd think Allah has preferred seating in heaven and the bigger the bomb, the better the accommodations. ... Lest I malign a whole race of people, let me be more specific. I am talking about Arab men. They have treated women like dirtbags since Ishmael was a pup. The ladies have to wear long dresses and totally cover their faces. They can't drive, wear mascara, watch MTV or color their hair green and spike it like their American counterparts. Women also are expressly forbidden to blow themselves up to gain favor with Allah. That's strictly a guy thing. I suspect that's one reason women agreed to cover their faces – to keep the men from seeing them snicker. My favorite ranting to come out of the Arab world is their pledge to 'eliminate the nation of Israel'. Yeah, right. If memory serves me correctly, the last time that was tried was 1967. The war lasted about two and a half minutes. The Israelis cleaned their clock and pushed them so far back they were in the outskirts of Alaska by nightfall.[6]

The Chicago Tribunal similarly quotes a message by a student of the University of Wisconsin to an Iranian student: 'Death to all Arabs, die, Islamic scumbag'.[7] As the article points out, image-makers often lump together Arab, Iranian or Turkish Muslims as 'dark complexion people flaunting beards or moustaches'.

The film *Rules of Engagement* in 2000 was one of a litany of films popular in the West that showed scant understanding of Arab culture. One critic wrote:

Would an Arab family allow young children, including girls, to carry and fire a gun at armed US marines? There is no explanation as to why this furious, bloodthirsty Arab rabble is bombarding the US embassy. The film's director, William Friedkin, explained that all this was an accurate depiction of Yemen and Yemeni society. The film castigates an entire society, not even a terrorist group, as is Hollywood's usual custom. They are hurling Molotovs, and shoot just because they all hate America and are naturally violent. At the end of the film, the script explains what happened to the various lead characters, implying that a fictional tale has a basis in fact.[8]

The American-Arab Anti-Discrimination Committee (ADC), founded in 1980 by former Senator James Abourezk, has collected other examples of anti-Arab racism in the West. The Rev. Franklin Graham, vice-chairman of the Billy Graham Evangelistic Association and son of the evangelist Billy Graham, made a series of extraordinarily comments at a televised revival in Kentucky on 14 October 2000. Graham, who is his father's designated successor as head of one of the largest evangelical associations in the USA, said 'The Arabs will not be happy until every Jew is dead. They hate the state of Israel. They all hate the Jews. God gave that land to the Jews. The Arabs will never accept that. Why can't they live in peace?' These remarks were broadcast to a huge television audience. The ADC also noted that a Republican nominee for the House of Representatives from central Florida had said on 12 October 2000, 'I think Palestinians are lower than pond scum.'

'This pattern of anti-Arab hate speech from otherwise respectable religious, journalistic and political figures', says ADC President Hala Maksoud, 'is shocking and deeply disturbing. It seems that many people in our country now feel entitled to defame and disparage any and all Arabs in a manner that would be unthinkable with regard to most other groups. I am not sure that any American community has endured an outpouring of raw hatred as vicious, flagrant and widespread as this in several decades. These are the sentiments that lead to hate crimes and serious abuse of Arab Americans and Arabs in the United States.'

Hanan Ashrawi tried to analyse the syndrome of victim turned oppressor in the Intifada of 2000.[9]

Whether battered wives, abused children, or Palestinians long subjected to the brutality of the horrendous Israeli military occupation, the first (and last) resort of the cowardly is in maligning the victim, in accusing him/her/them of having brought about the deserved cruelty of the crime. The battle between an Israeli army using live ammunition, tanks and helicopter gun ships is equated with the 'violence' of Palestinian civilians protesting with stones their victimization and continued loss of rights, lands, and lives.

Ashrawi sees the whole presentation as exhibiting the 'white man's burden'. Palestinians, she says sardonically, should be grateful for whatever 'generous offer' Israel chooses to grant them, regardless of the glaring injustice and illegality of the Israeli negotiating stance. 'Having compromised ourselves down to 22 per cent of historical Palestine, we are now being asked to be party to Israel's illegal annexation of Jerusalem and its settlement policies – i.e. an unholy partnership for the violation of international law and the relevant UN resolutions.'

She notes the instant scare tactics and panic politics coming into play with such labels as the 'terrorist' or 'dictatorial' or 'violent' Palestinians and a catch-22 situation visible: Arafat must 'control' his people and 'order' them to calm down and accept their enslavement and repression by the Israelis, otherwise he is no longer a 'peace partner' and cannot be considered a 'leader'. At the same time, says Ashrawi, Israel cannot deal with Arafat or the Palestinians because they are inherently 'undemocratic' and therefore have nothing in common with such 'civilized' democracies as Israel and the US. The historical and familiar slurs (including cockroaches, two-legged vermin, dogs) used by Israeli officials and public figures to describe Palestinians have been expanded, she says, to include 'snakes' and 'crocodiles.'

The murder by Israeli soldiers of the child Muhammad al-Durra [a terrified ten- year-old cowering in his father's arms before being killed by an Israeli soldier] shattered the complacency of those who had been comfortable with the anonymity of the Palestinians and the invisibility of their suffering. Even then, the Israeli propaganda machine tried to distort the truth even in the face of irrefutable evidence. First, it was said that he was killed by Palestinian 'gun men'. Then, he was 'caught in the crossfire'. The worst version was in the cynical depiction of the child Muhammad as a 'trouble-maker' or a 'mischievous' child who brought it upon himself. The last accusation involved a question: 'What was he doing there?' The real question should have been 'what was the Israeli army doing there?' in the heart of Palestinian Gaza shooting at civilians including a child and his father shopping together. Note the difference, however, when two Israeli under cover agents, belonging to the notorious Israeli death squads, were killed by Palestinian protestors. No Palestinian attempted to justify the act. Rather orders were issued to investigate and arrest those responsible. After all, there should be such a thing as the rule of law and due process. Instead, Israel moved its tanks and armies even closer to tighten the siege and strangulation of Palestinian towns, villages and refugee camps. Then it brought in its Apache helicopter gun ships and shelled Palestinian cities and towns in a most senseless and cruel form of collective punishment.[10]

The start of this new Intifada coincided with the Bush–Gore US Presidential elections. In a speech to the 39th Annual Policy Conference of AIPAC (American Israel Public Affairs Committee), on 18 May 1998 Gore had made no secret of his views:

> I want to salute you for your love of Israel, for your energetic and enduring support of the US–Israel relationship and partnership, and also for coming here every year to advocate for one of the most important cornerstones of American national security, and that is a strong and stable state of Israel … To begin with, every American citizen is better off because we have a loyal and committed friend in the Middle East that votes with us in the United Nations more often than any other country on the face of this earth. That is a partner. That is a fellow democracy that values what we value, a strategic ally and friend that we must support with the highest level of loyalty, and we will.
>
> …
>
> We meet tonight, of course, in the jubilee year of our great friend, Israel … to have the honor and the challenge of putting into words to the people of Israel, the bottomless reservoir of love and respect felt for them by the people of the United States of America and then to hear that love roared back, believe me, that was a joyous mission. … The Jewish love of justice has built a powerful democracy. The Jewish love of courage has built a powerful military and the Jewish love of knowledge and respect for learning has turned an infant nation state into a high-tech economic power house. … Today, Israel is a miracle. We in America believed in Israel and loved Israel from the beginning. We are intensely proud that 11 minutes after David Ben-Gurion declared the new state of Israel, the United States, under the wise leadership of President Harry S Truman, became the first nation in the world to recognize Israel. And on that auspicious day was born not only one of the most enduring nations in history but also the most enduring friendship between nations in history.

The influence of the Old Testament on many western Christians may have a significant impact on this unbalanced thinking. Historically, western antipathy to Islam is coloured by Ferdinand and Isabella's Reconquest of sophisticated Moorish Spain and by the Crusades. As Gore's speech demonstrates, since the creation of Israel in 1948 there have been more modern motives for supporting such denigration. European medieval images of Islam could verge on the comic. Muhammad was seen as a magician or even, says Albert Hourani, as 'a Cardinal of the Roman Church who, thwarted in his ambition to become Pope, fled to Arabia and there founded a church of his own'.[11] Peter Clark notes that the USA sees civilization starting with Sumeria and ending with the USA, an ideal of history which allows Islamic civilization no place. The US frontier tradition also sees the Israelis as frontiersmen by proxy. 'The language of Israel echoes this. The settlers are "pioneers".'

When his forces were defeated by the 'Abbasid army in the late eleventh century, Byzantine Emperor Alexius I called on Rome to liberate Jerusalem, leading to the initiation of the Crusades by Pope Urban II. The Crusades took Jerusalem but their influence was short-lived. The new threat was the Ottomans whom the Elizabethan historian Richard Knollys described as 'the present terror of the world', an unjust judgement of a dynasty that proved more tolerant to religious sects than the Byzantines it replaced. Indeed, so fearful was the Eastern Orthodox church of control by the Vatican that a saying was soon prevalent in the Balkans 'Better the turban of the Turk than the tiara of the Pope'. On the other hand, as John Esposito points out, the Ottoman threat contributed to the development of Europe as the focus of a common identity 'within a European Christendom torn apart by the Reformation, so that Erasmus was to exhort the nations of Europe to crusade against the Turks'.[12]

The feeling among Muslims that they are conspired against today was reflected in the 1999 scandal surrounding the origins of the great American-Palestinian sociologist Edward Said. Said is actually a Christian Protestant but is greatly respected by Muslims as a militant defender of the culture of the Islamic world. Did Said truly live in Jerusalem, was he a refugee and did either question affect his ability to defend the Palestinians? Said is the most eloquent spokesmen for the Palestinian Diaspora. Born in Jerusalem into a prominent and wealthy Jerusalem family, Said was brought up in luxury in Cairo, Jerusalem and Lebanon but has lived most of his adult life in the USA where he has for long been the darling of left-wing New York literary circles. The London *Observer* journalist Ed Vulliamy calls him 'one of the leading literary theorists of our century'. Said is an expert on classical music, a subject which has created a profound bond of friendship with the pianist Daniel Barenboim, who is extremely sensitive – as was Yehudi Menuhin – to the plight of the Palestinians.

Said is professor of English and Comparative Literature at New York's Columbia University but much of his energy has been spent putting to the western world, through books, articles and radio and television broadcasts, the story of what happened after 1948. He is by far the Palestinians' most credible Arab spokesmen. The new attack on Said had come in the form of an article, '"My Beautiful Old House" and Other Fabrications' by Justus Reid Weiner, a Jerusalem-based scholar, in a right-wing US magazine called *Commentary*. *Commentary* describes itself as 'general yet Jewish' and as 'one of the main centres of neoconservative thought' and is committed to the defence of Israel. In 1981 it launched a long attack on Said when it reviewed his book *The Question of Palestine*. At the end of the 1980s it published an article calling him 'The Professor of Terror' because of his membership of the Palestine National Council. In this third piece Mr Weiner, who was questioning Said's memories of his early life in Jerusalem, claimed to have spent three years researching Said's past. One wonders why, and who funded the research?

The arguments against Said seemed petty but they had been repeated with vehemence by writers with intellectual reputations to preserve like Daniel Johnson in the UK in the *Daily Telegraph* and *Sunday Telegraph*. They clearly aimed to breed doubt in people's minds in advance of the publication of Said's autobiography *Out of Place*. 'It is an attempt', Said told Vulliamy, 'to pre-empt the process of return and compensation for the Palestinians. It is a way of furthering the argument that the Palestinians never belonged to Palestine ... If someone like Edward Said is a liar, runs the argument, how can we believe all those peasants who say they were driven off their land?'

SEVENTEEN

The Role of al-Azhar University

Al-Azhar is the supreme authority: when it states an opinion we must all fall silent.

(Farouk Hosni, Minister of Culture, Egypt.)[1]

You write, then you are a criminal. You are trying through writing to change your society for the better, then you are a criminal ... Egyptian sheikhs want to burn books and burn their authors. Every intellectual is now likely to be accused of being an atheist.

(Adel Hamouda, Managing Editor,
Rose al-Youssef, August 1997.)

The Cyprus-based *Middle East Times* published titles of articles that had been banned in Egypt in 1998 and 1999. They illustrate Egypt's line on censorship today fairly accurately, including titles such as 'Coptic campaigns upset regime', 'Increasing violence among Egypt's dispossessed', 'Did Egypt kill fundamentalist preacher in Yemen?', 'It's easy trying to convert to Islam, but don't try changing back' and 'Torture victim's wife calls for justice'. Other articles worried the censor for their moral values. 'Stella in bed with the Army' and 'Call-girl ring for the rich and famous' were other titles that were banned. The bans had all come as initiatives from the Islamic Research Council (IRC), part of Islam's oldest religious institution, the tenth-century al-Azhar University in downtown Cairo. Al-Azhar has venerable roots which makes its present-day image distressing to Muslim liberals. Law 102 of 1985 allowed the IRC to recommend the banning or censorship of any book that may be judged to be blasphemous. Its role soon covered plays and novels as well as academic works.

The Fatimid version of Ismaili Shi'ism was a dynastic cause which established the right of the descendants of the children of Fatima – the Prophet's eldest daughter – to the leadership of the Islamic community, over that of the ruling Baghdad Caliphs. In 969 the Fatimids founded Cairo and established al-Azhar University and mosque, then a *dar al-hikma* (house of wisdom), in 972 as an institution of *da'wa* (propaganda). It became a bureau for the propagation of Fatimid ideas. There was little pressure on the Sunnis and Copts to convert and Sunni Muslims, Christians and Jews were able to hold the highest office under the Fatimids. The *da'wa* of Ismaili preachers spread revolutionary ideas throughout Syria and Arabia and Fatimid influence spread until in 1059 the sect briefly controlled Baghdad. But as Fatimid power and its revolutionary zeal declined new movements emerged such as the Druze in the 1020s and the Assassins in the 1090s. With the replacement of the Fatimids by the Ayyubids al-Azhar ceased to be a centre for Shi'a study and became an orthodox Sunni stronghold, which it has remained ever since.

In the early nineteenth century European encroachments on Egypt started ignobly, despite the good intentions of Napoleon and his scientists and literati whose *La Description d'Egypte* was to become a seminal tome, today to be found in smart Cairo drawing-rooms. The historian al-Jabarti was enraged by the treatment of al-Azhar by Napoleon's troops in 1798. 'Those goats entered the mosque riding their horses', soiling the area, drinking wine, ruining manuscripts, killing or molesting students. 'They did things in al-Azhar which it was impossible to exaggerate, for they are the enemies of religion, an opponent who is triumphing, an adversary who is gloating. They are like hyenas raging about.'[2]

After consolidating his power in the wake of the humiliating departure of the French soldiery, Egypt's charismatic new ruler Muhammad 'Ali co-opted the Azharis with jobs and became responsible for the *awqaf* (religious endowments). He created a modern system of schooling using *awqaf* money to finance new building projects. He sent teams of scholars to study abroad and encouraged the translation of European texts into Arabic.

Towards the end of the nineteenth century the great liberal Muhammad 'Abduh led a movement for reform at al-Azhar. As a result, a new law was passed in 1896 that extended subjects taught to include modern ones and reformed the curriculum to bring it closer in line with European universities. But there was always a tendency for al-Azhar to make pronouncements well beyond its accepted brief.

In 1926 the eminent Egyptian writer Taha Hussein was attacked by al-Azhar for his *Fi l-Shi'r al-Jahili* (On Pre-Islamic Poetry) in which he claimed that pre-Islamic poetry had been fabricated in the post-Islamic period. Although Hussein repented and rewrote his book, he was dismissed from his university post by then-prime minister Ismail Sidki in 1931. Azharis led demonstrations against him that culminated in book-burning. He was harassed over a two-year period and deprived of state employment.

It is probably appropriate to date the first modern banning of books in Islamic societies under the direct influence of al-Azhar to 1959 when Naguib Mahfouz's *Awlad Haratina* (translated as *Children of Gabalawi*) was serialized in *al-Ahram*. The *'ulama* accused Mahfouz of causing offence to the prophets of Islam from Abraham onwards. An article by Fauzi Najjar in the *British Journal of Middle Eastern Studies*[3] shows how violent the attacks were on this allegory of human history from Man's creation to the present day. The principal characters in the novel are Gabalawi (God), his sons Adham (Adam), Iblis and Idris, and Idris's offspring, Jabal (Moses), Rifa'a (Jesus) and Qasim (Muhammad). In 1988 Mahfouz won the Nobel Prize for Literature and a new edition of *Awlad Haratina* was quickly published in Beirut.

Then came the drama over Louis Awad's *Muqaddima Fi Fikh al Lugha al Arabiyya*, published in 1980. On 6 September 1981 the IRC asked for the book to be banned. Dr Awad challenged the decision in the courts but the courts upheld the ban. Those who objected appear to have based their criticism on the fact that Awad was attempting to prove that some Arabic words were based on the language of Ancient Egypt. Unfortunately, this affected sensitive words with religious connotations. The next notorious case was that of Alla Hamid whose novel *A Distance in a Man's Mind* got him an eight-year prison sentence on Christmas Day 1991. It was al-Azhar that called for his trial for blasphemy. At the Cairo Book Fair in 1992 several books by Judge Said al-Ashmawi were banned. Then came the withdrawal from the market of Hasan Tilib's book of poetry *Ayat Jim* (The Verse of Jim) which had won the critics award in 1992.

In 1983 the young comic actor Said Saleh was imprisoned after a trial before the Offences Court of Alexandria on charges of diverging from the story during a performance of *A Game Called Money*. He said: 'My mother has been married to three men. The first made whey cheese [a cheap form of cheese consumed by the poor]. The second told lies and the third was incapable of doing anything.' The men clearly referred to Nasser, Sadat and Mubarak.

Egyptian human rights groups see a more dangerous development unfolding. Al-Azhar, increasingly challenged by the courts, has begun to use the telephone to advise publishers and book distributors directly of their displeasure, rather than issuing a formal request for a book to be banned, a move which would involve state security or the courts to rule on the request. The state-owned General Book Organization (GEBO) has withdrawn several titles under pressure from al-Azhar in this way.

Al-Azhar first become formally involved in censorship in 1985 when Law 102 of 1985 gave it the authority to regulate publications of the Qur'an and the Hadith. Its powers began to grow.

In June 1992 the admired academic Dr Farag Foda was gunned down outside his office two weeks after an ad hoc committee of al-Azhar decided that 'everything he does is against Islam'. In open court his killers cited this condemnation as their justification for the murder. The Gama'a Islamiya (The Islamic Group) stated, 'Yes, we killed him ... Al-Azhar issued the death sentence and we carried out the execution.' Among Foda's last written words were, 'Terrorism has developed its own culture, for there are the journalists who defend it and the philosophers who justify it and there are those who finance it. There are those from the clergy who meet it halfway and those senior figures in the press who hesitate before embracing it.'[4] In June 1993 the Islamic preacher Sheikh Muhammad al-Ghazali issued a *fatwa* stipulating that any Muslim who argued for the suspension of the Shari'a should be considered a *murtad* (apostate) and could be killed with impunity. Early in 1990 Foda's book *To Be Or Not To Be* was condemned by the Islamic Research Foundation of al-Azhar University as offensive to Islam. He told his interrogators from the State Security Services:

> If the rules of Islam are to apply to everybody equally – and the Prophet said of his own daughter 'If Fatima were to steal I would cut off her hand' – then I say that the Sheikh of al-Azhar has slandered others and the punishment for that is flogging. He has called some intellectuals including myself, enemies of Islam and 'flies feeding off the table of Islam'. Hasaan Ibn Thabit, who was the Prophet's companion, was flogged for slander. Is the Sheikh of al-Azhar better than a companion of the Prophet?[5]

In July 1993, al-Azhar's Sheikh, Gad al-Haq, sent a letter to the head of the *fatwa* and legislative section of the national administrative court requesting a clarification of al-Azhar's role in 'confronting artistic works, audio and audio-visual artefacts that deal with Islamic issues or that conflict with Islam ... preventing them from publication, recording, printing and distributing'. On 10 February 1994 the Council of State issued ruling 58/1/63 legitimizing al-Azhar's role in censoring what are termed 'artefacts of sound and sight and sound' – films, music and video cassettes – and stipulating that al-Azhar's opinion was 'binding' on the Ministry of Culture. 'The Islamic Research

Centre has the right to track and examine publications and arts that deal with Islam ... the Sheikh of al-Azhar is the final arbiter in the assessment of the Islamic factor.'[6] Although the ruling limited the application to Islamic issues it also made clear that it was up to al-Azhar to define such limits.

Another target of the censors was Sayyed el-Qemni whose works describe the interplay of ancient myths and their influence on religious texts. In an article Qemni originally published in *Adab wa Naqd* in 1994, he explained that the mythical origin of woman from the rib of a man is the result of mistranslation by the writers of the Hebrew Torah (Old Testament). He explained that there is a story similar to the Old Testament's Garden of Eden in a Sumerian creation myth. The legend holds that the first man, Angi, was told by his mother, Mema Mamhoor Sag, not to eat a certain fruit in a land called Delmon. Because of ignorance, Angi disobeyed and developed an illness in one of his ribs. Angi's concerned mother created a woman to nurse his rib. Her name was Anti. Qemni argues that the mistranslation of this myth is the basis of the creation story in the Old Testament. In another article, Qemni explained that Arab women played prominent roles in pre-Islamic society and engaged in pagan rituals. He describes how Arabian women seeking fertility would walk around the Ka'ba in Mecca, later to become Islam's most holy site, touch their menstruation blood and then touch the black stone with their bloody fingers.

On 18 August 1997 Egypt's state security police raided Cairo's printing houses to confiscate Qemni's novel *Rab al-Zaman* (Lord of the Times). The Egyptian press promptly launched a wave of protest against the IRC. Cairo's weekly pro-government tabloid *Rose al-Youssef* and its managing editor Adel Hamouda (some of whose own books are banned in Egypt) led the attack on the IRC. *Rose al-Youssef* claimed that it had uncovered an al-Azhar plot to ban 196 Egyptian books. Hamouda added that many of them had nothing to do with religion. 'You write, then you are a criminal,' he wrote. 'You are trying through writing to change your society for the better, then you are a criminal. If you try to confront corruption, you are a criminal. If you try to escape life, then you are a criminal. Egyptian sheikhs want to burn books and burn their authors. Every intellectual is now likely to be accused of being an atheist.'[7]

Ironically, Egypt's artistic censor, 'Ali Abu Shadi, was popular among intellectuals who were pleased to have an enlightened man in this highly sensitive position but it seemed obvious from the confiscation of *Rab al-Zaman* that the IRC saw itself as answerable only to the *'ulama* in al-Azhar. Hamouda targeted the head of the IRC, Sami Sharawi, who was also the son of the popular televangelist Sheikh Mutawilli Sharawi. '[Sami Sharawi] has found the chance to take revenge on those who contradict his father's opinions about religion,' he wrote. 'These sheikhs are totally separated from the societal problems surrounding them ... they just stay in air-conditioned places thinking about banning what does not suit [them]. They do not contribute at all in all the problems threatening our country,' he added.[8]

'The opinion of the administrative courts is taken by the state as a law, but we have other departments working on censorship like 'Ali Abu Shadi, state security and the press censors,' said Amir Salem, Qemni's chief lawyer. 'They are really confusing us. When the Islamic Research Centre finds an offensive book, either on its own or via a complaint, it begins a review and prepares a report. In the case of Qemni, the IRC handed the report directly to the state security police at the Ministry of Interior.' The state security police, however, passed the report to its office in charge of censorship, al-Musanafat al-Faniyya. This office mainly deals with confiscating pornographic magazines and films and collecting controversial music cassettes. The Musanafat al-Faniyya, however, passed the report on to the state security prosecutors who issued a decision to send Qemni to the North Cairo Court and confiscate his book. The prosecutors at the state security are empowered to confiscate materials before a court decision because of the Emergency Law which has been in place since the assassination of Sadat in 1981. 'The state security prosecutors sent Qemni to the North Cairo Court in order to give the case a legal [veneer]. The state says we respect law and the legal system so they wanted to give it a legal decoration so that it would not seem like a decision [that] comes directly from al-Azhar or prosecutors at the state security,' said Salem. According to Salem, the North Cairo judge was not clear under what authority he was trying Qemni. 'I think that al-Azhar is trying to get the state directly involved against these kinds of writers. Otherwise they would have sent their report to one of the established censorship bodies,' speculated Salem.[9]

Today, al-Azhar is taking an increasingly interventionist role in deciding what can and cannot be shown on television. *Rose al-Youssef* reported that television scripts are 'as a matter of routine sent to al-Azhar for approval'. According to the Egyptian Organization for Human Rights the reason most frequently given for refusal is that it is an offence to Islam to portray any of the Prophet Muhammad's companions or the prophets mentioned in the Qur'an on television. In 1982 the Egyptian film-maker Yousuf Chahin's film *Le Caire* was shown at the Cannes Film Festival. The newspaper *Akhar Sa'a* called it 'obscene' while *Akhar Sa'a*'s umbrella newspaper *al-Akhbar* called for Chahin's prosecution. As a Christian he was safe, at least, from accusations of apostasy. The fundamentalists, often themselves foreign educated, refer contemptuously to Chahin's francophone education. In 1982 the Egyptian Minister of Information banned 'films of violence and sex', and increased television time for religious programmes.

Disturbingly, al-Azhar's powers to block the truth have spread beyond the borders of Egypt. In 1976 al-Azhar had called the leader of the Sudanese Republican Movement, an elderly, peace-loving cleric, Mahmoud Muhammad Taha, an apostate. He was also attacked by the Ikhwan, both in Egypt and Sudan. He and his followers attacked Nimairi's Islamization programme. They also challenged Nimairi's violation of the rights of the animist Christian Sudanese of the south. Taha was tried for apostasy in January 1985 and was hanged without even being offered the chance of repenting. Most Sudanese were appalled and this revulsion contributed to the downfall of Nimairi's increasingly brutal regime in April of the same year. Taha had led a liberal school of thought, claiming that much of what was considered timeless Shari'a had in reality been legislation relevant to the period of the early Islamic community. He rejected Shari'a rules that violated the norms of modern human rights. He and his followers believed that Islam, correctly interpreted, supported full equality between men and women and between Muslims and non-Muslims.

EIGHTEEN

Fatwas

It is high time we [Arabs and Muslims] re-examined our conditions, and liberated ourselves, not only from the authority of the religious texts, but also from every power that impeded human progress. We must do that now, and immediately, before we are swept away by the deluge.

(Nasr Hamid Abu Zayd, *al-Imam al-Shafi'l wa Ta'sis al-Idiolojiyya al-Wasatiyya*, Cairo, Sina' li-Nashr, 1992.)

What does [Abu Zayd] have in mind for the [Islamic] *Umma*, after it throws away the Qur'an and the Sunna?

('Abd al-Sabur Shahin, (ed.) *Qissat Abi Zayd wa Inhisar al-'Alamniyya*, Cairo, Dar al-I'tisam, 1995.)

Some modern writers of Muslim birth in the West seem openly to have courted *fatwas* over the past few years on the grounds that no publicity is bad publicity. As Oscar Wilde remarked, 'There is only one thing in the world worse than being talked about, and that is not being talked about.'' Writers in Egypt are even known to advertise in newspapers, drawing attention to the banning of their books, prompting a dramatic increase in sales. However, for one young, avant-garde Arab writer in London, who allowed the rumour to spread that a *fatwa* was about to be launched against him, the policy misfired badly. The publishers became so frightened that they allowed his second novel to sink without trace.

The first copies of *The Satanic Verses* reached Iran in September 1988 and Khomeini in February 1989 issued his *fatwa* declaring Salman Rushdie an apostate whose blood could and, indeed, should be shed. Even Dr Zaki Badawi,

Britain's leading Islamic scholar, told the *Guardian* newspaper, 'What he has written is far worse to Muslims than if he had raped one's own daughter. It's an assault on every Muslim's inner being. Muslims seek Muhammad as an ideal on whom to fashion our lives and conduct, and the Prophet is internalized into every Muslim heart. It's like a knife being dug into you – or being raped yourself.' But he went on to say:

> Yes, Khomeini reflects the entire Muslim religious view that Rushdie is on the face of it an apostate, a heretic. But neither he nor any Muslim authority has the power to sentence Rushdie to death. I must state with all the authority under my command that anyone who seeks or incites anyone to kill Rushdie is committing a crime against God and the Islamic Shari'a.[2]

In his Friday sermon on 16 February 1989 President Khamenei suggested that 'if he [Rushdie] apologizes and disowns the book, people may forgive him'. On 18 February Rushdie issued a statement regretting 'profoundly the distress the publication has occasioned to the sincere followers of Islam. Living as we do in a world of many faiths, this experience has served to remind us that we must all be conscious of the sensibilities of others.'[3] Khomeini's reply was chilling 'Even if Salman Rushdie repents and becomes the most pious man of all time, it is incumbent on every Muslim to employ everything he has got, his life and wealth, to send him to Hell.'[4]

Many other writers, including the great French Arabist Maxime Rodinson, had questioned the divinity of the Qur'an. As already noted in Chapter 4, it was partly the timing of the publication of *The Satanic Verses* that had caused the outcry against Rushdie. Khomeini's health had plummeted from the moment he had had to accept the 'poisoned chalice' of defeat in the form of UN Security Council Resolution 598 calling for a cease-fire in Iran's bloody war with Iraq. Iran's economy was in ruins and radicals and pragmatists were at each others' throats. Iran was liberalizing in exchange for economic carrots from the West, as it is now doing once again, and discussions were under way on how to free western hostages in Beirut.

All this infuriated the radicals who, with the help of Muslims in Bradford and Leicester, drew Khomeini's attention to crudely extracted excerpts from the novel. *The Satanic Verses* is a Pandora's box of literary magic in which Abraham, a revered Prophet to Muslims, is called 'the bastard', Muhammad becomes Mahound ('false prophet' in Christian medieval slang), the Qur'anic revelations were 'well-timed' to suit the Prophet when 'the faithful were disputing', the namesakes of his wives ply their trade as whores in a brothel, Mecca become Jahilia (the place of 'Ignorance') and sodomy is approved by the archangel (Gibreel). There are resonances here of traditional European Islamophobia. Derek Hopwood notes in his book *Sexual Encounters in the Middle East* that in the seventeenth century 'sodomy was called the Persian or Turkish vice'. He says that in 1704 Joseph Pitts wrote that the Turks practised sodomy so much that they 'loath the Natural use of the Woman'.[5]

Other books besides *The Satanic Verses* have challenged the same preconceptions, but their authors were not threatened because they were not Muslim. 'When Gamal Rahman's scandalous novel is publicly burned by the incensed Muslims of Bruddersford, a world falls apart. While the claims of wives and daughters fuel the flames, young men embrace the Sons of Allah, dedicated to the execution of the apostate author.' This is the book jacket blurb for *Fatima's Scarf* by David Caute, published by Totterdown Books in 1998. As nobody would publish the novel Caute published it himself and sold tens of thousands of copies.

In Egypt the artist is increasingly vulnerable to censorship by the fundamentalist tendency. According to Karim Alrawi, Deputy Secretary-General of the Egyptian Organization for Human Rights,[6] cassette tapes on sale have titles such as 'The filth of the artistic community' or 'Art is filth'. Writers and artists are frequently picked on by name and damned as 'corrupters of youth', 'atheists and apostates', with such charges theoretically punishable by death. They are not interested in Islam's religious message of tolerance, says Alrawi, but in cynically exploiting its broad appeal for political ends.

The fundamentalists had picked on Abu Zayd and on the novelist Ihsan Abdul Qudous, who even on his death-bed was being denounced by them as an apostate. According to Alrawi the attack was led by the Saudi-financed *al-Muslimoun* newspaper. The trouble that such writers face is that since Arabic is the very word of God they risk Islamic wrath merely by using the Arabic language. Alrawi points out that headline-seeking politicians attack writers in the press regularly. The government's response, meanwhile, is to increase censorship. Films and plays are banned 'in the higher interests of the state' while pop songs must be submitted for a recording licence. The government is seen to be trying to steal the clothes of the Islamic militants to the extent that many writers are surrendering to what they see as the inevitability of an Islamic regime in Egypt.

The Abu Zayd affair was the most curious example of the direction political Islam is taking and is told in detail in an article in *Index on Censorship*.[7] At the heart of the affair are the politics of the interpretation of the Qur'an. In the eyes of orthodox Islam, the Qur'an is the eternal, uncreated word of God revealed to the Prophet Muhammad in the seventh century. However, a rationalist school, the Mu'tazilites (see Chapter 8) believed in a created Qur'an, distinguishing between God's essence, which they held to be eternal and beyond human understanding, and His word, which is created and accessible to reason. Their thought influenced the writings of Nasr Hamid Abu Zayd himself who applied contemporary methods of textual criticism to his study of the Qur'an, contextualizing the book in its historical setting. This challenge to orthodoxy, he argued, had been used as a pretext by his enemies.

Abu Zayd's troubles began when he was turned down for a professorial post at Cairo's Dar al-Ulum University. In the introductory pages to his *Critique of Islamic Discourse* Abu Zayd criticized the so-called 'Islamic investment companies' that had been set up as alternatives to the modern, western banking sector. It happened that the dissenting voice among the Islamic experts consulted by the university's selection committee, Dr 'Abd al-Sabur Shahin, was also the religious adviser to one of these 'Islamic' institutions, al-Rayan Islamic Investment Company, that had featured at the centre of a great public scandal in 1988. The company was accused of misappropriating the savings of Muslim investors. Abu Zayd accused Shahin of using Islam to justify Islamic financial and economic investments. 'This huge swindle', wrote Abu Zayd, 'could not have been accomplished without the ground being prepared by the Islamic discourse, which sanctions myths and fables, and stifles reason.'[8] On 2 April 1993, two weeks after the university's decision not to confer a full professorship on Abu Zayd, Shahin used the pulpit of a central Cairo mosque publicly to proclaim Abu Zayd an apostate. The following Friday, mosques throughout Egypt followed suit. Shahin called Abu Zayd's works 'cultural AIDS' and a 'Marxian-secularist attempt to destroy Egypt's Muslim society'. His 'reprehensible' works did not deserve to be called 'academic research' and his Marxian writings testified to the 'atrophy of his religious conscience'. He belonged, said Shahin, to a gang of writers who believed in 'intellectual terrorism.'[9] Studying Abu Zayd's publications Shahin claimed that Abu Zayd had 'enthusiastically' championed *The Satanic Verses*, 'known for its depravity and hallucination'. He accused Abu Zayd of overlooking the 'rottenness that issues from the bowels of an apostate *kafir*', and betraying lack of intellectual integrity by comparing *The Satanic Verses* with Naguib Mahfouz's *Awlad Haratina*.[10]

He argued that any Muslim who maintains that the Qur'an is created (*makhluq*) is a *kafir*. As we have seen the Mu'tazilites believed that it was created and are, thus, considered apostates by orthodox Muslims. Abu Zayd maintained that it had two natures. One was divine in that it was the word of God. The other was that it was human in so far as it revealed a human, Arabic language. Abu Zayd was defending his freedom of thought and told the court that tried him, 'I refuse to defend myself against such charges [of apostasy] because I do not allow anyone, whoever he is, or any authority, whichever it is, to define my faith.'[11]

The plot to prove that Abu Zayd was a *kafir* was hatched in a mosque near the Giza Pyramids. Abu Zayd's opponents took advantage of a loophole in the Family Code, otherwise integrated within the Secular Egyptian Civil Code, to introduce cases in Islamic personal status law or *hisba*. On the precedent of a centuries-old Islamic ruling that disallows the marriage of a Muslim to a non-Muslim, a group of Islamist lawyers petitioned for the divorce of Abu Zayd from Dr Ebtehal Yunes, an associate professor of French civilization in her husband's faculty at the university.[12] Such a ruling would confirm Abu Zayd's status as an apostate and allow his opponents to press for his dismissal from the university. As Fauzi Najjar points out, the Abu Zayd case was 'unique in the current conflict between Muslim fundamentalists and liberal-secular intellectuals. Never before has an Egyptian court ruled that a husband must be separated from his wife on grounds of apostasy.'[13]

The clash was between those who were threatened by change and development and those like Abu Zayd who were forward thinking and interpreted the Qur'an in this light. Islam 'is no longer the system of spiritual and moral values, which permeates the individual's being and society, rather it has been used as a political slogan to mobilize the masses, exploit the simple minded, deceive the semi-educated, and arouse the emotions of many professionals.'[14]

On 15 April 1993, the supposedly moderate Islamic weekly *al-Liwa al-Islami*, founded by the ruling National Democratic Party to counter religious extremism and terrorism, ran an editorial fulminating against the 'heretic' Abu Zayd who had endangered the faith of his students and urging the rector of the university to fire him. A week later, the same paper counselled the government that execution was the only fitting penalty for Abu Zayd and that it should apply the provisions of the Islamic penal code immediately. On top of this came the pronouncement from Sheikh Muhammad al-Ghazali, a leading authority among Islamists, during the trial of the assassins of Farag Foda, that if the state did not do its religious duty, then it was the duty of every Muslim to execute the punishment.

The Egyptian Writers Union came out in open support of Abu Zayd. In a statement entitled 'We refuse the inquisition of conscience', more than 200 intellectuals 'having been dismayed by Cairo's Appeal Court's decision ... declare their complete solidarity with, and support for, Abu Zayd and his wife, in defence of freedom of belief, expression, scientific research and sanctity of personal life'. They continued: 'it is inadmissible for anyone to violate the human conscience by probing into it, seeking to incriminate and accuse [thinkers] of *kufr*, and terrorize society as a whole. Dr Nasr Hamid Abu Zayd's crime is that he has used reason and free thinking, and exercised *ijtihad* in an age that rejects *ijtihad*.'[5]

In an address to the American University in Cairo on 17 June 1999 Edward Said said, 'The whole notion of academic freedom underwent a significant downgrading during the past three decades. It became possible for one to be free in the university only if one completely avoided anything that might attract unwelcome attention or suspicion.'

The covert aim of the Islamists seems to have been to have Abu Zayd legally killed in the name of Islam. On 27 January 1994, the judge in the First Grade Family Court ruled the case inadmissible because the plaintiff had insufficient personal grievance with Abu Zayd. The decision was challenged in the court of appeal and overturned. The Islamists succeeded in having Abu Zayd's apostasy confirmed and his marriage officially annulled. Abu Zayd took his case to the Court of Cassation, Egypt's final court of appeal, but it failed again. His case generated widespread public protest and attracted media and human rights interest worldwide. By now the real danger came from militant fundamentalists. Jihad, the armed Islamist group which had assassinated President Sadat in 1981, said that Abu Zayd should be killed for apostasy. The price he and his wife paid for taking on their enemies in court and opposing any manipulation of Islam was flight from Egypt into exile in Europe.

After Taslima Nasrin's novel *Lajja* was banned she had travelled to France to speak at a meeting marking International Press Freedom Day. When she returned to Bangladesh she gave an interview to the *Statesman* newspaper in Calcutta which quoted her as calling for changes in the Qur'an. This claim revived calls in Bangladesh for her death. When she tried to clarify her statement by saying that she had intended changes in Shari'a law that would improve women's rights, this refuelled calls for her arrest. In June 1993 the Bangladeshi government issued an order for her arrest for 'insulting religious sentiments'. She went into hiding for two months. Tens of thousands of Bangladeshis took to the streets, calling again for her death. They carried a portrait of a young woman with a rope around her neck. 'Yes, yes, we want this and nothing but this,' they chanted. They described her as 'an apostate appointed by imperial forces to vilify Islam'. In August she was brought before the courts again, bailed and ordered to appear for trial at a later date. A week later she went to Stockholm where she became the guest of the Swedish PEN Centre. She told *Index on Censorship* in 1994, 'The Qur'an can no longer serve as the basis of our law ... It stands in the way of progress and in the way of women's emancipation.'

She argued that religion is the root and fundamentalism the tree. She said that Muslim women should be allowed four husbands. She smoked a cigarette on television while handling the Qur'an. She criticized Rushdie for appearing to seek reconciliation with his accusers and offended many with her calls for sexual freedom and attacks on male dominance. Her critics claim that her outspoken views have given fundamentalists the opportunity to mobilize themselves on a common platform and have imperilled causes such as women's rights that others have worked for years to achieve. When asked if she was a Muslim, she replied in an interview, 'No, I am an atheist. All forms of religion are anachronistic to me.'[16]

NINETEEN

Publish it Not: Media and Censorship

In most of the Islamic world press freedom remains a dream. In Libya, Iraq and Saudi Arabia almost complete control by the government ensures a compliant press. In Iran the atmosphere is more populist but newspapers such as *Salam*, which do not toe the line, are axed despite the popular anger this can cause, leading to social instability and riots. In Algeria, Egypt, Sudan and the Israeli-Occupied Palestinian Territories emergency legislation gives the authorities draconian powers of censorship. The head of state, the ruling party and, of course, the Islamic environment itself are usually forbidden targets for the writer.

Some countries belonging to the Islamic world do not have clear constitutional guarantees of the right to freedom of expression while others such as Saudi Arabia and Oman do not have a constitution at all. Some have provisions for the freedom of expression but severely restrict this fundamental right in law and practice. The Iranian constitution claims that 'publications and the press are free to publish their ideas unless they are injurious to the founders of Islam or public rights'. Syria's 1963 State of Emergency Law empowers the Prime Minister to impose 'censorship of letters and communications of all kind. Censorship of newspapers, periodicals, drawing, printed matter, broadcasts and all means of communication, propaganda and publicity before issue; also their seizure confiscation and suspension and the closure of the places in which they are printed.' In Iraq Article 26 of the 1968 Constitution guarantees 'freedom of opinion, publications, meeting, demonstration and forming political parties, unions and societies.' In practice, as Article XIX points out laconically, 'censorship [in Iraq] is near total and enforced by terror'.

In Lebanon an independent press of thirty daily, twice-weekly or weekly newspapers heralded in 1976 what they believed was the end of the civil war. In fact it was the beginning of a fifteen-year war, by the end of which Lebanon had become a Syrian satellite in all but name. The weekly magazine *Beirut al-Masa'*, financed by Libya, had been closed down in 1975 because it published an article critical of its Libyan sponsor. Other newspapers were chameleon in character. *Al-Moharrer* started as the organ of Lebanon's Arab Nationalist Movement, then it embraced the cause of the Palestinian Rejectionist Front, before becoming a mouthpiece of the Iraqi Ba'ath Party. In December 1977 it was closed by the Syrians for its pro-Iraqi stance. The pro-Iraqi *al-Dastour* newspaper, published and edited by 'Ali Balout, was also closed down but it moved that same month to London.

The period was dominated by a decision on Lebanon and on media coverage of the war taken in October 1976 in Riyadh. The resolution, signed by King Khaled of Saudi Arabia, Amir Sabah as Salem al-Sabah of Kuwait, President Hafez al-Asad of Syria, President Anwar Sadat of Egypt, President Elias Sarkis of Lebanon and Yasser Arafat, stated chillingly that 'Information campaigns and negative attitudes by all parties should cease; and that information be carried in such a way as to consolidate the cease-fire, promote peace and raise the spirit of cooperation and fraternity among everyone.' To give the rigorous censorship law a stronger sense of legitimacy the 1965 Arab Solidarity Pact was resuscitated. The pact called for the Arab mass media to 'be placed in the service of the Arab cause' and prohibited 'any writing or action that goes beyond objective discussion and constructive criticism and which seeks to harm relations among the Arab states or between Arab heads of states'.

Lebanon's importance to the region was obvious: it was press freedom. Syria would now suppress a free press in Lebanon largely for fear of 'contaminating' Syrians inside Syria who had long been protected from the truth. Syria's foreign minister is said to have told a Lebanese politician 'It is the Lebanese press or the Syrian army; one or the other must go.' Some papers went into exile to Nicosia, Paris and London. *Al-Hayat* was one of the most important to take up residence in London. Others simply went under entirely.

In the post-war era Islamic fundamentalist interference has increased in Lebanon with the condemnation of Marcel Khalifa, and of the Maurice Bejart dance company for wearing improper clothing in a ballet dedicated to the late, adored Egyptian diva, Umm Kulthum. In principle freedom of speech is protected by Lebanon's constitution, both by the original constitution of 1926 and by the amended constitution agreed at the crucial Ta'if Conference of 1989 which anticipated the war's end. In Lebanon today laws governing publishing and broadcasting do not involve prior censorship for locally published books and media products. However, it is forbidden to criticize foreign heads of state or to instigate 'confessional rivalries' and both the import and export of books, newspapers, magazines and films are controlled. In addition to this, newspaper readership has dropped dramatically over the years in the face of competition from television.

These days Lebanese newspapers are controlled by 'political money', above all from political figures such as the Prime Minister, Rafiq al-Hariri. Journalists tend to avoid critical subjects and indulge in a code based on understatement and allusion and avoid crossing certain red lines. However, the worst times are over; there is an increasing sense of freedom and the threat of violence to journalists has diminished. Even the term 'Syrian occupation' can be used at last.

The Lebanese civil war caused great tension in Kuwait where some 270,000 Palestinians lived. On 29 August 1976 the Kuwaiti Amir suspended the Constitution and the National Assembly and new articles were introduced in the Press and Publications law. The amendments allowed the Council of Ministers to withdraw printing licences and suspend for two years any newspaper 'if it serves the interest of a foreign power'. In May 1977 the Kuwait Appeal Court allowed the Kuwaiti press to reveal the shortcomings of the administration as long as character assassination was not involved. When a newspaper criticized the 'sub-standard services offered to patients by the Ministry of Public Health' the court judged that such criticism was constructive.

The media of the Middle East has its roots in nineteenth-century idealism. By the mid-nineteenth century French had replaced Italian as the lingua franca of trade and of the cities of the Near East and North Africa. In 1875 the Jesuits founded their Université St Joseph in Beirut. Newspapers and periodicals began to play an important role in the 1860s and 1870s. The most important were *al-Muqtataf* produced by two Lebanese Christians in Cairo, Ya'qub Sarruf and Faris Nimr, and *al-Hilal* by Jurji Zaydan. The earliest newspapers were published under official sponsorship in Istanbul, Cairo and Tunis but unofficial newspapers developed as a new educated generation sought for more general knowledge and the telegraph made it possible to satisfy their curiosity. The size of the reading population and the greater extent of intellectual freedom made Cairo the centre of the daily press although the most successful journalists were still immigrants from Lebanon. One such, *al-Ahram*, founded in Cairo by the Lebanese Taqla family in 1875, was to become the foremost newspaper in the Arab world.

The fear of the influence of Zionism spread by Jewish immigrants to Palestine at the turn of the century led to reaction in the Arab press. With the overthrow of Sultan Abdul Hamid in 1908 Palestinian publishers began to take advantage of new freedoms. *Carmel*, an Arabic newspaper published in the Palestinian city of Haifa, had taken up the highly inflammatory issue of land sales by Palestinian families such as the Sursocks to Jews. Its editor published a series of treatises on the struggle. Anti-Zionist organizations were established in Palestinian towns and in Constantinople, Cairo and Beirut.

By the beginning of the First World War there were cinemas in Cairo and other cities. In 1930 the first Egyptian film was made, based on the first authentic Egyptian novel *Zaynab*. In 1932 the first talkie was produced in Egypt and by 1939 Egyptian films were being shown all over the Arab world. By that time, too, there were local radio stations broadcasting talks, music and news and some European countries were broadcasting to the Arab world in competition with each other. By the early 1960s television was only just beginning to appear in Arab countries but cinemas were numerous; there had been 194 in Egypt in 1949 and by 1961 there were 375. In 1959 60 feature films were produced in Cairo, not merely musicals and romantic films but also serious films aimed at raising the Arab sense of national and cultural identity. By 1959 there were 850,000 radios in Egypt and half a million in Morocco, with each set, as today, listened to by dozens of people in cafés.

The most influential radio station of Nasser's Egypt was *Sawt al-Arab* (The Voice of the Arabs) but translated by some lampoonists as Sowt al-Arab – The 'scourge' of the Arabs – expressing the grandiose dreams of pan-Arab nationalism led by Nasser. After the emergence of Nasser in 1952 the Egyptian press, led by *al-Ahram*, began to lose its comparative freedom and was nationalized in 1960. It was still widely read if only because its editor, Hasanayn Haikal, a close friend of Nasser, expressed the opinion of the President. The freest press in the region was still in Beirut.

In 1961 male singers were first heard in Saudi Arabia, to the horror of the zealots, and when in 1963 a woman's voice was heard for the first time on Radio Mecca a deputation was sent to King Faisal. He responded calmly that the Prophet himself had been enchanted by the voice of the poetess al-Khansa and added that they would soon be 'seeing the faces of women on television'. In the face of bitter resistance television was introduced in 1967. A long series of tests was shown at first to prepare the public and when broadcasting started anything resembling a love scene was forbidden. Even Mickey Mouse was not allowed to give his spouse an affectionate kiss.

Nevertheless, in 1965 a grandson of Ibn Saud, Khaled ibn Musaid, led a group of fanatics in an attack on Riyadh's television station. They tried to destroy the transmitter and rejected the overtures of the King. When Khaled drew a revolver he was promptly shot dead by the senior policeman there. Faisal ruled that there was no question of the boy's father, Faisal's half-brother Musaid, being entitled to blood money since the policeman had merely been doing his duty. However, the King would pay dearly for the boy's death.

In 1966 a blind preacher, and the Kingdom's leading cleric, Sheikh 'Abd al-Aziz ibn Baz challenged the theory first propagated by Copernicus that the earth revolved around a fixed sun. 'Hence I say', he announced loftily, 'the holy Qur'an, the Prophet's teaching, the majority of Islamic scientists and the actual fact all prove that the sun is running in its orbit, as Almighty God ordained, and that the earth is fixed and stable, spread out by God for his mankind and made a bed and a cradle for them, fixed down firmly by mountains lest it shake." Anyone, he said, who believed otherwise would be guilty of 'falsehood towards God, the Qur'an and the Prophet'. These absurdities enraged Faisal who ordered the immediate destruction of all undistributed copies but it was too late to prevent Nasser's press in Egypt from ridiculing its ideological enemies. To illustrate the Kingdom's cultural contradictions, in 1985 Saudi Arabia's Prince Sultan Al Saud was to become the Arab world's first astronaut on Arab Satellite Communications Organization's second satellite, Arabsat 1B.

Despite his desire for reform, Faisal found himself increasingly forced to compromise with the Ikhwan. The sale of Christmas trees was forbidden and after the age of nine girls were segregated and forced to wear the veil. Cinemas and other similar forms of entertainment remained banned and women were forbidden to drive cars. Little has changed today. In many ways the development of fundamentalism has strengthened the hardliners. In the 1970s many foreign visitors expected a new, western-educated generation to emerge. The opposite has happened, with the encouragement of Islamic education and an increasing wariness of western values, although the issues are complex and deserve further study.

In 1962 Faisal established a Ministry of Information and two years later issued a new Press Code by royal decree which gave the government more authority to intervene when necessary. The establishing of the Saudi News Agency (SANA, not to be confused with Syria's news agency) in 1971 was aimed at helping journalists report on the daily activities of the monarchy. They did almost no investigative reporting. One critic dubbed SANA 'a bulletin board for the modern sector'. Events such as Mu'ammar Qadhafi's coup in Libya in 1969 or the Civil War in Jordan in 1970 were downplayed or ignored entirely. Attentive readers were obliged to read between the lines. They supplemented this by tuning in to the BBC, Voice of America (VOA) and other channels. A survey carried out among adults of Jeddah and Dammam showed that 32 per cent were tuning in to the BBC and 19 per cent to VOA in 1976.

Entertainment came in the form of films from Egypt or singers such as Umm Kulthum and Fayruz as well as American programmes such as *I Love Lucy*. Women were rarely seen in the newspapers or on television at this stage. Soon, however, clothing fashions appeared and quickly began to influence women. In 1967 a children's programme was narrated by a very modestly-dressed woman, something of a break-through. High-school girls were soon also included although fundamentalist criticism led to the abandonment in 1968 of women on television for a period. It is worth mentioning that women were reading television news in Kuwait before they were doing so in the UK. As Rugh notes in *The Modernization of Saudi Arabia* boys used to kicking stray dogs suddenly began to treat them kindly once they had watched a few episodes of Lassie.[2] Neil Armstrong's moonwalk in 1969 provoked a lively theological discussion.

But all these reforms were to be brought to an end when, on 25 March 1975, King Faisal was assassinated by his nephew Prince Faisal, the brother of Khaled ibn Musaid who had been shot leading the abortive attack on the radio transmitter in 1965. The King was succeeded by his half-brother, Crown Prince Khaled, and Fahd became heir apparent. During the new king's reign, economic and social development continued rapidly, revolutionizing the infrastructure and educational system of the country, but news continued to be heavily controlled.

By 1973 there were estimated to be some half a million television sets in Egypt, half a million in Iraq and 300,000 in Saudi Arabia. Television transmitted news presented, as Hourani points out, in such a way as to win support for the government, religious programmes, films and serials imported from Europe and America and plays and musicals made in Egypt and Lebanon. Significantly, by 1988 there were over 16 million radio receivers and 4 million television receivers in Egypt, 2 million radio receivers and 860,000 television receivers in Lebanon, and 5.5 million radio receivers and 1.6 television receivers in Algeria.

During the post-1981 communist period in Afghanistan television – which began broadcasting in Kabul in 1978 – and newspapers were only seen in Kabul and the major cities. Opposition currents were represented in clandestine 'night-letters' (*shabnamah*). According to the late Anthony Hyman, the writers and printers of these night-letters were lecturers at the universities, teachers at high schools, civil servants, and journalists paid by the state but working secretly for the opposition. They enjoyed widespread collaboration from the army and the police but in the Taliban's Afghanistan even these simple media offerings vanished.

TWENTY

The Averted Gaze: Love and Death in Iranian Cinema

Until the revolution in 1979, going to the cinema was a highly popular pastime for Iranians. By the early 1970s a new wave of young directors was emerging. Trained abroad and with liberal educations, they drew on Iran's history to produce allegorical films with a message which often only just managed to escape the censor's pen. There were resonances of Soviet *samizdat* cinema. During the first three years after the Islamic Revolution in Iran, 513 of a total of 898 foreign films were rejected and out of 2,208 locally produced films 1,956 were denied exhibition permits. The new rulers were not against cinema *per se* but against what Khomeini called its 'misuse' by the Shah's regime which aimed, he said, to corrupt and subjugate Iranians.[1]

A pioneering Iranian cinema actress and singer, Delkash, appeared in London's Queen Elizabeth Hall in October 1999 as part of a European tour which brought her back to the stage for the first time in almost twenty years. Women have been banned from performing in public in Iran since the revolution and Delkash's tour marked the first time she had sung in public since then. Now in her mid-seventies, she is remembered for her energetic and dominant voice. The very appearance of the diminutive, hunchbacked woman leaning on a stick provoked a standing ovation from her nostalgic admirers. 'We have aged together,' she said wryly to a packed hall of over a thousand Iranians. Delkash is from Babol on Iran's Caspian Sea. Her distinctive voice and acting style helped ensure the popularity of Iran's nascent cinema in the 1940s. She sings of innocent love, of nostalgia and of her home town. She has never been political but her very presence in a London concert hall, after twenty years of silence, was profoundly significant to her admirers.

There are about 300 directors making films in Iran today, of which a dozen are women. But it is largely the films of about ten elite film-makers that account for almost all Iranian festival representations. Despite restrictions and because of their simple and direct messages and metaphors, Iranian films have fascinated audiences in international arenas over the past ten years. Abbas

Kiarostami, Iran's biggest name in cinema, enjoys the support of directors such as Jean-Luc Godard, Nanni Moretti and Akira Kurosawa. Moretti made a short film about opening one of Kiarostami's films in his theatre in Rome. Kurosawa said of Kiarostami's films: 'Words cannot describe my feelings about them and I simply advise you to see his films ... When Satyajit Ray passed on, I was very depressed. But after seeing Kiarostami's films, I thanked God for giving us just the right person to take his place.'[2]

Before the First World War the few Iranian films that were made were sponsored and viewed by the Qajar royal family and the aristocracy, according to Hamid Naficy who teaches cinema at Rice University, Texas.[3] Cinema was a private affair. The first public cinema was the non-commercial Soleil cinema set up by Catholic missionaries in Tabriz. By the early 1930s Pathe and other foreign sound newsreels were playing. The first Persian language sound newsreel showed the Iranian Prime Minister Mohamed 'Ali Foroughi talking with Kemal Atatürk and delivering a speech in Persian. This astonished audiences unaccustomed to hearing Persian spoken on the screen.[4]

The first Persian-language talkie, *Dokhtar-e Lor* (The Lor Girl, 1933), was the first of several feature films made in India by an Iranian expatriate, Abdolhosain Sepenta, for the Iranian market. However, censorship stunted the growth of Iranian cinema during the 1940s. In 1940 nearly 253 films were censored, 159 of which came from the USA, 32 from Germany, 32 from France and 19 from Britain. Censorship, according to Naficy, was imposed in films showing revolutions, riots, and strikes, as well as indecency, pacifism and anti-Islamic attitudes. After the Second World War, film production in Iran resumed in 1949. It was encouraged by the US Information Agency as part of its policy to win the hearts and minds of non-communist countries. A group of US professors and film buffs from Syracuse University visited Iran in the early 1950s to establish 16mm film-processing laboratories and train Iranians to make documentary and educational films. They also developed a pro-Shah, pro-American newsreel called *Akhbar-e Iran* (Iran News), 402 issues of which were shown in public theatres throughout Iran. The low-quality melodramas and comedies made in this period set the foundation for a purely commercial cinema which dominated the Iranian screens for the next thirty years.

Naficy notes that the 1960s represented a conflict between financial freedom fuelled by petrodollars and restrictions placed by the Shah.[5] The state security apparatus, set up by the CIA and the Israeli Mossad, acted as censors of the film industry. In particular, says Naficy, socially conscious films made by young, European-educated film makers met with disapproval and confiscation. For example, Farrokh Ghaffari's *Junube Shahr* (South of the City, 1958) which described the reality of life in the poverty-stricken district of south Tehran was not only banned but also had its negatives mutilated. Meanwhile, under the Shah's new modernization programme global interests replaced regional interests.

The decade preceding the revolution saw the quiet emergence of an Iranian New Wave. A group of artists and intellectuals denounced the existing escapist cinema and launched a movement producing indigenous films of high cinematic quality and social consciousness. Masoud Kimiai's Qaisar (Caesar, 1969) developed the good guy–bad guy genre by linking the good with Iranian tradition and the bad with its violations, which many associated with the West. The other key film in the New Wave period was Dariush Mehrju'i's *Gav* (The Cow, 1969), a disturbing tale of poverty and mental breakdown in which the mysterious death of the only cow in a village drives its owner insane. Ironically, *Gav* was sponsored by the Ministry of Culture and Art but then censored and banned for a year by the same ministry. The withdrawal of the ban was probably influenced by the international acclaim it won. As in the Soviet Union the government would sponsor films for international but not domestic screening where it might be inflammatory. Syria followed the same practice in the 1990s. Later came the *Dayereh Mina* (The Cycle, 1974), considered by many Mehrju'i's most important film. It exposed the blood trade in Iran's hospitals from which the poor made desperately needed extra cash.

Despite its poor box-office performance, the critical success of *The Cow* paved the way for a modest annual production of 'New Wave' films and an alternative film environment. It was this environment that helped breed a generation of film-makers that are now considered the grand masters of Iranian cinema. Naficy highlights this epoch's protagonists, in addition to Mehrju'i and Kiarostami, Bahram Bays who made *Bashu, The Little Stranger*, Amir Naderi who made *The Runner*, Parviz Sayyad who made *The Mission* and Sohrab Shaheed Saless who made *Still Life*. However, the New Wave film-makers were hampered in their efforts by a harsh system of censorship that essentially kept them from dealing directly with the unpleasant realities of Iranian life.

The Cow was banned originally because of its uncompromising depiction of despair in an impoverished village. The film was conditionally released only after it won praise at the Venice Film Festival. As with Soviet film-makers such as Andrei Tarkovsky, the codes in the Islamic Republic of Iran forced the film-makers either to resort to symbolic communication in exploring social and political issues or to make less complicated films about simple characters and ordinary situations. This explains the symbolic complexities of some films and the marvellous simplicity of others. It included the emergence of a peculiar genre of films with child characters that were made for adults as much as for children.

The 1970s saw a downturn in the economy while, says Hamid Naficy, the censorship of political themes meant that completed films often had to wait for months or even years to obtain an exhibition permit. Directors became timid. Audiences beguiled by the New Wave were then disappointed because it could not satisfy their expectations. Unsatisfied by films that were heavily compromised or used abstruse language to deceive the censor, they turned back to foreign films.

The Islamic Revolution in 1979 initially struck a near-fatal blow to cinema in Iran which the ayatollahs perceived to represent the Shah and his corrupt era. It was seen to represent the West and became a target of revolutionary wrath. The Rex Cinema fire in 1978 (in which 400 perished) set a pattern. By the time of the revolution some 180 cinemas had been burnt. Film production came to a halt; many film-makers were indicted, on charges such as 'corrupting the public', and purged; nearly 2,200 previously shown domestic and foreign films were reinspected and just over 200 of them received screening permits. Some of these films had to be cut extensively before returning to screens. In an attempt to establish an 'Islamic, anti-imperialist' cinema, a new set of highly restrictive censorship codes brought film production under the tight control of the government. Most of these codes were aimed at the representation of female characters.

Nudity and immodesty were condemned. When cutting confused the narrative the offensive body parts were blocked off with markers applied to every single frame. Strict Islamic dress codes required women to cover their hair in public, and wear loose-fitting outer garments to cloak their body curves. Also, women could only be intimate with the immediate members of their family. Therefore, actors playing couples could not even touch each other's hands on the screen unless they were married in real life. Even today female characters' hair must always be covered, even when they are asleep in the privacy of their house. The restrictions, causing the unrealistic presentation of women, have forced many film-makers to give up on the idea of making films about couples and their relationships altogether. This explains why so many films are about children (See Chapter 2).

In June 1982 the cabinet approved a series of regulations governing cinema, charging the Ministry of Culture and Islamic Guidance with its enforcement. Currently, says Dr. Jamsheed Akrami,[6] film censorship is implemented in four stages: first, the script must be approved to ensure its content is appropriate; second, the list of cast and crew must be submitted to receive a production permit; third, the finished film is sent to the censorship board, which may approve it unconditionally, require changes, or ban it altogether; finally, the producers of the approved film must apply for a screening permit. The last stage subjects the film to a three-tier letter rating system – A, B, and C – determining the film's booking and its access to the media for promotion.

Film ratings in Iran, says Akrami, do not have the same meaning they have in the West. They have nothing to do with the content of the film; content is normally monitored at the script-approval stage. The ratings grade the quality of the films. An A-rated film would be allowed to be advertised on the government-controlled television, and shown in the best theatres at the most desirable times for a guaranteed period. C-rated films, on the other hand, not only would be denied promotion on television, but would be released for only a limited time in the worst theatres during the off-peak times of the film season. All these controls amount to a multi-layered system of film censorship that not only decides the content of a film, but also determines how the marketplace will react to it. American and European films are virtually impossible to import, says Akrami, since few of them would conform to these rules. The government is the sole importer of the limited number of films that are found appropriate for distribution.

Although Kiarostami emerged in the West as a major film-maker in the early 1990s with films like *Close-Up* and *Through the Olive Trees*, he had already been making films in Iran for two decades. In 1969 – the year that saw the birth of the Iranian New Wave with Mehrju'i's *The Cow* – Kiarostami helped to set up a film-making department at the Institute for Intellectual Development of Children and Young Adults. The department's debut production was Kiarostami's own first film, the twelve-minute *Bread and the Street*, the simple story of a small boy's perilous walk home from school. The department would go on to become one of Iran's most famous film studios, producing not only Kiarostami's films, but also such modern Iranian classics as *The Runner* and *Bashu, The Little Stranger*.

Kiarostami's wonderfully simple *Khaneh-ye Doust Kojast?* (Where Is The House Of My Friend?) is another example of using very simple techniques to create a profound message and beguile the viewer. A school boy in a remote village picks up the forgotten textbook of his friend and spends the rest of the film going from house to house to find him. According to the Iranian film-analyst Mir-Ahmad Mir-Ehsan, Kiarostami in his films develops the intel-lectually challenging notion of divine atheism, based on the mystical teachings of Hafez and Ibn Arabi as a foil to both intolerant atheism and its western mechanical negation, atheism.[7]

Akrami notes that although Kiarostami's films have been compared at various times to those of Satyajit Ray, Vittorio de Sica, Eric Rohmer, or Jacques Tati, they remain uniquely 'Kiarostami'. Effortlessly simple and conceptually complex in equal measure, poetic, lyrical, meditative, self-reflective and increasingly sophisticated, they mix fiction and documentary in unique ways, often presenting fact as fiction and fiction as fact. (Kiarostami has said 'We can never get close to the truth except through lying.') In the twenty-eight years since *Bread and the Street*, Kiarostami has made more than twenty films, including fiction features, educational shorts, feature-length documentaries and a series of films for television. He has also written screenplays for other directors, most notably *The White Balloon*, for his former assistant Jafar Panahi. But it was not until the late 1980s that his films began to be shown outside Iran. In 1998 he brought to the Cannes Film Festival *Taste of Cherry* and became the first Iranian director ever to win the Palme d'Or.

As in the Soviet Union it seems that the Iranian cinema has flourished under censorship and enjoyed much popularity, even in mainstream western cinemas.

Twenty-one

Censorship and Human Rights

Since the humiliating defeat of Arab countries in the 1967 Arab-Israeli war (often known as the Six-Day War), a distinction between the Islamic legal tradition based on the Shari'a and the concept of international human rights has become a serious factor. The Arab world, in particular, is passing through a process of transition from an era dominated by the ideology of Arab nationalism and governed by authoritarian regimes to an era dominated by the ideology of political Islam, itself led by authoritarian regimes whose most notorious model is Sudan. A similar pattern is emerging in other parts of the Islamic world.

In the modern debate on human rights and censorship, one of the most significant figures in the Islamic argument was the Iranian Sultanhussein Tabandeh, the leader of the Ni'matullahi Sufi order, who produced a human rights pamphlet in 1966 (translated into English in 1970). Tabandeh associated obedience to the Shari'a with deference to the will of the majority and the dictates of government. Article 3 of the Universal Declaration of Human Rights (UDHR), published in 1948, guarantees the general right to life, liberty and security of persons without qualifications but Tabandeh argued that those rights must be qualified by the requirement that they may not be 'contrary to the regulations of Islam nor molest the peace of others'.

Others, such as Maududi, founder of the Islamic Society, developed this Islamic argument. In 1976 Maududi published *Human Rights in Islam,* a book which won the King Faisal prize for 'outstanding services to Islam'. Muslim scholars have tended to condemn western concepts such as the critical Declaration of the Rights of Man and of the Citizen adopted by the French National Assembly on 26 August 1789, arguing once again that human rights in Islam must always put God first and Man second.

Nevertheless, the 1972 Charter of the Organization of the Islamic Conference (OIC), the international organization to which all Muslim countries belong, expressly endorsed international law and fundamental human rights, treating them as compatible with Islamic values. The Universal Islamic Declaration of Human Rights (UIDHR) produced in 1981 by the Islamic Council resembled UDHR, but deceptively so. Khomeini referred to the latter as 'nothing but a collection of mumbo-jumbo by disciples of Satan'. In its preamble the UIDHR says that 'by the terms of our primeval covenant with God our duties and obligations have priority over our rights'.

On the rule of law and on human rights issues Khomeini fell out with many of his followers, in particular with Bazargan and Montazeri, as we have seen. 'As soon as former Savak chief Nasiri's identity was established he had to be killed,' Khomeini said. 'Despite the fact that he deserved summary execution, he was kept for a few days and he was tried. Doesn't the human rights lobby think that criminals must be killed for the sake of human rights, in order to ensure the rights of man and those whom these people killed, tortured and destroyed? Nevertheless, we are trying them and we have tried them. Our belief is that criminals should not be tried and must be killed.'

Iran's representative to the UN Said Raja'i-Khorasani maintained that the UDHR represents a secular understanding of the Judaeo–Christian tradition, and thus cannot be implemented by Muslims and does not accord with the system of values recognized by the Islamic Republic of Iran. Iran, he said, would not hesitate to violate its provisions. In her book *Islam and Human Rights* Ann Elizabeth Mayer argues that the UIDHR opens the way to denying rights, including those guaranteed under international human rights law, in the guise of establishing Islamic duties.

The 1979 Iranian Constitution predates the UIDHR. It reflected Khomeini's view that man has no natural rights and that believers must simply submit to God's commands. It lays down that 'All civil, penal, financial, economic, administrative, cultural, military, political laws and regulations, as well as any other laws or regulations, should be based on Islamic principles. This principle will in general prevail over all of the principles of the constitution, and other laws and regulations as well. Any judgement in regard to this will be made by the clerical members of the Council of Guardians.' This meant that even rights guaranteed by the Constitution could be overridden by clerics representing the government. In fact, Khomeini made it clear that his Islamic state had the right to override Islamic law where necessary, even in such fundamentals as prayer, fasting and the Hajj.

Islamic writers in present-day Iran maintain that there is no censorship in Iran in the sense that people may talk and complain openly in the street and in shops. They justify media censorship by maintaining that there is no place for intellectuals in an Islamic revolution. The Islamic journalist Shahriar Zarshenaz considers intellectualism to be the product of modern western civilization which began with Renaissance humanism.[2] This puts man at the centre of things rather than God. Intellectuals are the product of the new secular universities and education system that emerged after the seventeenth century when the influence of the church declined. Progress in the West is limited to technical progress and material welfare. In Iran today, he says, professional journalism, secular intellectualism and religious intellectualism are all opposed to genuine religious thought. 'Journalism', he writes, 'is tolerant of the laxity that comes about when mankind turns its back on religion. Journalism was responsible for filling spare time and creating sensual joy and amusement for modern man frightened of being alone with himself.' He says that in modern civilization freedom means freedom from religion; and that humanist freedom allows man to reject the laws of God in favour of his own, man-made laws.

In April 1980 Khomeini attacked Iran's universities and some days later the universities closed down entirely and were not to reopen for two years. He banned the tenth-century Firdousi's monumental *Shah Nameh* (Book of Kings) and copies of it were burned. Significantly, Firdousi had revived the Persian language and Iranian nationalism after centuries of Arabic and Islamic influence. In February 1981, 133 writers, journalists and academics published an open letter to Khomeini in protest against illegal trials, the suppression of basic freedoms, the muzzling of the press, the burning of books and bookstores and other violations of the Constitution.

A decade later, in December 1990, however, the mood in Iran had softened and the celebrations for Firdousi's millennium were attended by international scholars and the General Secretary of UNESCO and were chaired by President Hashemi Rafsanjani. Several attempts had been made by zealous mullahs to remove the statue of Firdousi from central Tehran, but the statue remains. When the liberalising President Muhammad Khatami made his first visit to the UN (and his first to the USA) in September 1998 he quoted from the Qur'an, the New Testament and from the *Shah Nameh*, in arguing in philosophical language that dialogue was the key to understanding among nations. He had also made noises suggesting that the *fatwa* against Salman Rushdie might be lifted, although he spoke with caution as he remained locked in a fierce power struggle with the right-wing, fundamentalist hardliners led by the supreme leader Ayatollah 'Ali Khamenei.

Thinking after the Iranian Revolution had been encapsulated in Samuel Huntington's 1993 article 'The Clash of Civilizations', which saw Islamic and other Asian cultures set to replace Communism as the new threat to western civilization. Islam, he wrote in this highly controversial essay, 'has bloody borders'. Its culture is foreign to that of the West. 'Western ideas of individualism, liberalism, constitutionalism, human rights, equality, liberty, the rule of law, democracy, free markets, the separation of church and state', he writes, 'often have very little resonance in Islamic [and other] ... cultures.'[3]

In that same year the Cairo Declaration on Human Rights in Islam was presented at the World Conference on Human Rights in Vienna by the Saudi foreign minister. It had been endorsed in 1990 by the Organization of Islamic Conferences. In March 1992 the Basic Law of Saudi Arabia was drawn up, again placing emphasis on the supremacy of Islam. In Saudi Arabia today censorship is ubiquitous. The following are among forbidden topics: arousal of sexual excitement, women who appear indecently, women in athletics, unmarried couples in the same room with the door closed, references to Zionism, alcohol and gambling.

According to Mayer[4] Islamic criteria have regularly been used to cut back on freedoms guaranteed in international law, reflecting a culturally-based resistance to international human rights. Some governments have even claimed that Islamic authority has justified their human rights abuses. She points out that 'at the core of most efforts to delegitimize comparison of Islamic and international law is the conviction that they violate the principles of cultural relativism'.

In Sudan, Mayer points out, some academics complain that the rejection of President Nimairi's Islamization programme showed a lack of cultural relativism. She notes that these critics fail to see that Nimairi was not legally Muslim, that his record was not genuinely Muslim and that few Sudanese, even the most devout, were impressed by his experiment in Islamic government. The worst abuses took place during 1983–5. The West has often blatantly failed to condemn such violations. It was in 1985, shortly after the execution of Mahmoud Muhammad Taha for heresy, that Nimairi was welcomed in Washington by President Reagan.

Sickened by his abuses, the Sudanese themselves ousted him soon afterwards but even under President Omar al-Bashir the military continued to make common cause with the fundamentalists and the President continued to cooperate with Hasan al-Turabi and his National Front. In spite of his western education and sophisticated manners, Turabi backs crucifixions (cross amputations) for theft and other crimes according to his own, very narrow interpretation of the Shari'a.

In Iraq, meanwhile, President Saddam Hussein peppers his speeches with Islamic slogans and rules through terror. For him terror is by far the best form of censorship. Of the 4,000 people executed or tortured to death between 1968 and 1981 25 per cent were academics. During the Gulf War of 1990–1 the Iraqi government resorted to clumsy methods of propaganda. In an attempt to copy the British Second World War collaborator 'Lord Haw Haw' Iraqi radio broadcast exhortations such as, 'Your children are waiting for you. Your wife is waiting for you. Your wife has a lover. This is Radio Baghdad, the broadcasting service of the Iraqi republic.'

Of Iraq's population of 23 million 97 per cent are Muslim (Shi'a 60–65 per cent, Sunni 32–37 per cent). Formerly part of the Ottoman Empire, Iraq became a semi-independent kingdom in 1932. The king and the crown prince were brutally killed in 1958 and a republic was proclaimed. A series of military strongmen have ruled the country since, the latest being Saddam Hussein who emerged from the pan-Arab, secular Ba'ath Party. Territorial disputes with Iran led to an inconclusive and costly war (1980–88). In August 1990 Iraq seized Kuwait, but was expelled by US-led, UN coalition forces during January–February 1991. The coalition did not occupy Iraq, however, thus allowing the brutal regime to stay in power. Following Kuwait's liberation, the UN Security Council (UNSC) required Iraq to destroy all weapons of mass destruction and long-range missiles and to allow UN verification inspections. UN trade sanctions remain in effect on the grounds of incomplete Iraqi compliance with relevant UNSC resolutions.

In January 1997, according to Amnesty International, the government announced that the judicial punishments of amputation and branding had ceased and would be abolished by law. In March, Saddam Hussein reportedly ordered an end to the practice of ear amputation for army desertion and the release of hundreds of army deserters and draft evaders. In August, the Revolutionary Command Council, Iraq's highest executive body, reportedly issued Decree 81, formally abolishing the judicial punishments of ear amputation and branding for army desertion.

Meanwhile, Muslims were sensitive to the hypocrisy of a West which condemned Khomeini but was silent before the human rights abuses of the Shah. The USA enjoyed warm relations with Pakistan and its Islamizing President Zia ul-Haq and almost as an unwitting symbol of this friendship Zia died in a helicopter crash together with the US ambassador to Pakistan.

The 1980s and 1990s witnessed a dramatic growth in the influence of political Islam both through its civil and military factions in Arab and other Muslim countries. At times political Islam has become the equivalent of a shadow government, while in Sudan and Iran it is the actual government.

In Pakistan the first general elections on the basis of adult franchise and on party lines were held in 1970. Political parties calling for a theocratic agenda did very badly. In East Pakistan (later Bangladesh) the Jamaat-i-Islami put up 71 candidates but failed to win a single seat. In West Pakistan of 80 candidates only four won. Because they failed to win through the ballot box they had to turn to the military for their power base. After the downfall and execution of Zulfikar 'Ali Bhutto, General Muhammad Zia ul-Haq used as his excuse to remain in power his Islamization mission under the umbrella of martial law. As Malik Ghulam Jilani said in a speech to the Press Club in 1983,' 'This is why the General must remain, first to carry out his form of Islamization and then to keep a watch over the mischief he has unleashed.' The first laws Zia introduced were the Hudud Ordinances. Although even strict fundamentalists found the ordinances flawed, few were willing to repeal them, believing that to do so would undermine the overall interests of Islam. Many were entirely unacceptable to the educated mind. For example one could, in principle, be punished with the amputation of a limb if one stole a thousand rupees but embezzlement of any amount was not covered by the Hudud. Different weighting was shown to Muslims, non-Muslims and females, establishing discrimination on the basis of sex and religion. The underprivileged were especially threatened by the Ordinances.

Other regimes, meanwhile, tried to represent themselves in a more acceptable light internationally. After the overthrow of the Bourguiba regime in 1987, the new government in Tunisia announced in 1988 that it would establish an Amnesty chapter, the first one permitted in the Arab world. In 1988 even Libya's President Qadhafi issued a Libyan human rights charter, denounced the human rights abuses of his regime and showed willing to establish ties with Amnesty. A year later the Algerian government, shaken by riots, prepared a new constitution with human rights provisions along international lines and without Islamic qualifications. It accepted the innovation of a constitutional guarantee of protection for human rights advocacy, reflecting the power of grassroots calls for human rights in Algeria.

Nevertheless, a little more than a year later in free elections in June 1990 the FIS won control of most Algerian municipalities. In December 1991 it won the first round of national elections and in January 1992 the army moved in, smothering all hope of human rights in Algeria. As in so many Islamic countries Islam in Algeria has become the primary and most potent language of political protest against dictatorship.

Where power was won by Islamists it was a different story. Once in power in Iran the clergy prevented voters from throwing them out while in Pakistan and Sudan voters did throw out Islamic regimes as soon as they grasped what they represented. President Zia, who seized power in 1977 and executed President Bhutto, was more cautious and never allowed free elections. In reaction to this, in November 1988 Bhutto's daughter Benazir was elected, three months after Zia's death. She campaigned against Zia's Islamization programme and called for the restoration of the 1973 constitution but both her terms of office were to be disastrous.

In the West we are shocked to hear that in Saudi Arabia today there are neither defence lawyers nor juries in a Shari'a trial, but rather in the manner of the French *juge d'instruction* the Shari'a systems depends upon the integrity, piety, justice and wisdom of the judge himself. Nevertheless, according to Muhammad al-Awa, a former associate professor of law at Riyadh University, the relationship between the infliction of punishment and the evidence required to prove a crime is a very hard one. 'Where the court is not absolutely certain of the guilt of the accused', he points out, 'the punishment cannot be inflicted. Murder can only be proved where there is oral testimony of two adult males known to the judge as having the highest degree of moral and religious probity *('adala)*. This comes from the Qur'anic injunction "and call to witness two just men".'

TWENTY-TWO

Saudi Arabia

The reasons for banning books and newspapers in Saudi Arabia today are myriad. Criticism of the Saudi Royal family and its 20,000 princes and princesses tops the list of political taboos. Other subjects which the media cannot touch are corruption, the taking of commission or bribes, and arms-dealing. References to the kingdom's finances, above all the huge fortunes acquired by its princes, are equally forbidden. Even criticism of the rulers of Gulf and other friendly states is forbidden. An unveiled woman's face may not be published in the press and no woman singer is allowed to broadcast via television.

Saudi Arabia has, since the oil boom of 1973, increasingly acquired media organs internationally in order to control information, if not to stifle criticism. This was highlighted in 1996 by the closing down of the BBC Arabic service television whose transmission had been through the satellite broadcasting company Orbit which is owned by a member of the Saudi royal family. The station was shortly to rebroadcast a BBC *Panorama* documentary about the 'Death of a Princess' incident in 1980. Other issues of contention between the interests of the BBC and the Saudis had been the criticisms of the London-based Saudi dissident Dr Muhammad al-Mas'ari, head of the exiled Committee for the Defence of Legitimate Rights (CDLR).

The roots of the Saudi regime's tight control of expression lie in its recent history. The present Saudi dynasty is descended from Muhammad Al Saud, an eighteenth-century sheikh from the central region of Najd who formed a religio-military alliance with the fundamentalist Hanbali reformer, Muhammad ibn 'Abd al-Wahhab. The energy of the so-called 'Wahhabis' stemmed from conviction that it was the duty of the Muslim community to call the entire Islamic world to repentance for having broken away from the pure unitarianism of early Islam. Wahhab sought a return to the purity of the Prophet Muhammad and his companions. Exploiting the military might of the Saudi clan and its bedouin allies, he united with Muhammad Al Saud to create a puritan Islamic state. In 1802 the Shi'a of Iraq for the first time felt the sting of the Wahhabis when these militant fanatics sacked Kerbala and destroyed the Tomb of Hussein. In 1807 the Ottomans crushed this first Wahhabi state with the help of Ibrahim, the son of Muhammad 'Ali of Egypt. However, it was not until 1818 that the Wahhabi leadership surrendered and almost a year after this that their capital at Dir'iya was destroyed. They tormented one of the Wahhabi leaders, Sulayman, by playing a guitar to him (music is anathema to them) before executing him.¹ The Wahhabi leaders were forced into exile in Kuwait. However, at the turn of the century Saudi fortunes were revived by 'Abd al-Aziz ibn 'Abd al-Rahman Al Saud (commonly known to the world as Ibn Saud). Setting out from Kuwait with a handful of followers, he regained the stronghold of Riyadh from the Al Rashid clan and proceeded to recover all the former Saudi dominions.

However, a conflict of identity was to ensue between Ibn Saud, who remained a Wahhabi but sought to absorb the best of the modern world, and the Ikhwan die-hard extremists who rejected any deviation from the model of the Prophet's life based on the Qur'an and the Hadith and opposed innovations such as cars, telephones and the radio. His critics would argue that Ibn Saud depended upon these ferocious puritans for conquest and control. The Wahhabi *ulama* condemned Ibn Saud's tobacco tax because they forbade tobacco while he saw the trade as a valuable source of revenue. He feigned agreement but also stopped salaries to the Ikhwan on the grounds of his now 'straitened means', increasing their resentment.

The history of the Kingdom of Saudi Arabia begins properly on 18 September 1932, when the regions of the Hejaz and Najd were unified under the name of the Kingdom of Saudi Arabia. By the late 1940s the Kingdom's oil wells were flowing. This sudden access of wealth, however, was to be a mixed blessing. The more sophisticated Hejaz region with its seaport of Jeddah was to be the centre for culture and the media of newspapers and radio. Ibn Saud viewed this flood of wealth and the consequent changes in morality with anxiety although not by the standards of the Ikhwan who by now saw him as a dangerous modernizer. He had resorted to the ruse of a having a cleric recite the Qur'an through the telephone system to counteract Ikhwan protests and then to put forward a quaint scientific 'light and shadow' argument (light for spiritual light, shadow for spiritual darkness) to persuade them to accept television. At about this time al-Azhar issued a *fatwa* saying that photography might be permitted since it was 'reproduction' rather than 'creation'.

Although he had used the Ikhwan as a primitive tool to create his state, he was himself not averse to worldly pleasures. On a journey with companions one day he is said to have announced, 'There are no Ikhwan with us. He who has a good voice will now let us hear it.' Whereupon his companions began to sing their hearts out. Towards the end of his life St John Philby told of how music roared out on the King's parade ground and how the forbidden cinema appeared in the palaces 'to flaunt the less respectable products of Hollywood before audiences which would have blushed or shuddered at the sight but ten or fifteen years ago'. Liquor and drugs, wrote Philby in 1955, appeared in quarters where people had been killed for smoking tobacco. The motor-car allowed women, he said, to 'dance or frolic to the tunes of a gramophone [another prohibited article] in the latest summer frocks from Paris, or dine alfresco in strapless bodices'.[2]

Ibn Saud set to remoulding the relatively sophisticated coastal region of the Hejaz in the wake of the defeated Hashemite rulers to a Wahhabi puritan culture grown from the harsh deserts of the Najd Province. To execute this backward metamorphosis he created his Frankenstein monster, the Ikhwan-run committee for the Advancement of Virtue and Elimination of Vice (AVEV). His wars, says Aburish, a fierce critic of the House of Saud, involved 40,000 public executions and 350,000 amputations, affecting respectively 1 and 7 per cent of the estimated population of four million. 'Compared with his sword', he says, ' the accepted Arab notions of loyalty, brotherhood, hospitality, honour and beauty amount to very little. And the imported ideas of freedom, equality and representative government do even less. The word of the Qur'an is supreme: all is derived from it and everything is subordinated to it. The sword is how the Word is carried out.' The Ikhwan flogged people at random and people were punished for wearing western clothes, gold, perfume, or silk, for smoking and the men for not wearing a moustache or a beard, he says. Singing was forbidden. The Saudi writer Nasser al-Said remembers how AVEV zealots broke into his grandmother's house and flogged him in her presence when he was a boy of eight.[3]

Press censorship had, of course, pre-dated the Saudi state. An Ottoman-controlled press, the traditional guardian of the public interest and the only channel for public expression, already existed in the peninsula. *Al-Hejaz* was published in 1908 in Mecca and a year later *al-Raked* and *al-Qibla* were launched. Until 1924 they were all written by Ottoman Turks, Syrians and others. The Mecca newspaper *Umm al-Qura* (Mother of the Villages), run by St John Philby's prolific colleague K. Hussein, was founded in 1924 and remained virtually the only publication until 1932. The catalyst for Saudi dominion in the Hejaz had been the Sharrif of Mecca's extremely unpopular proclamation of himself as Caliph as soon as he heard that the Ottoman Caliphate had been abolished by Atatürk. The weekly newspaper in Mecca had begun publishing telegrams of congratulations which were allegedly pouring in from all over the world. Most of these messages, however, were invented.

Al-Hejaz, al-Qibla and *al-Raked*, which followed enlightened policies and encouraged healthy debate, were closed down by Ibn Saud shortly after he conquered the Hejaz in 1925. Initially he had ordered them to promote his policies but when they refused he ordered the arrest of people who read them and finally he confiscated their printing presses. By 1927 he had turned *Umm al-Qura*, now his official Wahhabi mouthpiece, into a purely propagandist newspaper aimed at defending the narrow tenets of Wahhabism. According to Aburish he had his own articles ghost-written by the Lebanese Amin Rihani and depended on the literary support of George Antonius, the famous author of *The Arab Awakening*, and Yusuf Yassin, author of a highly propagandist book called *Ibn Saud: Unifier of the Arabs.*

Ibn Saud was succeeded by Sa'ud, his eldest son, who proved incompetent and was soon in effect replaced in authority by his next son, the charismatic Faisal, the Prime Minister. Under Faisal's auspices, television was introduced in 1958 and education for women in 1960. Two years later Faisal was to abolish slavery at a cost to the government of $1,785,000 for 1,682 slaves in the central province to begin with. In 1964 Saud was deposed and Faisal was proclaimed king.

With Faisal came winds of change. He held regular and open press conferences and allowed businessmen, technicians, diplomats and even journalists to travel to remote parts of the Kingdom. David Holden notes that although the holy cities of Mecca and Medina remained closed to non-Muslims, 'on at least one occasion in 1963 the Anglican Archbishop of Jerusalem was seen in transit at Jeddah airport wearing his purple surplice and gold cross with never a Wahhabi eyebrow lifted in his direction'.[4]

Ibn Saud had established his own private radio network in 1932 to be kept informed of events. In 1948 the government set up a low-powered short-wave radio station in Jeddah, principally to broadcast Islamic programmes to Muslims. When broadcasting began from Jeddah in October 1949 Ibn Saud issued a royal decree on policy. This stated that, apart from Qur'anic recitals, (Wahhabi) religious sermons and historical lectures on Islam and the Arabs, international news was to be neutrally presented 'without defamation or irrelevant praise'. Domestic news was to 'abstain from broadcasting what we do not wish to broadcast, and to broadcast what we are accustomed to publish'.[5] However, the only existing radio station when Faisal became Prime Minister was Radio Mecca, which in 1954 had became the Saudi Arabian Broadcasting Service. Most Saudis depended on word of mouth for their news, although urban Saudis had been exposed to social mixing in Mecca during the Hajj.

At this time the Arab media had little with which to challenge Saudi ideology. The transmission signals of the Arab radio stations in Egypt, Iraq and Palestine were weak and only really accessible to the elite whose well-being depended on their rulers. Of course, later this was to change with the 'rebel princes' switching allegiance to Nasser in the 1960s. Once Nasser had launched his powerful if acid propaganda radio station, The Voice of the Arabs, the Saudis were forced to respond (see below).

The Saudi approach to government and censorship was to vary. During his eleven-year reign King Sa'ud had openly bribed journalists but allowed a reasonable degree of self-censorship. Faisal, on the other hand, was tough with the media within the Kingdom and began to use the Arab press outside Saudi Arabia to further Saudi interests and Wahhabi values. King Faisal's views were fairly straightforward. 'A constitution?' he asked in 1966. 'What for? The Qur'an is the oldest and most efficient constitution in the world.' Nevertheless, it was to be Faisal who developed the ministries of government and established for the first time an efficient bureaucracy. 'Like it or not', he said, 'we must join the modern world and find an honourable place in it.' His foreign policy was characterized by hatred of communism whose atheism was anathema to his Wahhabism and hatred of Zionism, largely because it had usurped Islam's third holiest city, Jerusalem. When asked about his attitude to socialism he returned to usual Wahhabi dogma: 'We have the Holy Qur'an and the Shari'a law. Why do we need socialism, capitalism, communism or any other ideology?'

Faisal was also sensitive to the fact that even modest reforms could provoke the wrath of the hard right. Having paid lip service to the need to maintain Islamic values in Point Six of his famous Ten-Point Programme for reform he promised 'to reform the Committees for Public Morality in accordance with the Shari'a and Islam's lofty goals, for which they were originally created, and in such a way as to extirpate to the greatest extent evil motives from the hearts of people'. In practice he wanted to limit the excesses of his religious police or *mutawi'in* who forced shops to close at prayer-time, broke dolls in the souk, whipped the exposed legs of European women and sometimes even entered private houses to smash record players. Despite the semi-nudity of sportsmen, sports escaped censure but public cinemas, which would bring groups of men, and even women, together, did not. They have remained banned ever since.

Faisal wanted 'to make available innocent means of recreation for all citizens.' When asked to elucidate he added, 'We do not of course mean the opening of cabarets, night-clubs, bars and gambling houses. The kind of recreation we have in mind is that which does not conflict with God's religion and with moral behaviour.' This seems to have included television which had been introduced in 1958 and which Faisal needed to counteract Nasser, particularly after the *coup d'état* in Sana'a which sparked off the Yemeni civil war in 1962. Faisal saw Nasser's socialism as a very real threat to his traditional, conservative kingdom. When Egyptian troops were sent to North Yemen in 1962, tension between the two countries became severe.

The war in Yemen brought Saudi Arabia into direct confrontation with Egypt's propaganda machine, above all its hugely popular Voice of the Arabs radio station in Cairo. These Egyptian broadcasts aimed to mobilize Saudis and other Arabs against a 'despotic' and 'reactionary' regime. King Faisal felt at a disadvantage in this 'radio war' and wanted to rectify this. He aimed to address the whole Islamic world from his position as protector of the two holy cities (Mecca and Medina). Ironically, many of the kingdom's journalists and broadcasters were Egyptians with strong sympathies with Nasser and when the Yemeni civil war began several of them went on strike in support of the Egyptian leader. The Saudi press was privately owned but politically passive and bland. When Nasser attacked Saudi Arabia Faisal encouraged it to bare its fangs and respond, saying, 'we have given the press freedom to express its views, and when it did so, it was described as aggressive. Who is the aggressor, brothers?'

However, in reality Faisal had little patience with a free press. In 1963 he described his frustration with journalists who began discussing 'socialism and other subjects ... when the discussion developed into what we feared might compromise certain governments or leaders, we advised our friends of the press to avoid discussing this subject'. Faisal was clearly more comfortable with a passive press which avoided controversial issues with dangerous social implications for his ultra-conservative kingdom.[6] He cancelled the right of individuals and families to own publications and turned all newspapers and magazines into limited-liability public companies whose licences were periodically renewed and subject to the King's personal approval. He also brought in laws involving who could and could not become a journalist, restricted the contents of publications and imposed large fines and imprisonment for those who broke the rules.

When Beirut became the centre of the free Arab press because of Nasser's dictatorial ways, hundreds of newspapers and magazines opened in Beirut. Faisal used Saudi money to try to prise them away from their support for Nasser's new world of socialism and pan-Arabism. The editor of the leading Lebanese weekly *al-Hawadeth*, Salim al-Louzi (who was to be killed, most likely by Syrian agents, in Beirut in 1979), divided the Lebanese who took Saudi money into 'pirates and beggars'; the first group 'threatened the Saudis until they paid them bounty, and the second just begged for money to do their dirty work'.

Journalists were co-opted through bribes but not all supported him for personal gain. Aburish notes that Kamel Mroeh, editor of *al-Hayat*, cooperated with Faisal because he opposed Nasser ideologically. 'Money', says Aburish, 'was a vehicle which allowed him to present his well-thought-out, elegantly presented point of view.' When Nasser's attempts to silence Mroeh failed he had him murdered but, by killing him, Nasser merely 'threw the door wide open for less able and less intelligent people', says Aburish.

Meanwhile, Faisal tried to replace Egyptian journalists with Saudis. In January 1964 he issued the new press code (Royal Decree No 62) which gave the Ministry of Information power to close newspapers (Article 8C), approve the hiring of a General Manager (Article 16) or require his dismissal (Article 18D). Articles 9 and 31 of the new press code demanded that each newspaper and magazine have a board of directors composed of fifteen Saudis and that each daily have at least five full-time editors, two foreign language translators, a photographer and 'correspondents residing in three major capitals'.

King Faisal was succeeded in 1975 by his half-brother, Crown Prince Khaled, and Fahd became heir apparent. During the new king's reign, economic and social development continued rapidly, revolutionizing the infrastructure and educational system of the country but news continued to be heavily controlled. When, at the end of July 1977, Princess Misha'il bint Fahd ibn Muhammad and her lover Khaled Muhalhal were executed for adultery, the story was not published. It was only picked up in the West the following January. When the story was highlighted by a British television documentary in April 1980 it led to a breakdown in relations with the UK and the British ambassador James Craig was forced to leave the Kingdom. The British government deplored the showing of the film but explained to the baffled Saudis that it could not override the British right to freedom of speech.

Until Egypt's catastrophic defeat by the Israelis in 1967 Nasser had to a large extent controlled the Arab press outside Egypt. After the defeat Saudi Arabia suddenly replaced Egypt as Pied Piper to Arab journalists and after the oil boom of 1973 Saudi financial influence over journalists became paramount. Saudi ownership of the pan-Arab press outside the Kingdom started in 1979 when the Arabic newspaper *al-Sharq al-Awsat* was launched in London and transmitted by fax to printing presses in the USA, Egypt and Saudi Arabia. Today it is printed daily in seven or eight cities in the world.

This was followed by the purchase of the Lebanese newspaper *al-Hayat* which had closed down in Beirut in 1976 during the early part of the civil war. Most of its shares were bought in 1988 by Prince Khaled ibn Sultan, the former commander-in-chief of the Saudi armed forces and a nephew of King Fahd. Under its new, largely Saudi, ownership it was to be edited from London but with publishing centres in Cairo, Casablanca, Frankfurt, Beirut and New York and a current circulation of 100,000. Although considered one of the best newspapers in the Arab world, *al-Hayat* has to censor itself severely wherever Saudi interests are concerned. When a group calling itself 'The Army of Liberation of the Islamic Holy Places' claimed responsibility for the bombs which hit the US embassies in Nairobi and Dar es Salaam in August 1998, the newspaper dropped the crucial word 'Islamic' in deference to the fact that King Fahd claims to be Custodian of the Two Holy Places.

After the signing of the Egyptian–Israeli peace agreement on 26 March 1979, Saudi Arabia had joined most of the other Arab nations in severing diplomatic relations with Egypt. The establishment of the Islamic Republic of Iran in 1979 and the subsequent Iran–Iraq War of 1980–8 also made a strong impact on the kingdom and on internal controls, including press censorship.

But the most dramatic domestic challenge to the monarchy since the Second World War took place when the Great Mosque in Mecca, the holiest site in the world for Muslims, was seized by followers of a Saudi religious extremist, Juhaiman ibn Muhammad al-Otaibi, on 20 November 1979. The Saudi press was very slow to respond to such a terrifying outrage. 'No, not in Islam', was the banner headline of a Damman newspaper when it was eventually permitted to publish what little it knew. The line the Saudi press followed was one which claimed godless fanatics were burning Qur'ans in the cellars of the mosque and solacing themselves with sex, a far cry from the truth. The rebels occupied the mosque for two weeks before they were defeated. Domestic unrest continued with rioting by Shi'i Muslims in eastern Saudi Arabia in 1979 and 1980. The Shi'a have always felt and continued to feel persecuted by the overwhelmingly Sunni-dominated regime.

As Holden and Johns point out in *The House of Saud* the press waited twenty-four hours before even mentioning the 1979 Mecca Mosque siege and when it eventually did report it, it laid the blame on Khomeini, Sadat of Egypt, Libya, the PLO and Zionism, in that order. The arrival of Jordanian, British and French troops to put down the revolt was never reported. Nor was it reported that French troops had been given special permission to enter Mecca, a city absolutely forbidden to non-Muslims. The subsequent Shi'i rebellion was not reported at all, nor was the fact that the leader of the Mecca rebellion was a Wahhabi, a Saudi and a former student of the Kingdom's leading cleric, Sheikh al-Baz. The distinct impression had been given that the coup leaders had been Pakistanis and other foreign Muslims. The decision to execute the coup leaders summarily was only announced on the actual day of the executions by beheading and after that the saga was never referred to by the press again. Nevertheless, in the spring of 1981 graffiti appeared in the lavatories of Riyadh

University: 'Juhaiman, our martyr, why didn't you storm the palaces? The struggle is only beginning.'[7]

Today the Saudi press is controlled by the 1982 Press and Publications Code which, as an Article XIX report points out, is far from conforming with international standards protecting freedom of the press.[8] Criticism of censorship has come from very senior levels. In 1981 Turki al-Sudeiri, a relative of the King, and editor-in-chief of the daily *al-Riyadh*, dubbed the Saudi Ministry of Information the 'Ministry of Denials' in a front page editorial. He was dismissed from his job but, thanks to his prominence, was later reinstated. In the same year Hamid Ghuyarfi, the editor of the daily *al-Yaum*, was dismissed and not reinstated and in the following year an *al-Yaum* reporter Muhammad al-Akli was arrested and detained for two years.

On 13 June 1982, King Khaled died, and Fahd, who had long been influential in the administration of affairs, succeeded to the throne. Fahd maintained Saudi Arabia's foreign policy of close cooperation with the USA. Oil revenues were crucial to Saudi society as its economy was changed by unheard of wealth. Urbanization, mass public education, the presence of over a million foreign workers and access to sophisticated new media all affected Saudi values. However, although Saudi society was changing profoundly, the political processes were not developing or liberalising. Although the political elite included increasing numbers of bureaucrats and technocrats, real power remained with the Saudi dynasty.

When Iraq invaded neighbouring Kuwait on 2 August 1990, the Kuwaiti government fled to Saudi Arabia and King Fahd denounced the Iraqis. Fearing that Saddam Hussein might invade the oil-rich Hasa Province next the Saudis invited the USA and other countries to send troops to protect the kingdom. The economic and social impact of the crisis was dramatic. Saudi Arabia played host to foreign troops as well as Kuwaiti civilians. It expelled Yemenis and Jordanians, as their countries had supported Saddam. King Fahd made few political changes but promised future reforms. In the ground war that began in February 1991, Saudi troops helped defeat the Iraqis. The impact of foreign, in particular, American troops had been considerable. Scantily dressed American women driving jeeps was an entirely new phenomenon as was the smell of bacon fried by US troops.

One of the first results of the social changes created by the war was King Fahd's decrees of 1 March 1992 called 'A Basic System of Government'. This mini-constitution involved new laws which altered the way in which the heir to the throne was chosen, established a right to privacy, forbade human rights violations without cause, and established the ground rules for a consultative council. The new council was able to initiate and review laws but the King held on to ultimate power, including the authority to dismiss the council. Such changes helped stave off opposition to the regime at a time when the regional atmosphere was being challenged by the fallout from the collapse of the Soviet Union and the challenge from Iraq.

One of the most dramatic concepts to hit the developing world has been satellite television. It was popular Algerian frustration with the economic success, capitalist greed and moral decadence of Europe through the myriad satellite channels beamed to Algeria, that helped to unleash the hideous civil war that started in 1991. European channels were already explicit in the sexual messages they sent. In 1980 Fahd had encouraged the establishment of Saudi Arabia's own satellite station, the Middle East Broadcasting Centre, which claims 30 million viewers. Knowing just how sterile an organ run by Saudi bureaucrats would be, Fahd set up in London the Middle East Broadcasting Corporation (MBC) and newspapers such as the UK-based *al-Sharq al-Awsat* and the Jeddah based *Jeddah News* as semi-independent organizations. As well as MBC the Saudis today own ANA, the Arab radio station in Washington DC, Radio Orient, the Arabic-language radio station in France and United Press International (UPI).

Law No 128 of 10 March 1994 bans the import and sale of satellite dishes. Instead, the Saudi Ministry of Information said it would 'assume responsibility for the establishment of a system for the reception of foreign television signals … and to deliver them via a cable network to viewers in the Kingdom in harmony with its religious and social values'. The penalty for importing a dish and initiating one's own television transmissions was set between 100,000 and 500,000 Saudi riyals or between 26,000 and 133,000 dollars although the ban was not particularly effective and could be circumvented by many. The Gulf War had just excited huge interest in the West. Some 150,000 satellite dishes were providing a million people in the Kingdom with television signals at the time that the government decided to ban the equipment.

Modern technology and increasing exposure to the West appears if anything to have strengthened controls and censorship in Saudi Arabia. Despite the difficulty in acquiring accurate information from within the kingdom, violations are energetically and regularly exposed by organizations such as Amnesty, Human Rights Watch and Article XIX but it is difficult to ascertain to what extent, if any, the Saudi government has responded to such indictments.

TWENTY-THREE

Awaiting the Imam: A Golden Age of Tolerance

Until his imprisonment in January 2001 Iran's foremost populist investigative journalist Akbar Ganji was mobbed in Tehran like a pop star. When he attended a lecture at Tehran University in February 2000 students whistled and chanted his name. At an election rally featuring the country's most popular reform politicians he brought the house down. 'Ganji! Ganji!' the crowd roared when he arrived. Once a functionary in the Revolutionary Guards and Ministry of Islamic Culture and Guidance, the 41-year old Ganji helped bring down one of the regime's most powerful figures, 'Ali Akbar Hashemi Rafsanjani, in the parliamentary elections in February 2000.

He received regular threats. 'I guess I'm a troublemaker,' he told *Time* magazine,' adding. 'I call it playing with death. One day something might happen to me. This fight for reform is lawful, but it has its price.' He was regularly tipped off about death squads targeting him. His scoops which began appearing early in 1999 linked Iran's Intelligence Ministry to the chain of murders of dissident authors and political activists in the autumn of 1998.

In what he described to *Time* as 'disclosure by drips', he published one article after another explaining how government death squads selected their victims and executed them. He avoided accusing specific officials of ordering the murders, fascinating readers by pinning the blame on anonymous figures such as 'Mr. Master-Key' and the *'éminences grises'*, terms widely thought to refer to former Intelligence Minister 'Ali Fallahian and other Iranian leaders. 'In the history of Iranian journalism, there is hardly a precedent for Ganji's bravery,' Ahmed Bourghani, a former Ministry of Islamic Culture and Guidance official, told *Time*. 'He has pulled back the curtain.' Ganji's first confrontation with the system some years ago landed him in prison for three months. His crime was a speech which the religious authorities said branded Iran's Islamic system as a form of fascism.

On 13 January 2001 Iran handed down long gaol terms to several leading reformists over their attendance of a German conference which prosecutors said aimed at overthrowing the clerical regime. Ganji was given a ten-year prison sentence and a further five-year exile from Tehran after he gets out of gaol. He was apparently given four years for attending the conference and six years for an array of other serious charges, including spreading propaganda against the Islamic regime. The conference had been disrupted by the Iranian opposition in exile and was considered 'un-Islamic' in Tehran, in part because a man undressed in protest against the Islamic regime.

There was a curious twist to this story, however, after an interview with the *Guardian*'s Genevieve Abdo in which Ganji warned of a possible social explosion in Iran in reaction to the theological 'fascism' being exercised. His friends and family accused her of deliberately distorting his views and threatened legal action against her under Iran's harsh press laws. The director-general of foreign press in the Ministry of Culture and Islamic Guidance told her it was illegal to interview a political prisoner. Abdo's husband Jonathan Lyons was Reuters bureau chief in Tehran and Reuters was told that the matter was under investigation. Fearful of prosecution as criminals, both made for the airport and flew to London. The following day Abdo was strongly attacked in a newspaper close to Khatami, the official *Iran Daily,* the newspaper of the state news agency Irna. As Abdo noted sadly, in the Guardian.

> More than any single event during my years in Iran, this experience brought home to me the autocratic tendencies of the reform movement that claims a democratic mantle – and how serious are the obstacles to political development in a country with a centuries-old history of authoritarian rule and limited experience of democracy's give-and-take.[2]

Many had pinned their hopes on Iran, a country that had so bravely experimented with an ideology that went to the very roots of Islamic idealism. Is this experiment now to fail like so many others or is Iran taking three steps forward and two steps back? Iran, Egypt and Algeria are all, in their own ways, role models for many in the Islamic world but do they deserve this honour? In June 2000 the beautiful Algerian–French actress Isabelle Adjani turned down an invitation to an Elysée Palace dinner in honour of the Algerian President Abdelaziz Bouteflika.

> How could they possibly imagine I'd want to be associated with the posturing of a man who wants us to forget what's going on in the country – the army's crimes, the injustice and the forced amnesia of the population as regards massacres and disappearances. They must have said to themselves:

whom could we invite who's in some way connected with Algeria? In other words, let's put wogs with wogs.[3]

In February 2001 at least a dozen books and other publications were confiscated at the Cairo International Book Fair. This followed withdrawal from circulation by the Ministry of Culture of a number of novels and the imprisonment of the Egyptian writer Salah al-Din Mohsen. Egypt had recently restated its commitment to human rights under the Euro-Mediterranean Barcelona Process. The books withdrawn included three by Nawal el Saadawi and three others on the grounds that they contained 'obscene ideas and terminology'. On 27 January 2001, Salah al-Din Mohsen was sentenced to three years' imprisonment with hard labour for defaming Islam and 'disseminating extremist beliefs with the intent of causing upheaval'.[4]

On 26 January 2001 Egypt and the European Union had initialled a draft Association Agreement as part of the Barcelona Process. The agreement included an explicit commitment to respect freedom of expression as set out in the Barcelona Declaration which Egypt signed in 1995. Egypt's other obligations to freedom of expression include Articles 47, 48, 49 of the Egyptian Constitution and Article 19 of the International Covenant on Civil and Political Rights, according to Article XIX. Indeed, on 30 July 2001 a judge on Cairo's Personal Status Court dismissed the lawsuit to forcibly divorce Nawal el Saadawi from her husband of thirty-seven years. Saadawi had for long provoked the traditionalist views of sexuality in books such as *The Hidden Face of Eve* and *Woman at Point Zero*. In March 2001 she gave an interview with the independent magazine *al-Midan* in which she was quoted as saying that the Hajj was a remnant of pre-Islamic paganism. This formed the basis of the suit against her which was thrown out on the grounds that her prosecution lawyers lacked standing to file the suit.

There are many ironies in the development of freedoms in the Islamic world today. As the head of the Muslim College in London, Dr Zaki Badawi, notes, nothing helps an author more than banning his books. Abu Zayd, forced to divorce his wife and go into exile in Europe, is co-editor of Leiden Press's Encyclopaedia of the Qur'an which will be widely distributed by al-Azhar – the very organization that had condemned him for apostasy – when it is published. The religious authorities used to be cautious; today they meddle whenever they can, says Badawi. Abu Nuwas is banned in Egypt today because of his praise for wine and homosexuality but he was hardly ever banned before in Islamic history. Taha Hussein's book on the Jahiliyya poetry, with its claims that these poems were written after the Qur'an and that the Qur'an was itself 'pre-Islamic', were available for a long time after they were published. Today they are banned. Some writers actually advertise in newspapers that their books are banned in order to ensure a run on the market. With this phenomenon in mind, Badawi encouraged the Sheikh of al-Azhar to ignore *The Satanic Verses*. His advice was not followed and Rushdie subsequently became rich and famous as a consequence of censorship.

With the rapid exposure of people to the Internet, censorship, says Badawi, is now impossible, in any case. Censorship in Egypt is as much a struggle for power as it is in Algeria where entire villages are destroyed in the name of Islam by grandees seeking title-deeds to real estate which are their killing fields. The secular governments are to blame for the rise of fanaticism. When governments absorb their Islamist opponents these latter are obliged to tackle immediate practical issues and moderate their policies. Islamophobia has for long been an unfortunate current in the West, fuelled easily by devastating incidents such as the dynamiting of the Buddhas at Bamiyan. Islamic society is going through a crisis similar to a nervous breakdown. If the cynical forces of western materialism and neo-colonialism allow it, it may survive a rite of passage leading towards catharsis, reform and renascence. Perhaps the sooner the sourness of these present dark ages are tasted and reassessed, the sooner a golden age recalling that of Moorish Spain can be expected.

The US President George W. Bush's immediate response to the terrible events of 11 September 2001 reflected the gut reaction of many westerners towards the challenge to their cherished values of democracy and fair play. 'We will rid the world of evil-doers', he said and embark on a 'crusade' against people who 'hate us because we are free'. It was a serious gaffe. To Muslims the word 'crusade' is entirely pejorative. A week or so later one of Osama bin Laden's right-hand men, Sulaiman Abu Ghaith, prefaced bin Laden's speech with references to 'the crusader war, promised by Bush'. A colleague of Bush was reported as saying that the President was 'getting his strength from his belief that he was doing God's will' in mobilizing the world against the Taliban.

The remarks were dangerously insensitive but true to form, for Bush's *Weltanschauung* is rooted in America's fundamentalist present and Puritan past. Both tend to be reinforced by the American media as symbols of patriotism. Bush is aware that nine per cent of Americans are Christian fundamentalists and that their 'Christian coalition' had played a major role in the election of both his father and himself. Half the American population is said to believe that the Bible is the literal word of God. Replace the word Qur'an for Bible and the Wahhabi fundamentalists who support Osama bin Laden would share this view.

In a hand-written letter in Arabic sent to al-Jazeera Television a month after the bombing of Afghanistan began bin Laden urged Muslims to stand up to the 'infidel' West of George Bush. 'The crusader war against Islam has intensified. The world is split into two. Part of it is under the head of infidel, Bush, and the other half under the banner of Islam. Standing against wrong will strengthen us.'[5]

Once articulated by Bush, the word 'crusade' was enough to fire up the angry crowds supporting the Taliban and bin Laden in Quetta long before the bombing started. The crowds immediately called for *jihad* against the USA and Britain. Bush's advisers may have reminded him that the first Crusaders in 1099 had slaughtered the entire population of Muslims and Jews in Jerusalem and it was only when Saladin defeated the Third Crusade that the Jews were allowed to return. On 25 September the USA changed the code-name of its military build-up from 'Operation Infinite Justice' to 'Operation Enduring Freedom' after objections from Islamic scholars. The expression Operation Infinite Justice translates into Arabic as *'adala ghayr mutanahiya'*. As Oxford University's Clive Holes noted in *The Times* on 23 October this phrase implied divine retribution being arrogated to itself by an earthly power; thinking that would strike any ordinary Muslim as blasphemous. The word 'crusade' had already been dropped but not by bin Laden who urged Pakistanis to fight any assault on Afghanistan by 'crusader Americans'. In 1998 bin Laden had grotesquely named his umbrella group 'The World Islamic Front for the Struggle against Jewish–Crusader Aggression', blithely ignoring Islam's tolerance for the People of the Book (Jews and Christians).

As spokesman for Bush's war effort, the British Prime Minister, Tony Blair, saw himself motivated by a profoundly moral world view. In his speech to the Labour Conference in Brighton he spoke of the need for all the 'children of Abraham' to unite and create a better world. For him defeating the Taliban was only the beginning of a process aimed at solving all the world's ills. However, he failed to say that the absence of universal anger over the September outrage was related to the world's terrible economic disparities. Meanwhile, bin Laden's brilliantly-timed videos portrayed himself as a man of calm amid the storm, condemning the arrogance of the West and its partiality in dealing with the Palestine–Israel conflict among Middle East woes. 'Here is America struck by God Almighty in one of its vital organs. Grace and gratitude to God.' These were the words of bin Laden but they sound more like the rhetoric of the Bush–Blair team. Bin Laden appeared to be in control of the exchange of language, with Blair constantly reacting to it in all his own speeches.

Blair countered bin Laden's electrifying video on al-Jazeera Television, insisting that the West was not fighting Islam but terrorism and was defending democracy, but he was given a grilling by the interviewer and failed to explain why the West employed double standards when it came to Israel. The Qatar-based channel is the only free television network in the Middle East and has succeeded, to its credit, in enraging every Arab regime, Israel and now the USA. As the defender of free thought, the USA had for long praised it for its Jeremy Paxman-style interviews and its investigative journalism. However, when al-Jazeera started giving bin Laden the kind of air-time that might increase his charisma, already immense on the Arab and Pakistani street, US Secretary of State Colin Powell asked the network to rein in on its freedom. This was on the quaint grounds that his cassettes might contain coded messages to terrorists. It was a rare commentator who reminded us that most fundamentalist movements were supported by America in its war against communism, that both Saddam Hussein and bin Laden were CIA protégés and that America had washed its hands of its religious allies once they were no longer needed.

When the western media turned to the threats of anthrax, smallpox and other possible terrorist attacks, the western democracies began to consider draconian methods of controlling their own populations. They had forgotten Thomas Jefferson's maxim written in 1776 to James Madison that 'Any society that would trade a little liberty to gain a little safety will deserve neither and lose both.' As panic swept America a former FBI director called for Americans to embrace Burke's idea of 'ordered liberty' and abandon our obsession with individual right. The British human rights lawyer Gareth Pierce noted that we in the democratic West were rushing to throw away the few last protections for people such as asylum-seekers that exist. She believed that in Britain a whole community had been made suspect and was enduring the stigma and the fear that the Irish community in Britain had endured for more than twenty-five years.

Bin Laden issued *fatwas* (the legal decisions of a mufti, an expert on the Shari'a) without any clerical authority. He regarded the Islamic clergy as discredited. Instead, he tapped into the world of popular preaching, particularly that provided by the Deobandi *madrasahs* in Pakistani refugee camps, which feed off marginalism and bitterness against the West. Bin Laden called the suicide killers *istishhadi*, 'martyr-like'. His al-Qaida movement sounded as if it were clear about the 'spiritual' goals it was fighting for. In his video bin Laden spoke of the 'Islamic nation groaning for more than 80 years under the weight of the joint Jewish–Crusader aggression.' At the wedding in February of his second oldest son Muhammad he read out a poem he had composed for the occasion: 'She sails into the waves flanked by arrogance, haughtiness and false power. To her doom she moves slowly ... Your brothers in the East readied themselves. And the war camels prepared to move.' The reference was obvious. So was the warning to the 'false power' of the USA. A few months earlier the USS Cole had been attacked in Aden harbour and 17 US servicemen had been killed.

Bin Laden's real battle was against Arab regimes for supporting the infidel West. These are regimes which have imported western goods and western technology but have remained inured from outside political and ideological goods such as democracy, secularism, the state of law, the principle of rights and, above all, the nation state. The nation state, in the view of the *al-Hayat* journalist Hazim Saghie,[6] was seen as a conspiracy to fragment the Ottoman Empire. In the nineteenth century (the Arab world's 'liberal age') religious reform was tried and failed, partly because it was tarnished with western ideas. This failure led to more extreme versions of Islam. As Saghie notes, efforts to modernize Arabic and bring the classical and spoken Arabics closer together did not materialize. Public spheres such as a free press, trade unions and civil societies for debating matters relating to the common good were not established. Above all Muslims and Arabs failed to resolve the question of political legitimacy. This failure of rulers to legitimize themselves created a vacuum that is filled today by populist politicians and extremist groups. It may be worth leaving the last word with Saghie, who writes:

> Arab intellectuals who ought to encourage change, have largely failed in that role. For the most part they did not detach themselves from the tribal tradition of defending 'our' causes in the face of the 'enemy'. Their priority has not been to criticize the incredible shortcomings that they lie with. They tend ceaselessly to highlight their 'oneness'. Thus they help stereotype themselves before being stereotyped by any enemy. It is in this particular history and this particular culture, and not in any alleged clash of civilizations, that the roots of our wretched present lie.[7]

Notes

Introduction
1. David Hirst, 'How friendly Arab states fell out of favour with US', *Guardian*, 8 November 2001.
2. Ibid.
3. Ibid.
4. Salman Rushdie, 'A war that presents us all with a crisis of faith', *Guardian*, 3 November 2001.
5. In an interview with Mona Eltahawy, *Guardian*, 20 October 1999.
6. Justin Huggler, 'They celebrated to the beat of trashy pop tunes. For now Kabul can go back to work and school', *Independent*, 14 November 2001.
7. Samuel Huntingdon, 'The Clash of Civilisations', *Foreign Affairs*, Summer 1993.

Chapter 1
1. *Index on Censorship*, No. 4, 1995.
2. *Guardian*, 11 November 1994.
3. *Independent*, 2 September 1994.
4. Quoted by J. Richardson, *Théophile Gautier: His Life and Times*, London, Reinhardt, 1958, in Derek Hopwood, *Sexual Encounters in the Middle East*, London, Ithaca Press, 1999, p.103.
5. Ann Elizabeth Mayer, *Islam and Human Rights*, Boulder, Westview Press, 1991, p.88.
6. 'The Unbelievers', *The Qur'an*, 109:6, translated by Arthur J. Arberry, Oxford, OUP, 1964.
7. Ann Elizabeth Mayer, *Islam and Human Rights*, p.65.
8. *Index on Censorship*, No. 2, 1985.
9. Judith Miller, *God has Ninety-Nine Names*, New York, Simon and Schuster, 1996, p.317.
10. Hasan al-Banna, 'Between Yesterday and Today', from *Five Tracts of Hasan al-Banna: a Selection from majmu'at rasail al imam al shahid hasan al-banna*, translated by Charles Wendell, Berkeley, University of California Press, 1979, pp.27–8, quoted in Derek Hopwood, *Sexual Encounters in the Middle East*.
11. Nizar Qabani, *Index on Censorship*, No. 6, 1981, p.71. See also No.3, 1984, p.31.
12. Attributed in S.G. Tallentyne, *The Friends of Voltaire*, 1907, p.199
13. Oscar Wilde, *The Picture of Dorian Grey* , 1891, Preface.
14. Khalid Kishtainy, *Arab Political Humour*, London, Quartet Books, 1985, p.136.
15. David Hirst, *Guardian*, 12 August 1999.
16. Hamid Naficy, 'Veiled vision/powerful presences: women in post–revoloutionary

Iranian cinema', Chapter 3 in *Life and Art: the New Iranian Cinema*, edited by Rose Issa and Sheila Whitaker, London, National Film Theatre, London, 1999, p.52.

17. From *Zan va Mas'aleh-ye Zan*, quoted in Naficy, p.54,
18. *Sahifeh-e Nur*, Vol. 5, p.236. Quoted in Baqer Moin, *Khomeini: Life of the Ayatollah*, London, I.B. Taurus, 1999.
19. Moin, *Khomeini: Life of the Ayatollah*, p.280.
20. Ibid, p.272.
21. Moin, *Khomeini: Life of the Ayatollah*.
22. Maxime Rodinson, *Muhammad*, London, Penguin, 1996, p.213.
23. Genevieve Abdo, an article in *Guardian*.
24. 'Punishment' by Ahmed Shamloo, in *The Gardens of Mirror*, Tehran, Morvarid Publishers, 1967.
25. *Toronto Globe and Mail*, 24 October 1994.
26. Ibid.
27. *The Polmear Ambache Duo*, website: www.polmearambache.co.uk

Chapter 2
1. *Index on Censorship*, No. 5, 1982.
2. Marilyn Booth, 'Sheikh Imam the singer: an interview', *Index on Censorship*, No. 3, 1985, p.18.
3. Ibid.
4. See her entry in *The New Grove Dictionary of Music and Musicians*, Second Edition.
5. *Agence France-Presse (AFP)*, 18 April 2000.
6. Fatima Mernissi, *Islam and Democracy: Fear of the Modern World*, Reading, Mass., Addison-Wesley, 1992, p.5.
7. 'Ali Amir Hoseini, Bani Sadr's adviser, in an interview with Moin, London, 1986, quoted in Baqer Moin, *Khomeini*, p.219.
8. Shaul Bakhash, *The Reign of the Ayatollahs: Iran and the Islamic Revolution*, London, 1985, pp.127–8, quoted in Baqer Moin, *Khomeini*, p.219.
9. Jason Burke, 'Baghdad settles war scores on celluloid', *Guardian*, 23 January 2001.
10. Rose Issa and Sheila Whitaker (eds.), *Life and Art: the New Iranian Cinema*, London, National Film Theatre, 1999.
11. Ibid.
12. *Kayhan*, 26 September 1985.
13. Judith Miller, *God has Ninety-Nine Names*, New York, Simon & Schuster, 1996, p.316.
14. Ibid, p.317.
15. Ibid.
16. *Guardian*, 11 August 1999.
17. Judith Miller, *God has Ninety-Nine Names*, p.104.

Chapter 3
1. Muhammad Asad, *The Road to Mecca*, Tangiers, Dar al-Andalus, p.297.
2. Stephen Runciman, *The History of the Crusades*, Vol. 1, London, Penguin, 1990.
3. Norman Daniel, *The Arabs and Medieval Europe*, Harlow, Longman, Beirut, Librairie du Liban, 1979, p.118.
4. Karen Armstrong, *A History of Jerusalem*, London, Harper Collins, 1996, p.228.
5. S. Fisher, *A History of Europe*, London, Edward Arnold, 1941, p.368.

Chapter 4

1. *Guardian,* 4 February 1990.
2. Taslima Nasrin, *Shame,* New York, Prometheus Books, 1997, Preface p.14.

Chapter 5

1. Said Soltanpour, from *On this Shore of Fear* quoted in *Index on Censorship* 6, 1982.
2. Hadi Khorsandi, *Asghar Agha,* No. 144, 5 February 1983, quoted in *Index on Censorship,* No. 2, 1986, p.25.
3. Voice of Iran Radio, 11 June 1999.
4. Genevieve Abdo, *Guardian,* 13 September 1999.
5. Genevieve Abdo, *Guardian,* 30 September 1999.
6. *Index on Censorship,* No. 4, 1999.
7. 'Ali Ansari, 'The World Today', *Journal of The Royal Institute of International Affairs,* London, October 1999.
8. *Guardian,* 29 November 1999.

Chapter 6

1. *Index on Censorship,* No. 4/5, 1994.
2. Ghania Mouffok, 'Etre Journaliste en Algérie', *Reporters sans Frontières,* Paris, 1996.
3. Judith Vidal-Hall, 'A Gig too Far', *Index on Censorship,* No. 6, 1998, p.117.
4. Abdenour Kilou, 'Obituary of Matoub', *Guardian,* 29 June 1998.

Chapter 7

1. Adel Darwish and Haifaa Khalafallah, 'Lebanon: last refuge of the written word destroyed', *Index on Censorship,* No. 6, 1982.

Chapter 8

1. *Index on Censorship,* No. 5, 1997, p.13 and *Banipal,* London, 1998.
2. Robert Irwin, *Night and Horses and the Desert, the Penguin Anthology of Classical Arabic Literature,* London, Penguin, 1999, p.59.
3. Israel Shahak, *Jewish History, Jewish Religion,* London, Pluto, 1997, p.57.
4. Qur'an, LIII: 9–23.
5. Qur'an, XI:51.
6. Derek Adie Flower, *The Shores of Wisdom: the Story of the Ancient Library of Alexandria,* Isle of Man, Pharos, 1999, p.195.
7. William Dalrymple, *From the Holy Mountain: a Journey in the Shadow of Byzantium,* London, Harper Collins, 1998, p.279.
8. Karen Armstrong, *A History of God,* New York, Knopft, 1993, p.163.
9. Baqer Moin, *Khomeini: Life of the Ayatollah,* p.17.
10. Daryush Shayegan, *Cultural Schizophrenia: Islamic Societies Confronting the West,* London, Saqi Books, 1992, p.101.
11. Ibid, p.102.
12. *Poems of al-Mutanabbi,* selected and edited by A.J. Arberry, Cambridge, CUP, 1967. p.112.
13. Phillip Hitti, *History of the Arabs,* London, Macmillan, 1974, p.446.
14. Francis Robinson (ed.), *Atlas of the Islamic World since 1500,* Cambridge, CUP, 1982, p.135.

Chapter 9
1. Haifaa Khalafallah, *Index on Censorship*, No. 3, 1984, p.30.
2. Nizar Qabbani, 'Footnotes to the Book of the Setback', translated by Abdullah al-Udhari, *Index on Censorship*, No. 6, 1981.
3. From Adonis's speech 'The Poet as Historical Witness', given at the ICA, London in June 1981, in *Index on Censorship*, No. 6, 1981.
4. *Victims of a Map: a Bilingual Anthology of Arabic Poetry)*, [Samih al-Qasim, Adonis, Mahmoud Darwish] translated by Abdullah al-Udhari, London, Saqi, 1984.

Chapter 10
1. Samih al-Qasim, 'Slit lips and other poems', *Index on Censorship*, No. 6, 1983, p.30.
2. Mahmoud Darwish, 'Three Poems', translated by Abdullah al-Udhari, *Index on Censorship*, No. 4, 1984, p.30.
3. Patrick Cockburn, *Independent on Sunday*, April 1998.
4. Said K. Aburish, *Arafat: from Defender to Dictator*, London, Bloomsbury, 1998, p.316 and *passim*.
5. The quotations from Naji el-'Ali are taken from an interview subtitled: 'From Lebanon to Kuwait, the cartoonist has so far survived attempts to stop his work', *Index on Censorship*, 1984.
6. Naji el-'Ali, *Index on Censorship*, 1984.
7. Ibid.
8. Ibid.

Chapter 11
1. Muslim: *Mukhtasa sahih Muslim* (Collection of Hadiths).
2. *British Journal of Middle East Studies*, Vol. 27, No. 2, 2000.
3. Olivier Roy, *The Failure of Political Islam*, London, I.B. Tauris, 1994, p.45.
4. From Luc Barbulesco and Philippe Cardinal, *L'Islam en Question*, Paris, Grasset, 1986, p.116, quoted in Daryush Shayegan, *Cultural Schizophrenia: Islamic Societies Confronting the West*.
5. Mohammad Hashim Kamali, *Freedom of Expression in Islam*, Cambridge, Islamic Texts Society, 1997, p.28.
6. Malise Ruthven, *Islam: a Very Short Introduction*, Oxford, OUP, 1997, p.131.
7. Mohammad Hashim Kamali, *Freedom of Expression in Islam*, p.190.
8. Fariba Adelkhah, *Being Modern in Iran*, London, Hurst, 1999, p.106.
9. Olivier Roy, *The Failure of Political Islam*, p.45.
10. Ibid.
11. Qur'an, XVI:106.

Chapter 12
1. Ahmad ibn Hanbal, *Masnad*, 3/446.
2. Nawal el Saadawi, 'The truth sometimes shocks', translated by Miriam Lowi, *Index on Censorship*, No. 3, 1982.
3. Fatima Mernissi, *Islam and Democracy*, p.78.
4. Qur'an, XXIV:30,31.
5. Interview with Libby Brooks, *Guardian*, 2 August 1999.
6. Daryush Shayegan, *Cultural Schizophrenia, Islamic Societies Confronting the West*, p.91.
7. Ahmed Rashid, *Taliban, Islam, Oil and the New Great Game in Central Asia*, London,

I.B. Tauris, 2000, p.116.

8. Baqer Moin, *Khomeini: Life of the Ayatollah*, p.30.
9. Qur'an, IV:3.
10. Ameer Ali, *The Spirit of Islam*, University Paperbacks, Methuen, London, 1967, p.255.
11. Peter Jackson, *The Delhi Sultanate: A Political and Military History*, Cambridge, 1999.
12. Wijbrand Schaap, 'Aisha in trouble', *Index on Censorship*, No. 2, 2001, p.171.
13. Fatima Mernissi, *Islam and Democracy*, p.78.
14. *Index on Censorship*, No. 2, 1985.
15. Ibid.
16. Farida Abdelkhah, *Being Modern in Iran*, p. 83.

Chapter 13

1. Simi Wali, 'Statement on Afghanistan' to the US Congressional Human Rights Caucus, October 1997. Quoted in Ahmed Rashid, *Taliban, Islam, Oil and the New Great Game in Central Asia*, p.111.
2. Reuters, 'Iranian leader accuses Taliban of defaming Islam', 4 October 1996. Quoted in Ahmed Rashid, *Taliban, Islam, Oil and the New Great Game in Central Asia*, p.116.
3. Ahmed Rashid, *Taliban, Islam, Oil and the New Great Game in Central Asia*, p.115.
4. 'Taliban restricts music', 18 December 1996, quoted in Ahmed Rashid, *Taliban, Islam, Oil and the New Great Game in Central Asia,* p.118.
5. I have relied on *The New Grove Dictionary of Music and Musicians*, second edition, for much of this background to music in Afghanistan.

Chapter 14

1. From 'Akhbar al-Hallaj and other sources', *Anthology of Islamic Literature*, edited by James Kritzeck, London, Penguin, 1964.
2. Baqer Moin, *Khomeini: Life of the Ayatollah*, p.32.
3. Letter written on 22 February, published in Resalaat, 25 February 1989, in Baqer Moin, *Khomeini, Life of the Ayatollah*.
4. Baqer Moin, *Khomeini*, p.40.
5. Baqer Moin, *Khomeini*, p.8.
6. I have relied on *The New Grove Dictionary of Music and Musicians*, second edition, for this background to music in Islam.
7. Ibid.
8. Ibid.
9. Ibid.
10. Ibid.

Chapter 15

1. Robert Irwin, 'Is this the man who inspired Bin Laden', *Guardian*, 1 November 2001.
2. Alain Gresh, *Le Monde Diplomatique*, 4 April 2000.
3. *Index on Censorship*, No. 3, 1996, p.9, quoted in Gresh, *Le Monde Diplomatique*, 4 April 2000.
4. Baqer Moin, *Khomeini*.
5. Baqer Moin, *Khomeini*, p.30.
6. Daryush Shayegan, *Cultural Schizophrenia, Islamic Societies Confronting the West*, p.111.

Chapter 16

1. Olivier Roy, 'After the Fall: Afghanistan', *Index on Censorship*, No. 5, 1999.
2. Ibid.
3. Tariq 'Ali, 'Try and disarm us, if you can', *London Review of Books*, 15 April 1999.
4. Hanan Ashrawi, 'Anatomy of racism', 18 October 2000.
5. Juan Goytisolo, *Index on Censorship*, No.5, 1999, p. 65.
6. Dick Yarbrough, 'Arab terrorists are big cowards', *The Neighbor*, November 2000.
7. 'Free speech versus greedom from bigotry, an article in the *Chicago Tribune*', 8 March 1991, p.2.
8. A letter from Chris Doyle, Information Officer for the Council for the Advancement of Arab–British Understanding, published in the *Independent*, 19 August, 2000.
9. Hanan Ashrawi, 'Anatomy of Racism', 18 October 2000.
10. Ibid.
11. Albert Hourani, *Arabic Thought in the Liberal Age 1789–1939*, Cambridge, CUP, 1962.
12. John L. Esposito, *The Islamic Threat, Myth or Reality*, Oxford, OUP, 1995.

Chapter 17

1. Quoted in *Index on Censorship*, Vol. 21. No 2.
2. A.R. al-Jabarti, *Tarikh muddat al-fransis bi-misr*, ed. S. Moreh, Leiden, 1975, p.75.
3. *Journal of Middle East Studies*, May 1998.
4. Farag Foda, *Index on Censorship*, No. 2, 1992, p.23.
5. 'In the name of God, go', Ibid.
6. Tarek al-Bishri, Ibid.
7. Richard Engel in the *Middle East Times*, August, 1997.
8. Ibid.
9. Ibid.

Chapter 18

1. Oscar Wilde, *The Picture of Dorian Grey*, 1891, Chapter 1.
2. Dr Zaki Badawi in an interview with Paul Martin, *Guardian*, 27 February 1989.
3. Malise Ruthven, *A Satanic Affair*, London, Chatto & Windus, 1990, p.113.
4. Ibid.
5. Quoted in Derek Hopwood, *Sexual Encounters in the Middle East*, p.175.
6. *Index on Censorship*, No. 1/2, 1999.
7. *Index on Censorship*, No. 4, 1996.
8. Abu Zayd, quoted from varous sources by Fauzi Najjar in *British Journal of Middle East Studies*, Vol. 27, No. 2, November 2000.
9. 'Abd al-Sabur Shahin (ed.), *Qissat Abu Zayd wa Ihnisar al-'Almaniyya*, Cairo, Dar al-L'tisam, 1995. Quoted in *British Journal of Middle East Studies*, Vol. 27, No. 2, November 2000.
10. *British Journal of Middle East Studies*, Vol. 27, No. 2, November 2000.
11. 'Abd al-Sabur Shahin (ed.), *Qissat Abu Zayd wa Ihnisar al-'Almaniyya*, Cairo, Dar al-L'tisam, 1995. Quoted in *British Journal of Middle East Studies*, Vol. 27, No. 2, November 2000.
12. *Index on Censorship*, No. 7, 1993.
13. *British Journal of Middle East Studies*, Vol. 27, No. 2, November 2000.
14. Ibid.

15. Memorandum of the Egyptian Legal Aid Centre for Humen Rights, quoted in *British Journal of Middle East Studies*, Vol. 27, No. 2, November 2000.
16. *Index on Censorship*, No. 4/5, 1994.

Chapter 19

1. David Holden and Richard Johns, *The House of Saud*, London, Pan Books, 1982, p. 262.
2. William A. Rugh, 'Saudi Mass Media and Society in the Faisal Era', from *King Faisal and the Modernization of Saudi Arabia*, edited by Willard A. Beling, London, Croom Helm, 1980, p. 136.

Chapter 20

1. Much of this chapter is based on *Life and Art, the new Iranian cinema*, edited by Rose Issa and Sheila Whitaker, and an article, 'Sixty years of film production in Iran,' by Dr Jamsheed Akrami, *The Iranian*, June 1999.
2. Dr Jamsheed Akrami, *The Iranian*, June 1999.
3. Hamid Naficy, 'Veiled vision/powerful presences: women in post–revolutionary Iranian cinema', Chapter 3 in *Life and Art: the New Iranian Cinema*, edited by Rose Issa and Sheila Whitaker, London, National Film Theatre, London, 1999, p.52.
4. Ibid.
5. Ibid.
6. Dr Jamsheed Akrami, *The Iranian*, June 1999.
7. Rose Issa and Sheila Whitaker, (eds.), *Life and Art, the new Iranian cinema*.

Chapter 21

1. *Sahifeh-e Nur*, Vol. 5, p.236, quoted in Moin, *Khomeini, Life of the Ayatollah*.
2. *Index on Censorship*, No. 3, 1992.
3. Samuel Huntington, *The Clash of Civilisations*, Ibid.
4. Ann Elizabeth Mayer, *Islam and Human Rights*, p.8.
5. Asma Jahangir and Hina Jilani, *The Hudood Ordinances – A Divine Sanction?*

Chapter 22

1. Elizabeth Sirriyeh, *British Society for Middle East Studies (BRISMES) Bulletin*, Vol. 16, No 2, 1989.
2. St John Philby, *Sa'udi Arabia*, 1955.
3. Saïd K. Aburish, *The Rise, Corruption and Coming Fall of the Home of Saud*, p.270.
4. David Holden, *Farewell to Arabia*, London, Faber, 1966, p.134.
5. Article XIX report, October 1991.
6. William A. Rugh, 'Saudi Mass Media and Society in the Faisal Era', from *King Faisal and the Modernization of Saudi Arabia*, p.133–4.
7. Quoted by Eric Roulean in *Le Monde*, 4 May 1981.
8. For example, Article 6 makes it a crime to publish anything which may disturb public order or morality; Article 7 is indiscriminately used to harass people exercising freedom of expression; Article 16 authorizes the Ministry of Information to confiscate without compensation any banned or unlicensed imported publication; Article 33 authorizes the Ministry of Information to confiscate without compensation any issue of any newspaper published in Saudi Arabia which contains

anything which may offend religious feelings or undermine public morality. Meanwhile, the King has absolute power to appoint and dismiss editors-in-chief and board members of the press.

Three government departments, the Supreme Information Council, the General Directorate of Publications and the Department of Domestic Press Censorship, have full authority to interfere with editorial decisions and to censor publications, films and cassettes. Government departments can prohibit the discussion of specific projects. One example was the ban issued in September 1988 on discussion of tradition and modernism in Arabic literature.

Only Saudi citizens are allowed to own bookshops, printing presses and other information outlets. Their operation requires a licence from the Ministry of Information (Article 3). Certain Qur'anic verses may nor be broadcast on radio or television or publicized in the press. One such banned verse states: 'Whenever kings enter a city they cause it to be corrupt, turning its honourable people into humiliated people. Verily, they do just that' (XXVII:34). According to Saudi journalists even words and expressions such as 'the oppressed', 'Islamic revolution' and 'imperialism'are forbidden.

Inside Saudi Arabia all radio and television with the exception of a concession granted to ARAMCO at Dhahran is controlled by the Ministry of Information. Neither news nor opinions may be broadcast which is inconsistent with government policies. Trade unions are banned and it is a criminal offence for three or more people to withdraw their labour. Royal Decree No. 12/2/23/2639 of 21 June 1956, imposes penalties of up to two years imprisonment for organising or attempting to organize a labour demonstration or strike. Saudi Arabia has so far refused to ratify the International Covenant on Civil and Political Rights (Article 19 of which protects the right to freedom of expression) and its First Optional Protocol (which allows individual petitions).

(Source: Article XIX)

Chapter 23
1. *Time Magazine*, 6 March, 2000.
2. Genevieve Abdo, 'We told you – no more scoops', *Guardian*, 5 February, 2001.
3. *Le Monde*, 23 December 2001.
4. The books reported by Article XIX to have been confiscated included:

   Lebanese poet Joseph Harb, *al-Sayeda al-Baida' wa Shahwatiha al-Koholeya*, Dar al-Rees, Lebanon.
   Dr Nawal el-Saadawi, *Suqut al-Imam*, Dar al-Saqi, Lebanon.
   Dr Nawal el-Saadawi, *al-Hobb Fi Zaman al-Naft*, Dar al-Adab, Lebanon.
   Dr Nawal el-Saadawi, *Awraq Hayati*, Dar al-Adab, Lebanon.
   Faris Sawah, *al-Shaytan wa al-Rahman al-Thanaweya al-Kawneya wa Lahot al-Tarikh*, Dar 'Ala al-Din, Syria.
   Yehya Ibrahim, *Hikayat Majnoon*, Dar al-Jamal, Germany.
   Muhammad Shukry, *al-Kheyma*, Dar al-Jamal, Germany.
   Muhammad Shukry, *al-Shutar*, Dar al-Jamal.
   Fatima Rees, *Hal Entom Mahsunoon Ded al-Horeya?*, Dar al-Saqq, London.
   Fatima Rees, *al-Khawf Men al-Herasa*, Dar al-Saqq, London.

Al-Jinns 'End al-'Arab, A book of heritage.
Torky Ahmed, *al-Siyassa Bein al-Halal wa al-Haram*, Dar al-Rees, Lebanon.

The three novels which were confiscated by the Ministry of Culture on the grounds of obscene ideas and terminology were:

Yasser Sha'aban, *Abna' al-Khata' al-Romancy.*
Muhammad Hamed, *Ahlam Muharama.*
Tewfic Abdel Rahman, *Qabl wa Ba'ad.*

Mr Mohsen was tried by the State Security (Misdemeanours) Court of the District of Giza. The prosecutions were brought under Article 98 of the Criminal Code and Article 304 Item 2 of the Criminal Procedures Code. His publications, *Musamarat al-Sama'* (Lecture of the Heaven), *Mudhakkirat Muslim* (Memoirs of a Muslim) and *Irti'ashat Tanwiriya* (Shivers of Enlightenment) were reportedly withdrawn from circulation.

5. *Guardian*, 2 November 2001.
6. Hazim Saghie, 'It's not all America's fault', *Time*, 15 October 2001.
7. Ibid.

Select Bibliography

Adelkhah, Fariba, *Being Modern in Iran,* Hurst, London, 1999.

Arberry, Arthur J., *The Koran Interpreted, The Unbelievers,* 109:6, OUP, Oxford, 1964.

Armstrong, Karen, *A History of God,* Alfred Knopf, New York, 1993.

Asad, Muhammad, *The Road to Mecca,* Dar al-Andalus, Tangiers, 1954.

Bakhash, Shaul, *The Reign of the Ayatollahs: Iran and the Islamic Revolution,* Basic Books, New York, 1984.

Esposito, John L., *The Islamic Threat, Myth or Reality,* OUP, Oxford, 1995.

The New Grove Dictionary of Music and Musicians, second edition.

Hitti , Phillip, *History of the Arabs,* Macmillan, London, 1974.

Holden, David & Johns, Richard, *The House of Saud,* Pan Books, London, 1982.

Hopwood, Derek, *Sexual Encounters in the Middle East,* Ithaca Press, London, 1999.

Hourani, Albert, *Arab Thought in the Liberal Age,* Oxford University Press, Oxford.

Irwin, Robert, *Night and Horses and the Desert, the Penguin Anthology of Classical Arabic Literature,* Penguin, London, 1999.

Kamali, Mohammad Hashim, *Freedom of Expression in Islam,* Islamic Texts Society, Cambridge, 1997.

Kishtainy, Khalid, *Arab Political Humour,* Quartet Books, London, 1985.

Mayer, Ann Elizabeth, *Islam and Human Rights,* Westview Press, Boulder, USA, 1991.

Mernissi, Fatima, *Islam and Democracy; Fear of the Modern World,* Addison-Wesley Publishing Company, New York, 1992.

Miller, Judith, *God has Ninety-Nine Names,* Simon and Schuster, New York, 1996.

Moin, Baqer, *Khomeini, Sign of God,* I.B. Tauris, London, 1999.

Mostyn, Trevor, *Coming of Age in the Middle East,* Kegan Paul International, London, 1987.

Mostyn, Trevor and Hourani, Albert, *The Cambridge Encyclopedia of the Middle East & North Africa,* Cambridge University Press, Cambridge, 1988.

Naficy, Hamid, *Veiled vision/ powerful presences, women in post-revolutionary Iranian cinema, Life and Art : the new Iranian Cinema,* edited by Issa, Rose and Whitaker, Sheila, National Film Theatre, London, 1999.

Nasrin, Taslima, *Shame,* Prometheus Books, New York, 1997.

Rashid, Ahmed, *Taliban, Islam, Oil and the New Great Game in Central Asia,* I.B. Tauris, London, 2000.

Richardson, J., *Théophile Gautier: his life and times,* London, 1958.

Robinson, Francis, *Atlas of the Islamic World since 1500,* Phaedon, Oxford, 1982.

Rodinson, Maxime, *Muhammad,* Penguin, London, 1996.

Roy, Olivier, *The Failure of Political Islam,* I.B. Taurus, London, 1994.

Rugh, William A., *Saudi Mass Media and Society in the Faisal Era,* from *King Faisal and the Modernisation of Saudi Arabia,* edited by Beling, Willard A., Croom Helm, London, 1980.

Ruthven, Malise, *Islam: A very short introduction,* OUP, Oxford, 1997.

Ruthven, Malise, *Islam in the Modern World,* OUP, Oxford, 1984, 2000.

Shayegan, Daryush, *Cultural Schizophrenia, Islamic Societies Confronting the West,* Saqi Books, London, 1989.

al-Udhari, Abdullah (trs.), *A Bilingual Anthology of Arabic Poetry; Victims of a Map [Samih al-Qasim, Adonis, Mahmud Darwish],* Saqi Books, London, 1984.

Index